SOUTH SHIELDS

From Old Photographs

JOHN CARLSON

AMBERLEY

This book is dedicated to South Shields people of goodwill everywhere (and also a few people from Jarrow who we don't mind really!) Also to all the new people we will meet in the future and all of the people from the past, who we hope to meet again.

First published 2017

Amberley Publishing
The Hill, Stroud
Gloucestershire, GL5 4EP

www.amberley-books.com

British Library Cataloguing in Publication Data.

A catalogue record for this book is available from the British Library.

ISBN 978 1 8486 8858 2 (print)
ISBN 978 1 4456 6424 8 (ebook)

Origination by Amberley Publishing.
Printed in the UK.

Acknowledgements

Welcome to a new book on South Shields. Hopefully inside you will find many photographs of the town you have not seen before, or if you have they will now be in colour.

This book is dedicated with thanks to the late Thomas Gibson, Uri Robarkidze and, by no means least, Denis Boad, a 'top bloke', as they say, who did so much to help us and has made an unsung contribution to preserving parts of historic South Shields.

Special mentions should also go to, in no particular order, Stuart Smith, Neil Mortson, Derick High, Geordie Atkinson, Keith Bardwell, Andrew Clark, Malcolm G. Charlton, Pauline Chu, Peter Headly, George Nairn, Harry Fitzsimons, Eddie Post and David Packer.

On a final personal note I am interested in tracking down any living relatives of the late Billy Walker, formerly of Marsden Road. You can contact me at johncarlson2@yahoo.com.

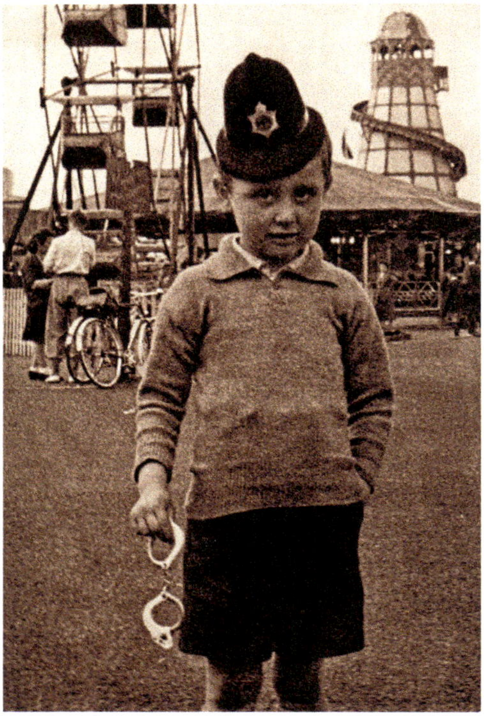

Ocean Beach Pleasure Park

Ocean Beach Pleasure Park used to be known as 'The Fair'. This image shows Frederick Stone, whose regalia had been bought at the fairground by his mother. (Photo courtesy of Dave stone)

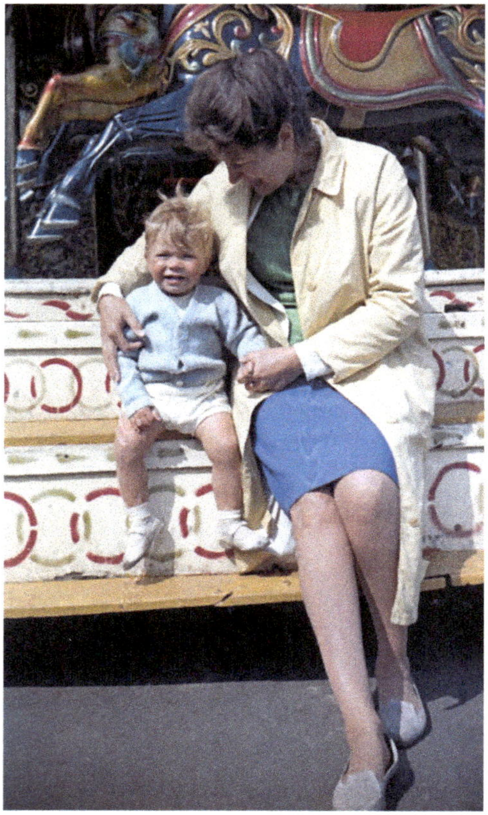

Ocean Beach Pleasure Park

John Carlson (author) with his mother Joyce around 1964.

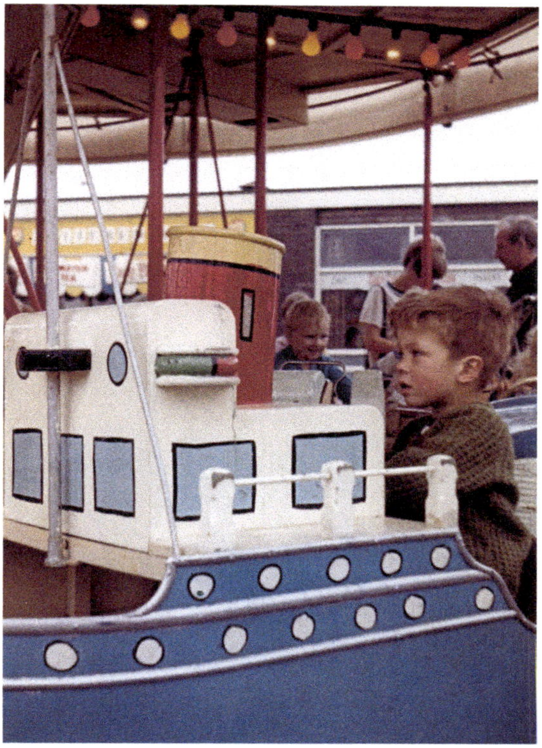

Ocean Beach Pleasure Park

The author at Ocean Beach Pleasure Park around 1957.

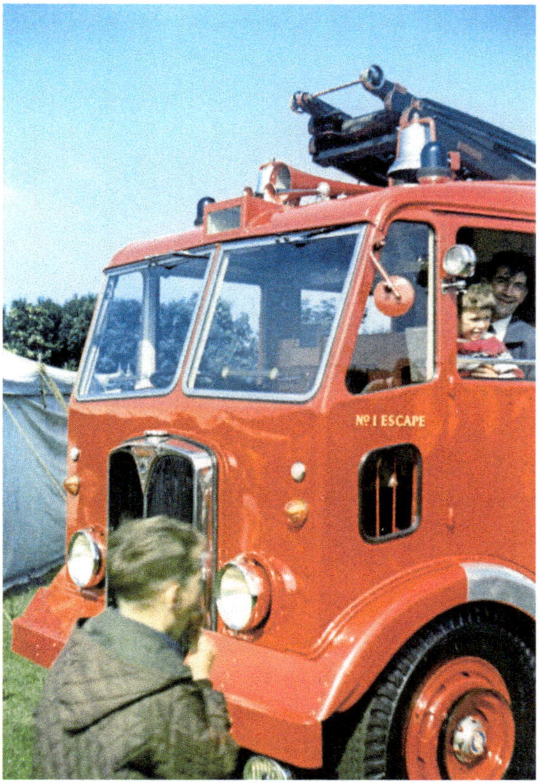

Fire Engine

The author with his father Charles in a South Shields fire engine *c.* 1968. This was taken at a flower show in Bents Park.

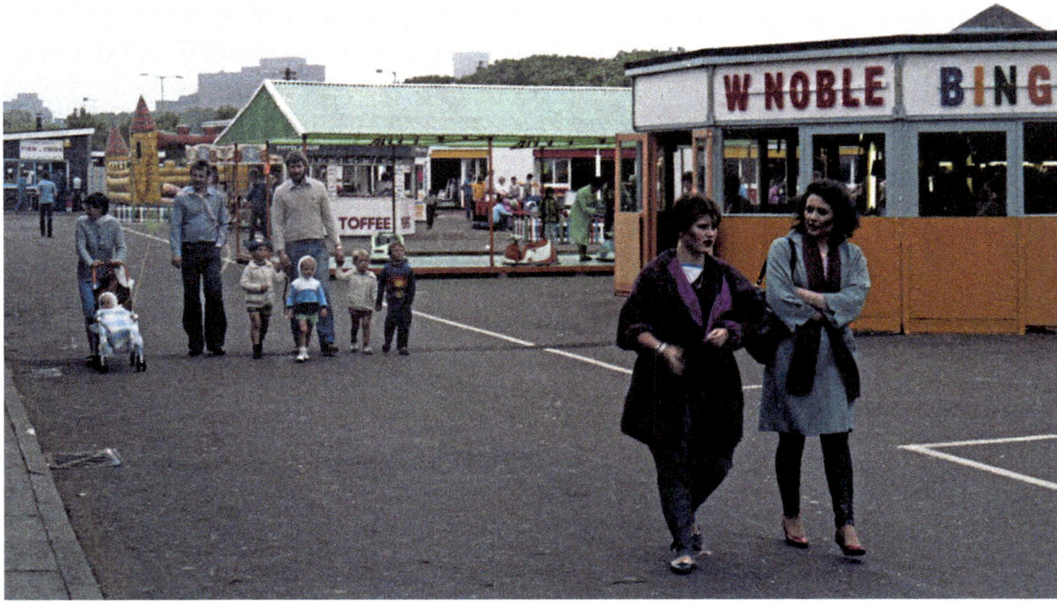

Above and below: Fairground

Images taken at the fairground on a cold day around 1982. Ocean Beach Pleasure Park, the town's fair, has been going from strength to strength.

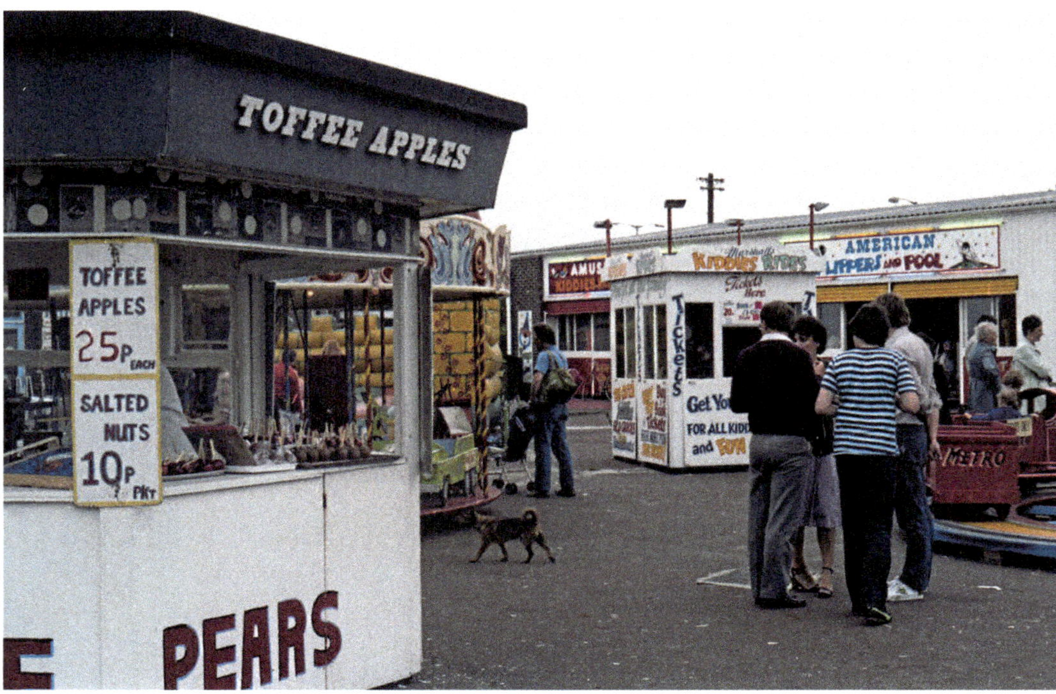

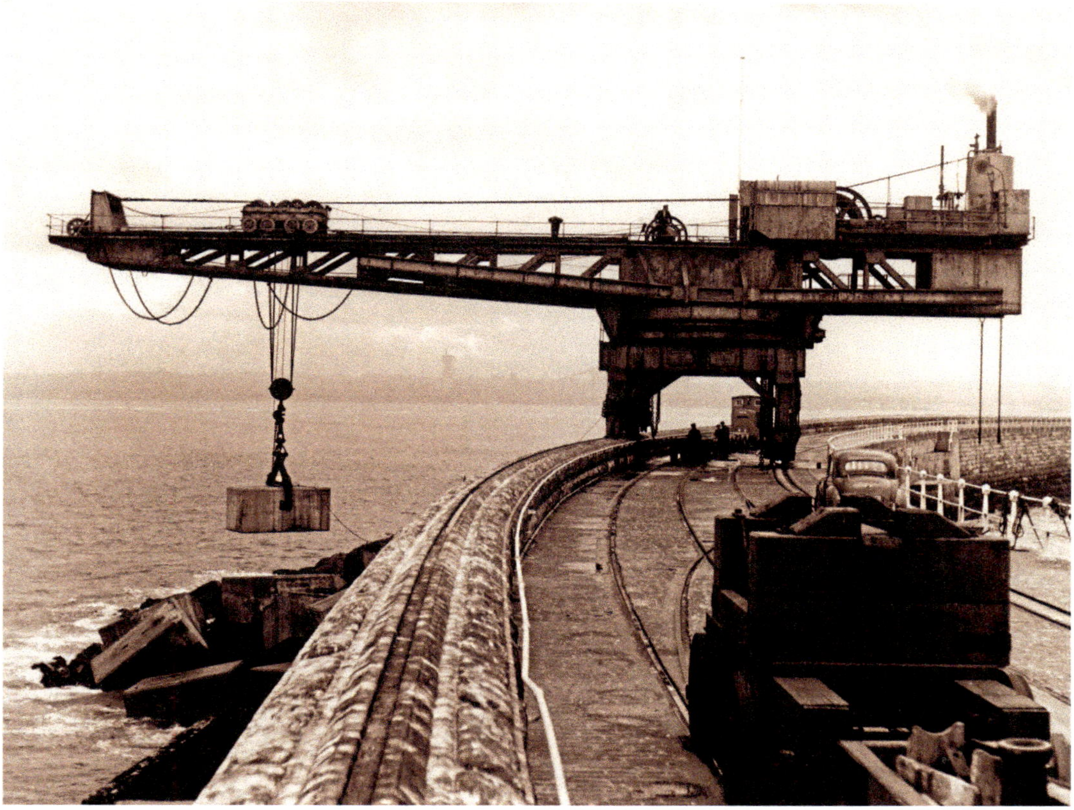

Crane on the Pier

The titan crane was used to drop 40-ton blocks of concrete over the side of the pier to form a defence against strong seas. Installed in 1899, we believe this was at least the second crane used on the pier and that the great storm of 1893 swept away a similar crane on the north pier. A short while later the south pier crane went the same way. We also believe that the crane pictured here was built by Stothert and Pitt of Bath and was originally intended for work at Gibraltar. One leg had to be retrospectively shortened to work on the pier.

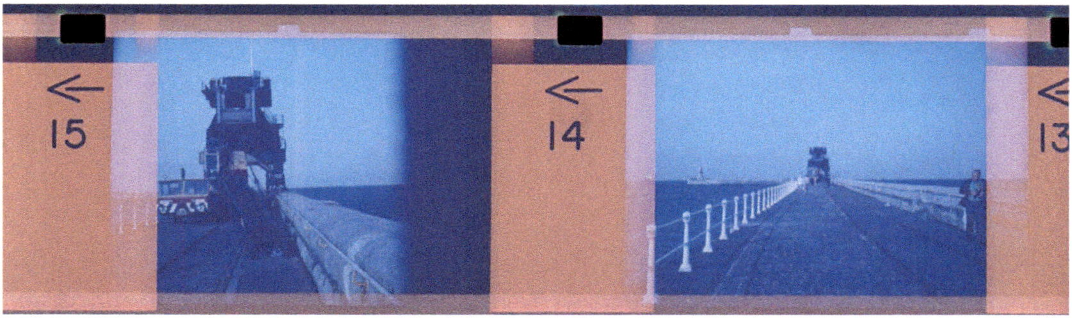

Crane's Demolition

During the 1960s the crane saw only limited use. These images, taken with a rather cheap instamatic, show its demolition in 1975.

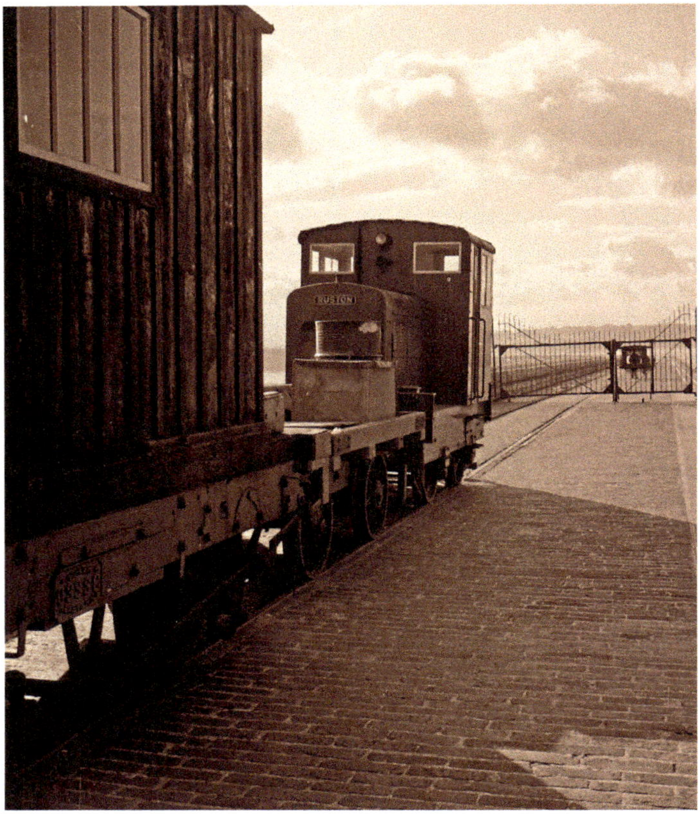

South Pier

In 1897 the pier commissioners barriered off the entrance to the piers, possibly with the intention of encouraging visitors to walk along them. South Shields councillors soon removed the barriers. However, as the cost of the South Pier was around £1million pounds it's understandable that the commissioners wanted to charge something. For a while pleasure boats sailed from a landing on the pier.

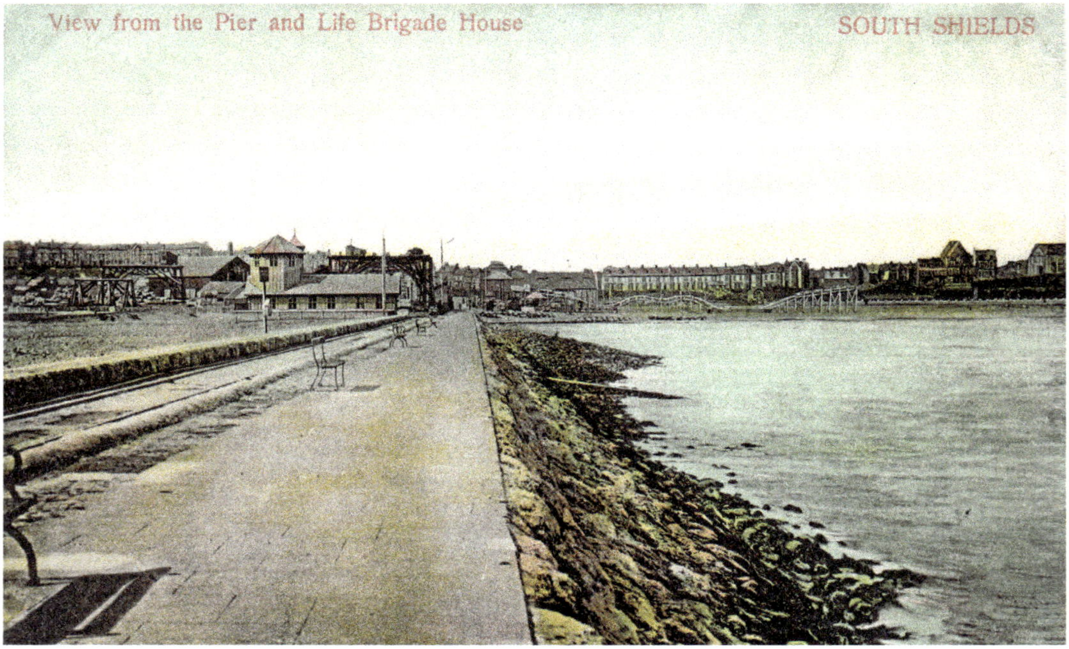

Pier Head

A colourised postcard of the pier head area.

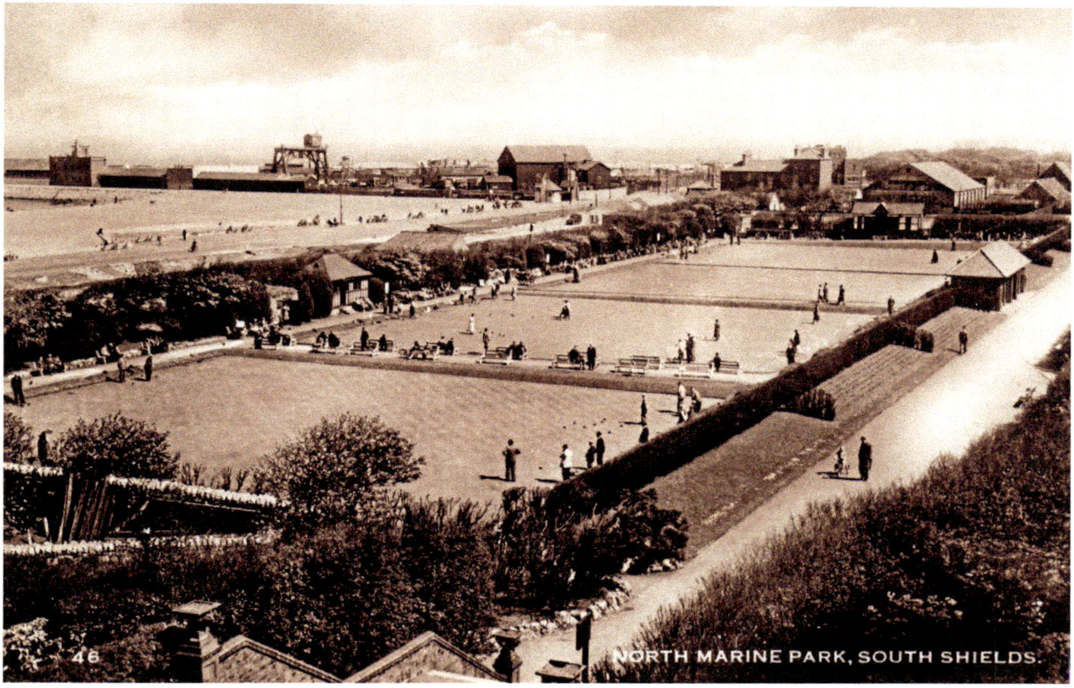

North Marine Park

The splendid bowling greens of the North Marine Park, a statement in municipal magnificence. For many years the area around the pier head was a curious mixture of entertainments, and a reminder that work was never far away from leisure is given by the cranes and sheds of the South Pier block yard. The more modem lines of the Sea Hotel are just visible towards the right.

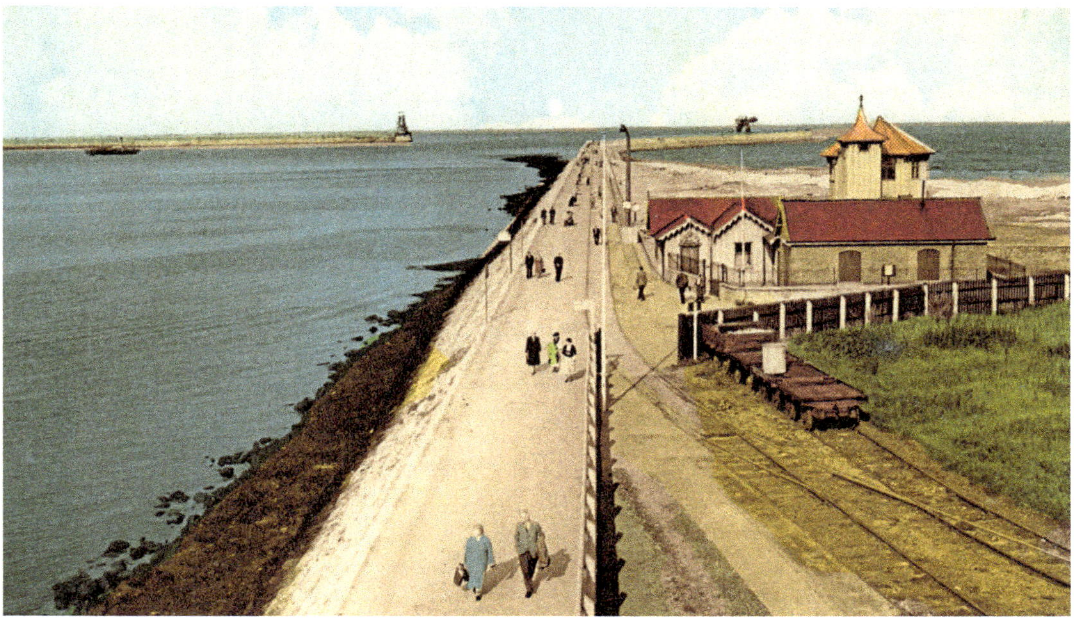

South Pier

Looking along the South Pier.

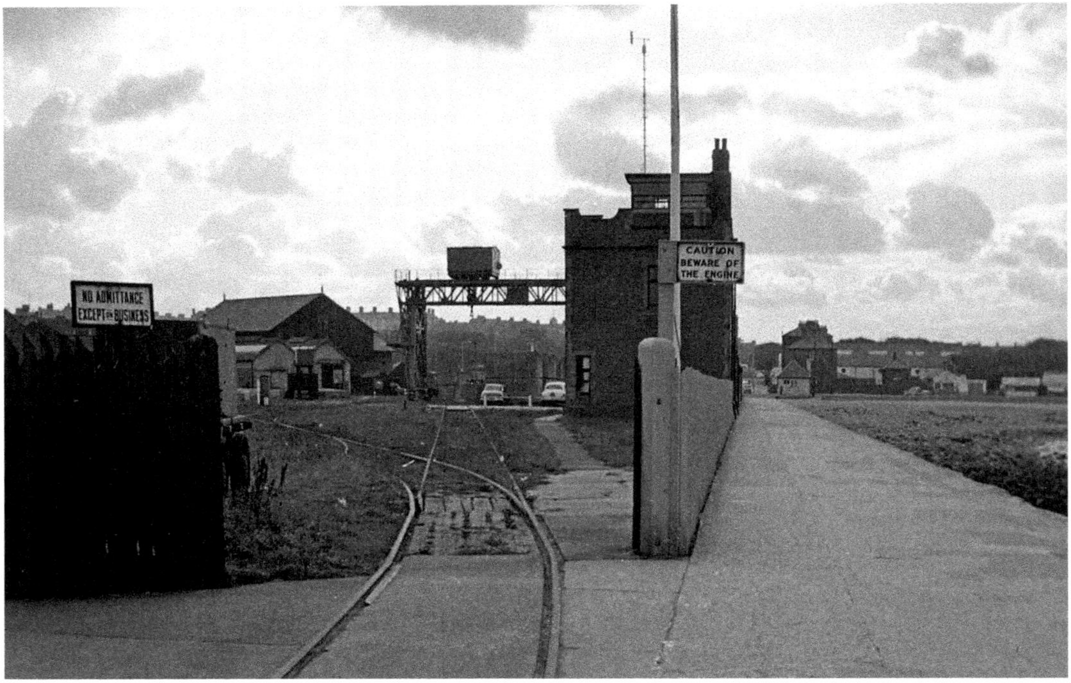

Pier Head, 1960s
A 1960s view of the pier head. The area to the left is now a coach park.

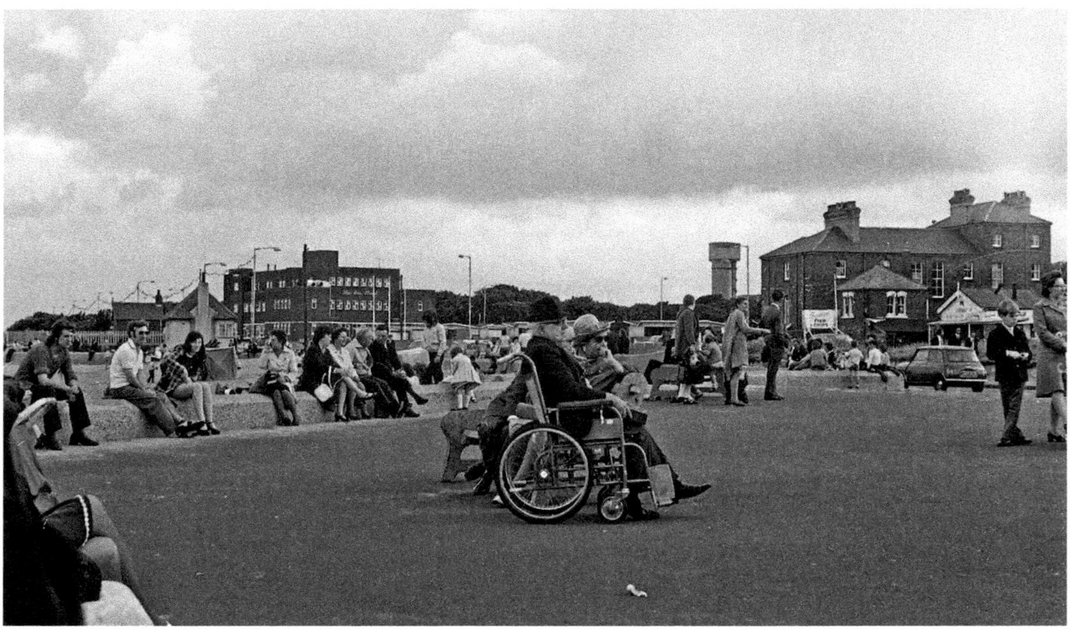

Pier Head, 1970
An image of the pier head taken sometime around 1970. The Sea Hotel (visible towards the left) is still around today, in a modified form. However the winding tower of Westoe Colliery went in 1994 and the building towards the right, which I believe was housing for coastguards and a pet monkey, is now also gone, to be replaced by a very modern swimming pool.

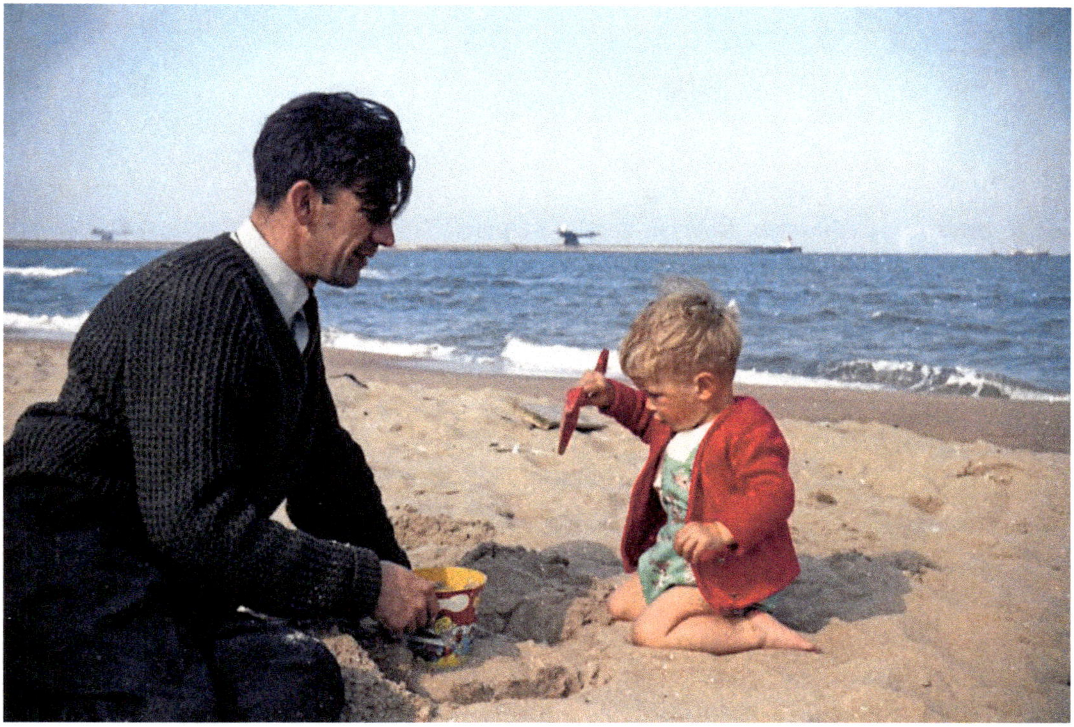

Above and below: The Beach

Colour images of John Carlson with father Charles Carlson on the beach in the mid-1960s. The formation of the sand dunes were a by-product of the building of the pier. The level of the sand was once a yard or so below the concrete balustrade visible at the lower right of the lower picture.

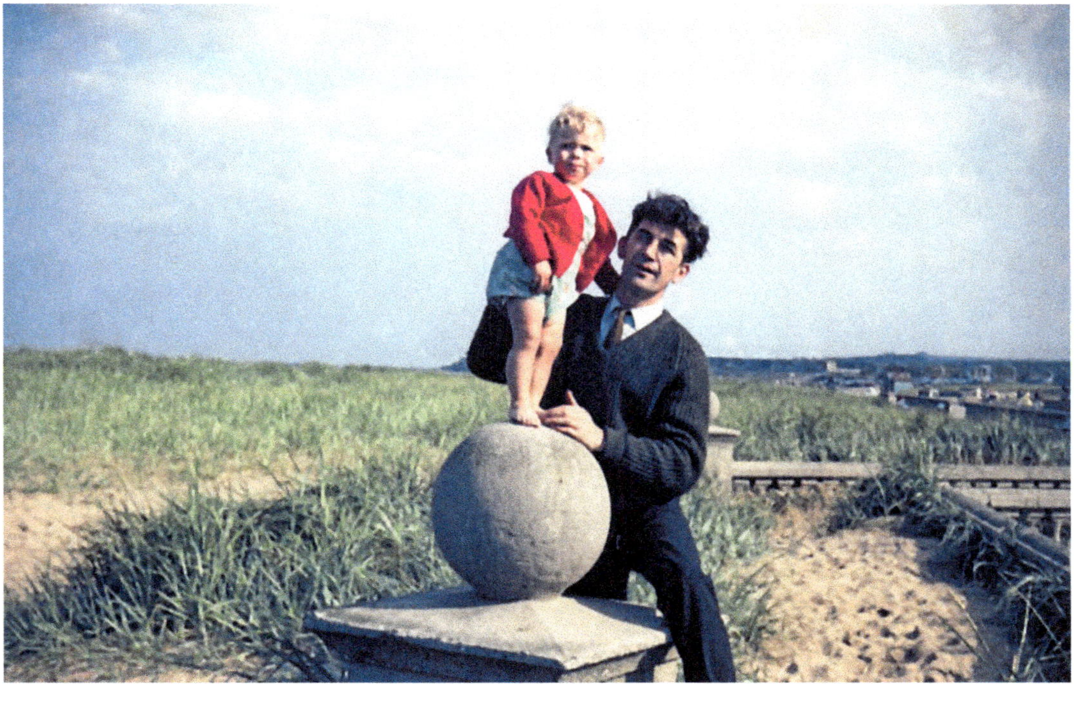

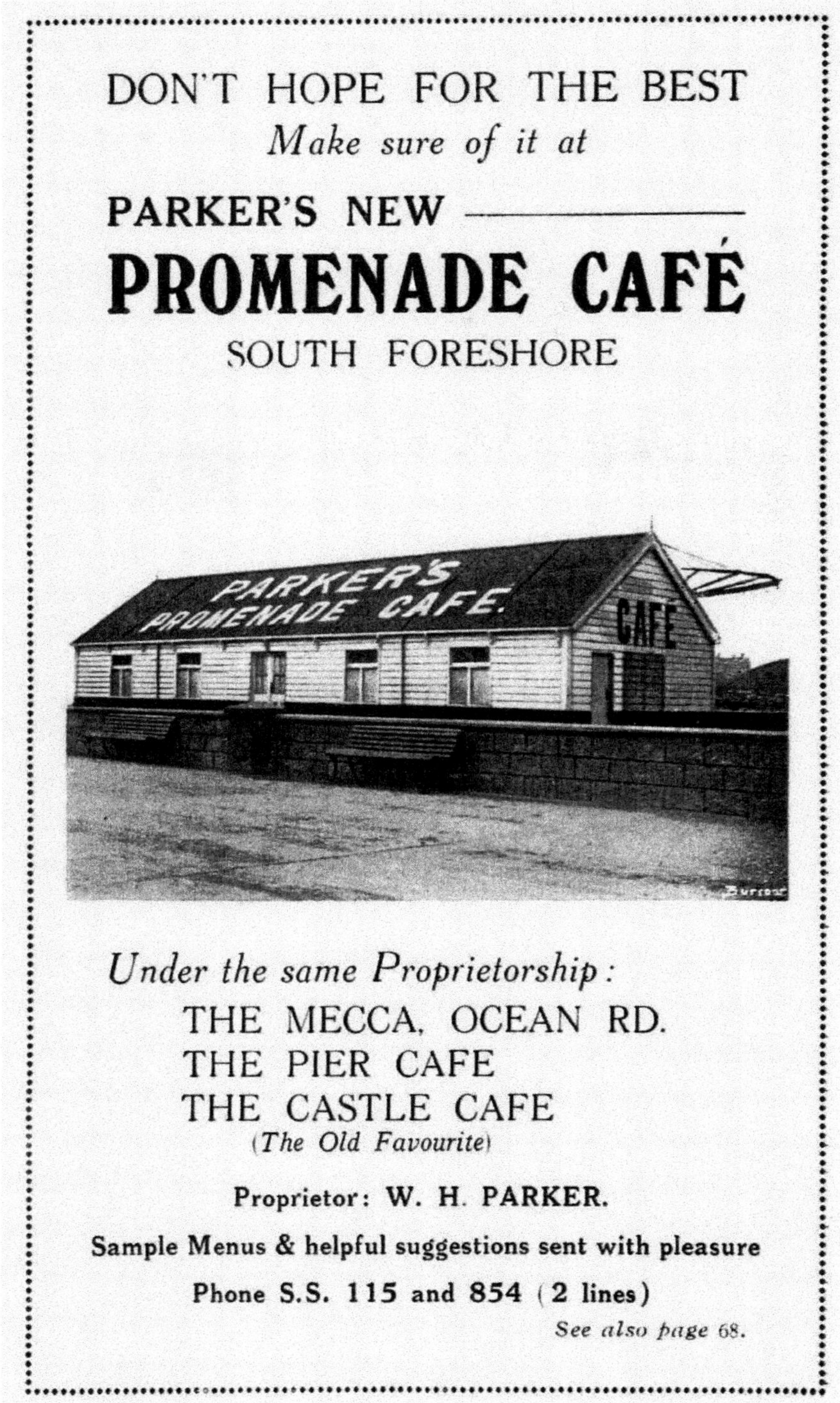

Above and opposite: Somewhere to Eat
There is no better companion to sea air than ice cream and coffee, or even fish and chips. In the early days of Minchella's and Colman's, both justifiably famous (at least in Souths Shields), there were a number of other establishments, two of which are illustrated here.

YOUR DAY OUT will be more enjoyable if you make THE

MARINE PARKS CAFE

PIER APPROACH

YOUR RENDEZVOUS

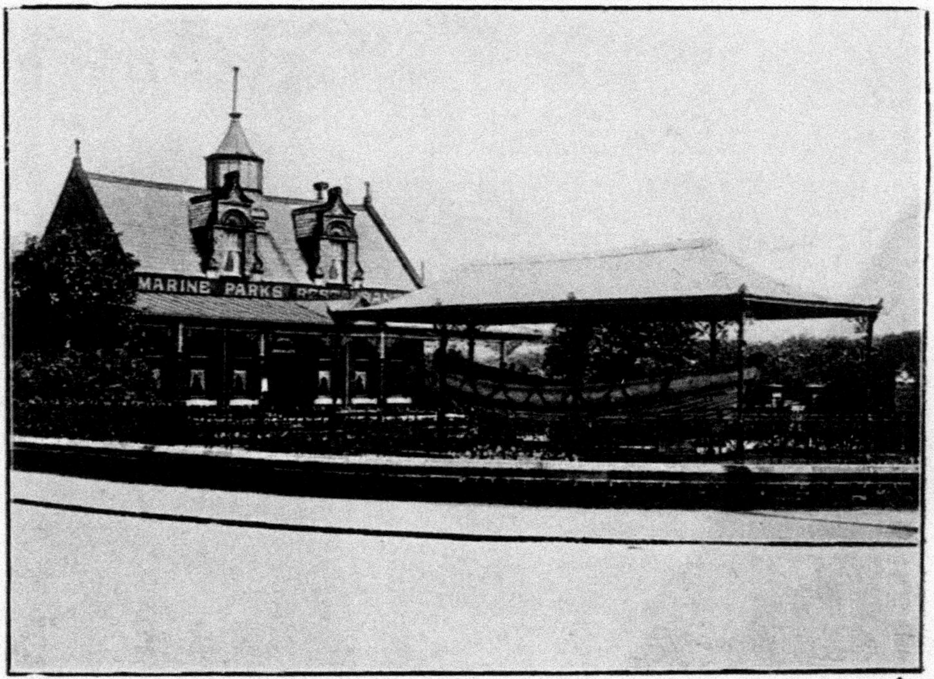

Cold Luncheons, Teas and Suppers.

All kinds of parties catered for.

Specimen Menu sent if desired.

Write for terms. *Ices a Speciality.*

Proprietor - - C. H. USHER

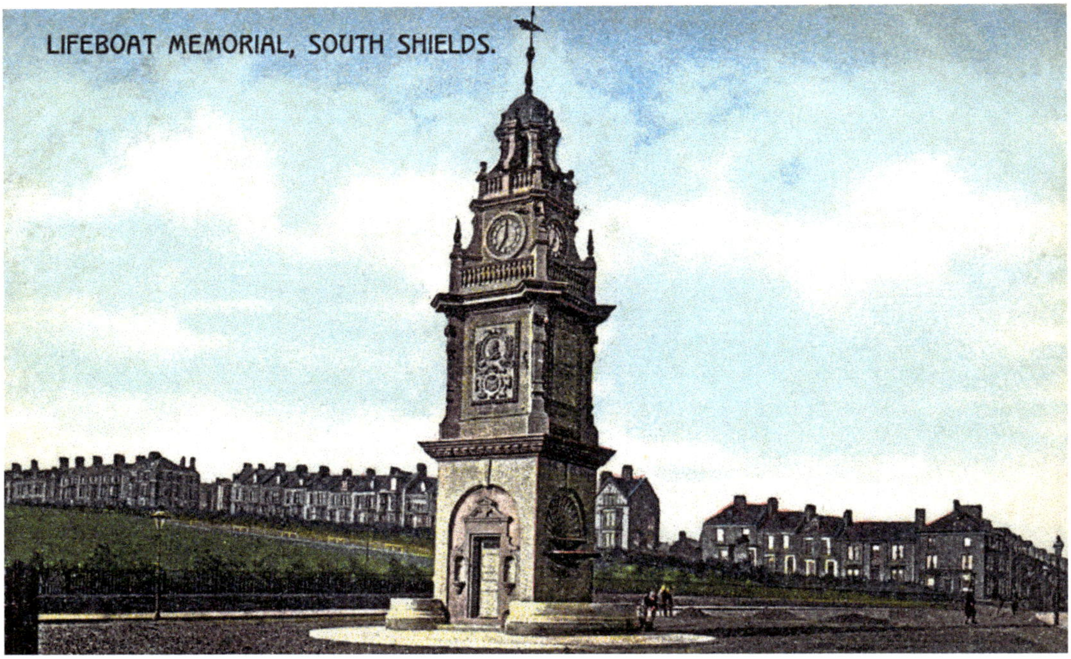

Wouldhave and Greathead Memorial

The Wouldhave and Greathead memorial at the pier head. There has been a great deal of debate over who was responsible for the invention of the lifeboat and we believe Wouldhave's claim was slightly undermined by his capacity for swearing.

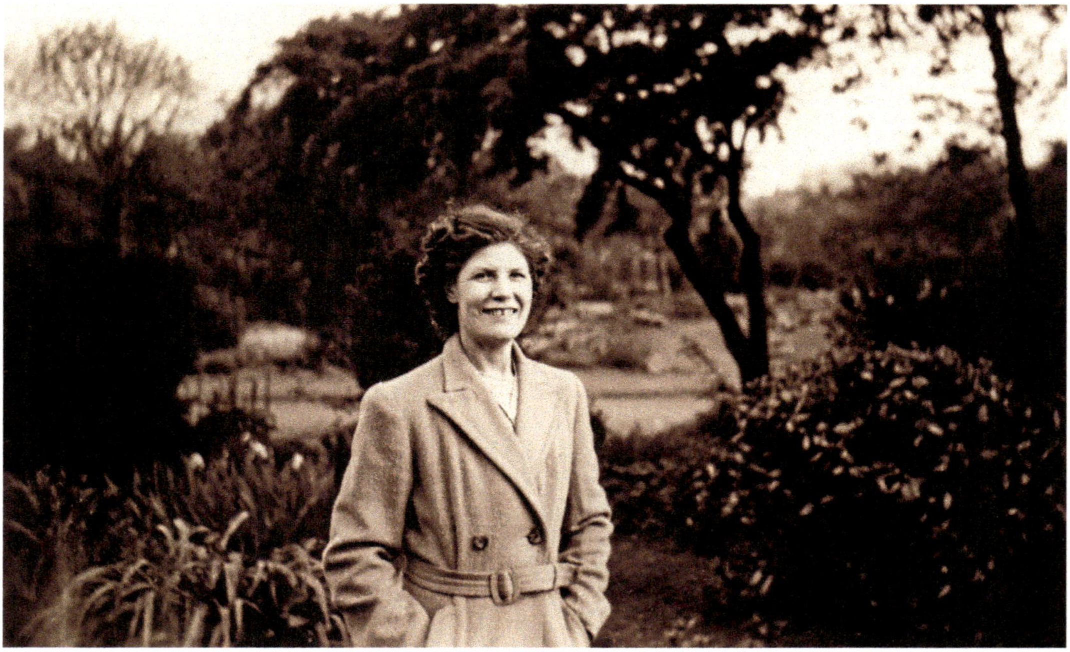

Elisabeth Wilkinson

The parks were a justifiable source of local pride with local people. Pictured is Elisabeth Wilkinson, a great believer in the benefits of the fresh air the parks afforded.

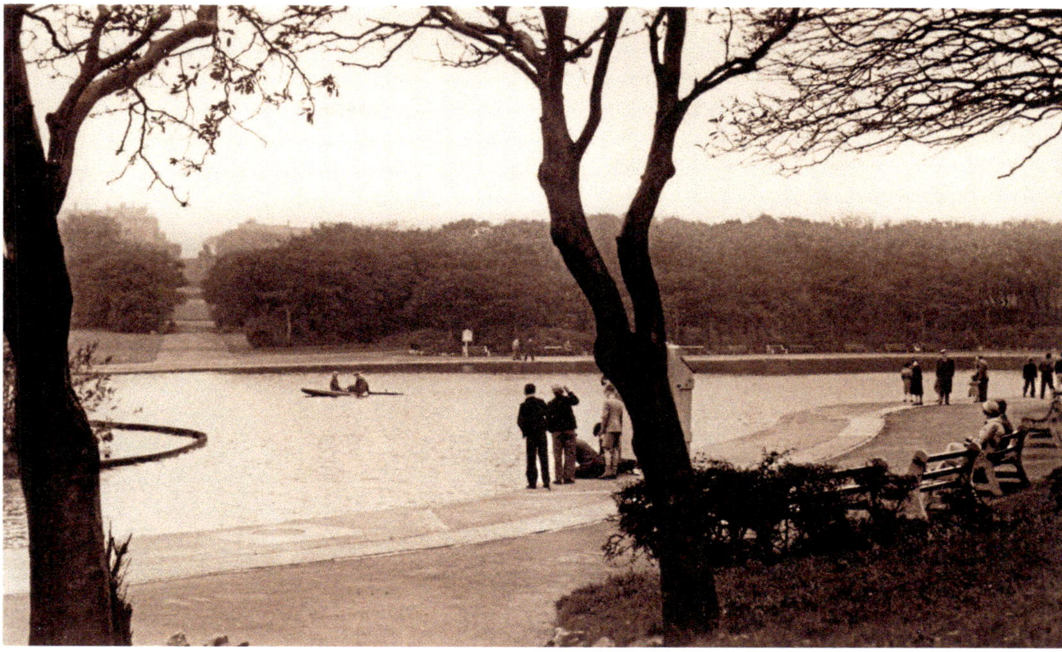

South Marine Park
A postcard view of South Marine Park.

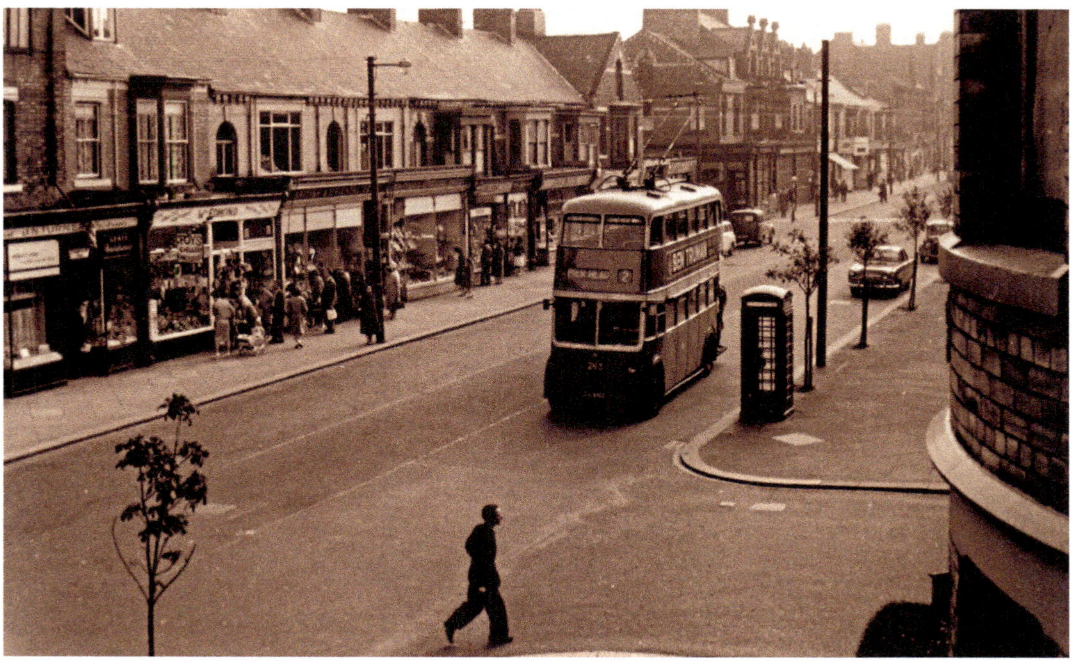

Ocean Road
A late 1950s view of the 'sunny side' of Ocean Road. The various souvenir emporiums into which visitors and townspeople once eagerly peered have now been replaced by a very well-regarded collection of restaurants. The image was taken by transport photographer David Packer, who was a frequent visitor to the town.

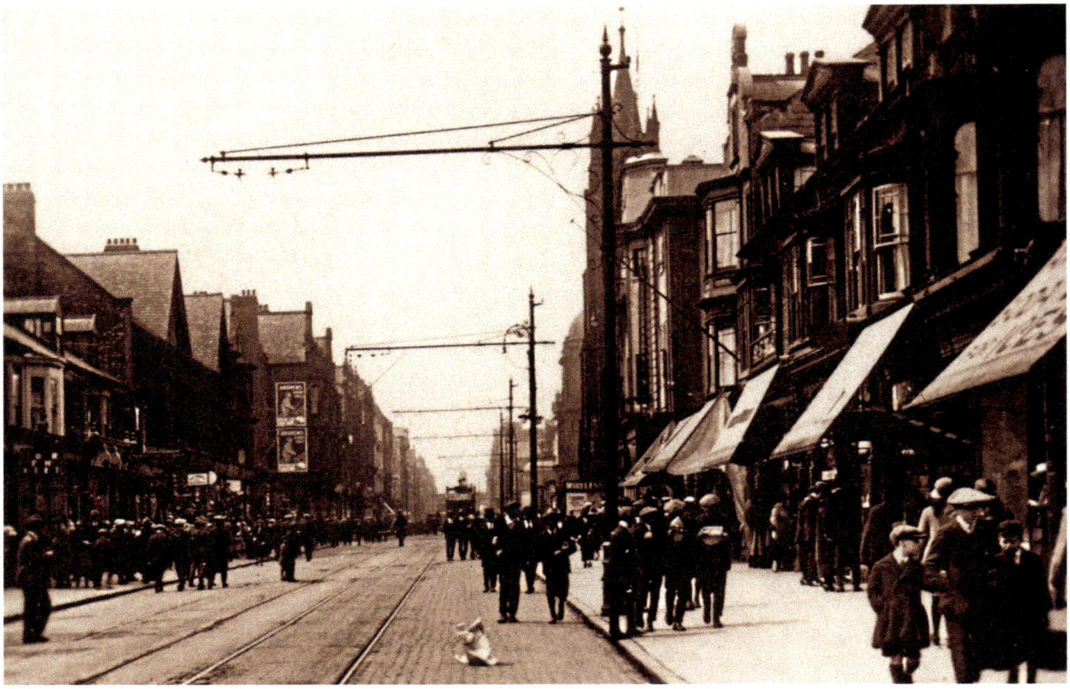

Ocean Road Towards the Market

Looking along the packed pavements of Ocean Road towards the market. Many of the buildings to the right, including the Congregational Church (whose tower is just visible), have now gone.

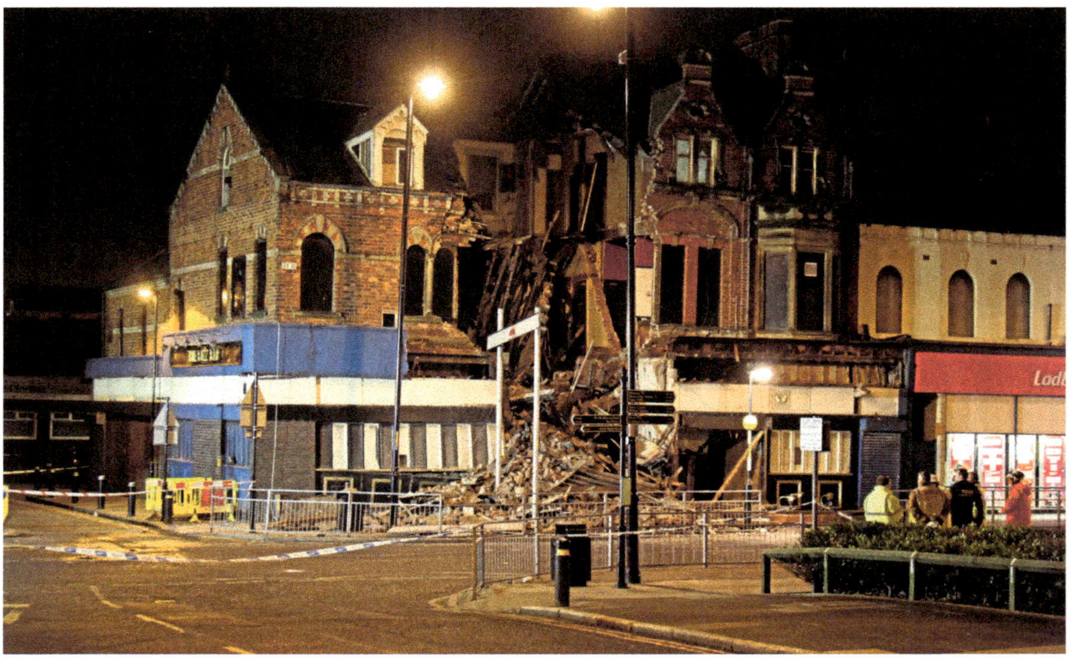

Ocean Road

Some of the formerly well-kept buildings of Ocean Road met their end when they collapsed on 9 March 2012.

Grand Electric Theatre

OCEAN ROAD

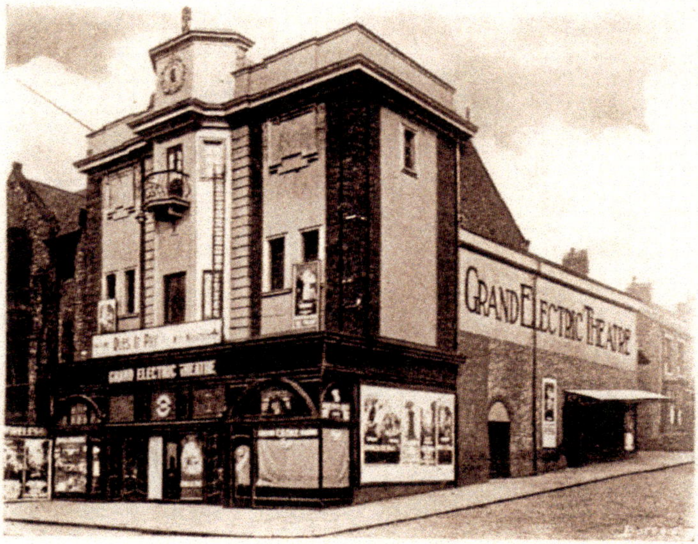

6.30——Twice Nightly——8.40

Matinee Saturday——2.

FOR PICTURES THAT ENTERTAIN & AMUSE

Telephone - - - **160**

Stalls **9d.** Circle **6d.** Pit **4d.**

Grand Electric Theatre

An image of the now long-demolished Grand Electric Theatre on the junction of Ocean Road and Pollard Street. It opened its doors on 23 May 1910 and was destroyed by fire on 11 March 1932. I wonder if they were happy neighbours with the adjoining Congregational Church? The site of the Grand Electric was used as a car park for many years. The site of the church remains undeveloped to date.

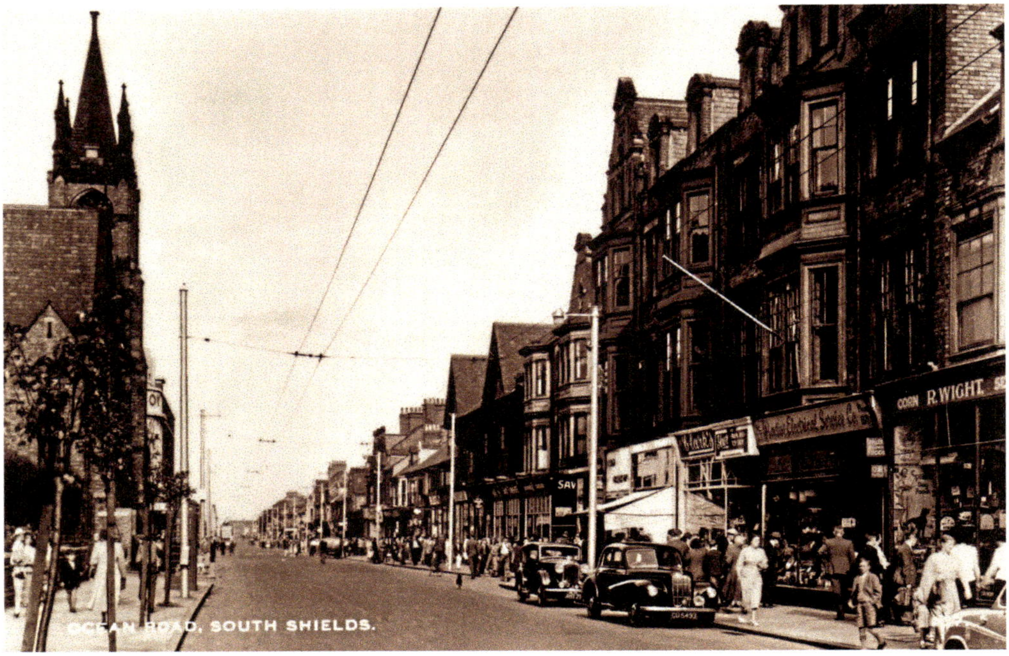

Ocean Road Towards the Pier Head

A 1950s postcard view of Ocean Road looking towards the pier head. Several of the buildings in the middle right have been swept away to be replaced by the junction with Anderson Street.

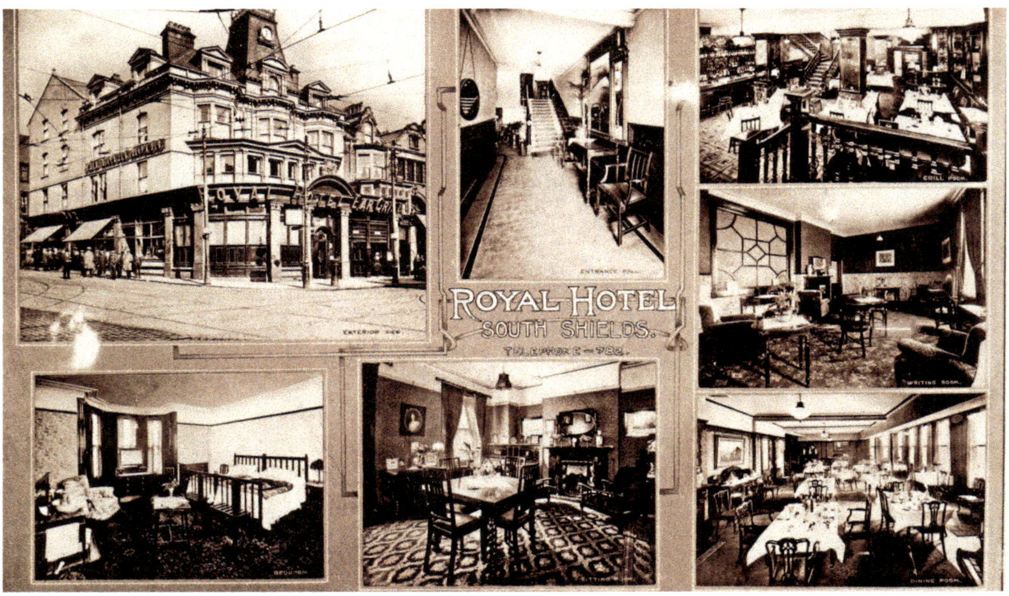

Royal Hotel

The Royal Hotel is still very much in business, although now simply as a pub. The building's profile is still largely unaltered, although the front has been modified to serve a variety of retail purposes including W. Marr & Sons tobacconists. For a while 'Marr's Courner' was a popular meeting place in the town.

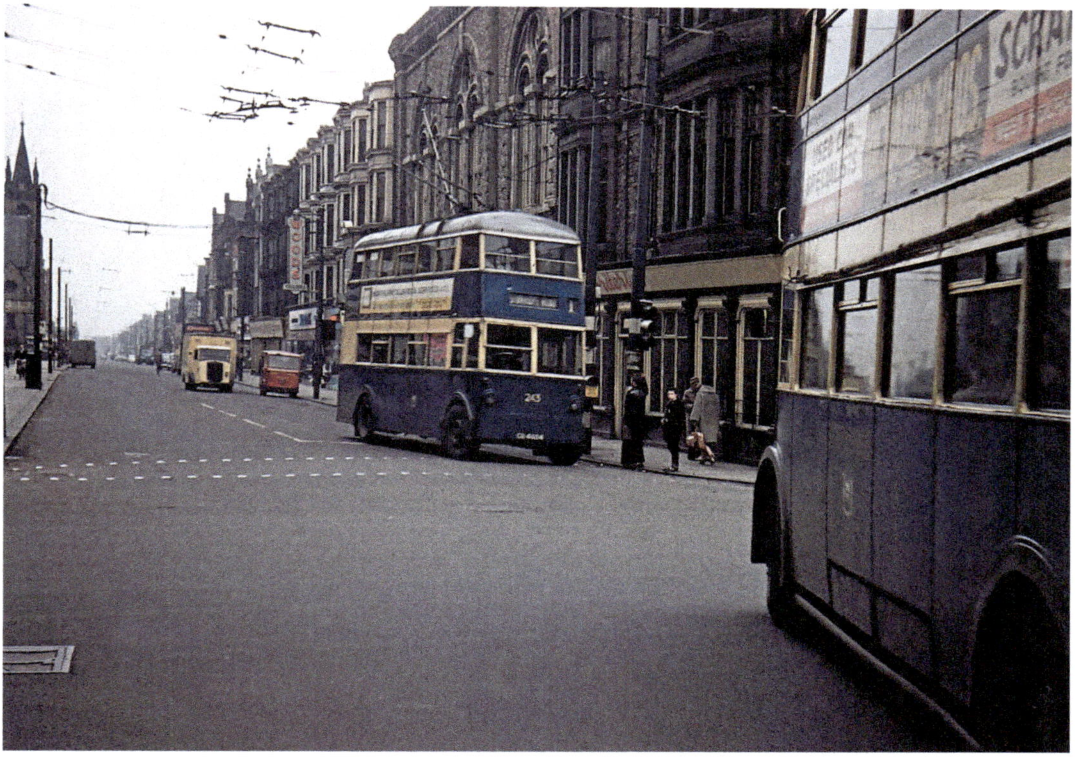

Above and below: Trolleybuses

Corporation trolleybuses in their twilight days on the junction of King Street and Fowler Street.

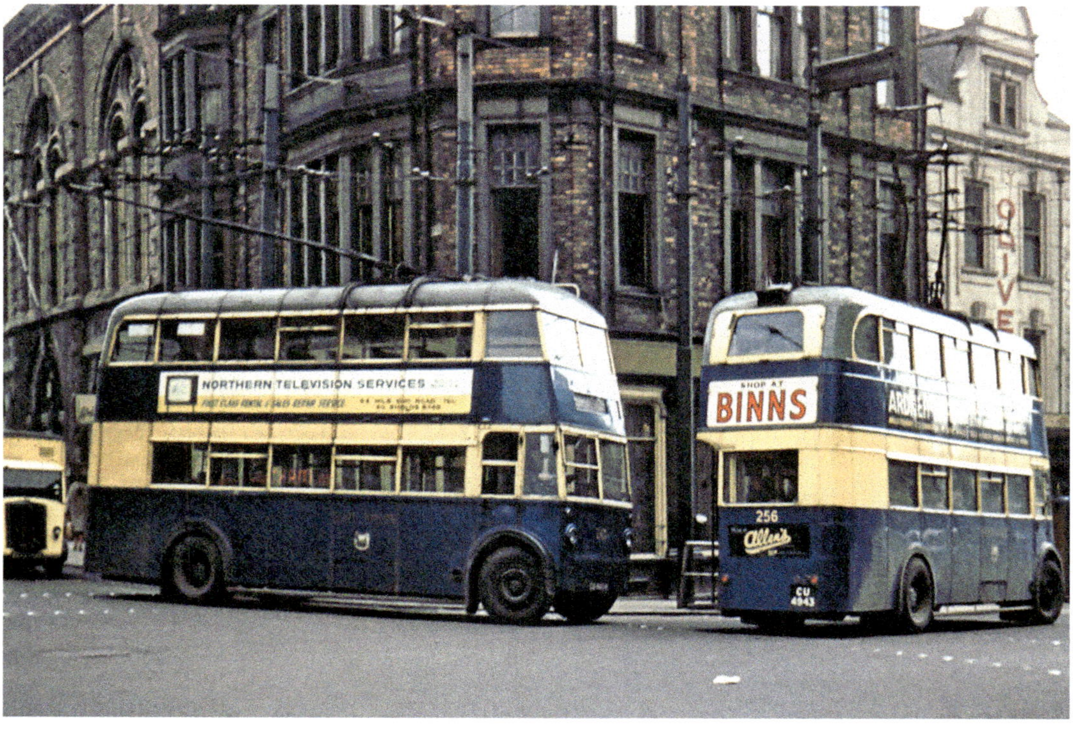

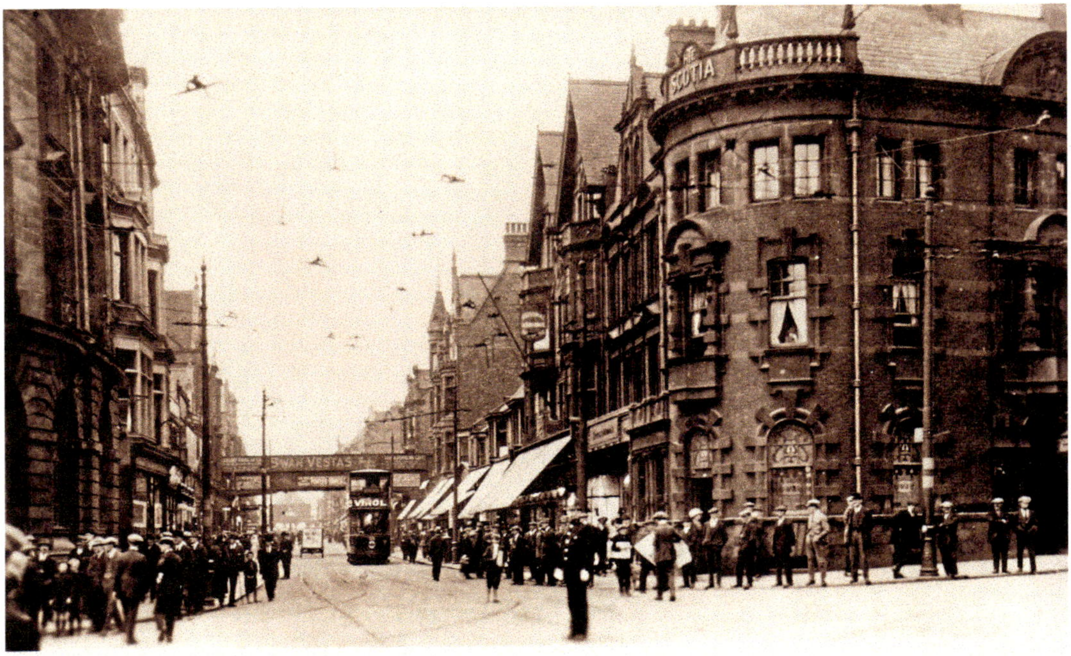

KING STREET, SOUTH SHIELDS.

Above and below: King Street

King Street in the 1920s with curious amounts of men standing on the street corner. I believe this corner was a popular meeting place for all kinds of activities. Below is a similar view *c.* 1960, but this time the scene is almost deserted.

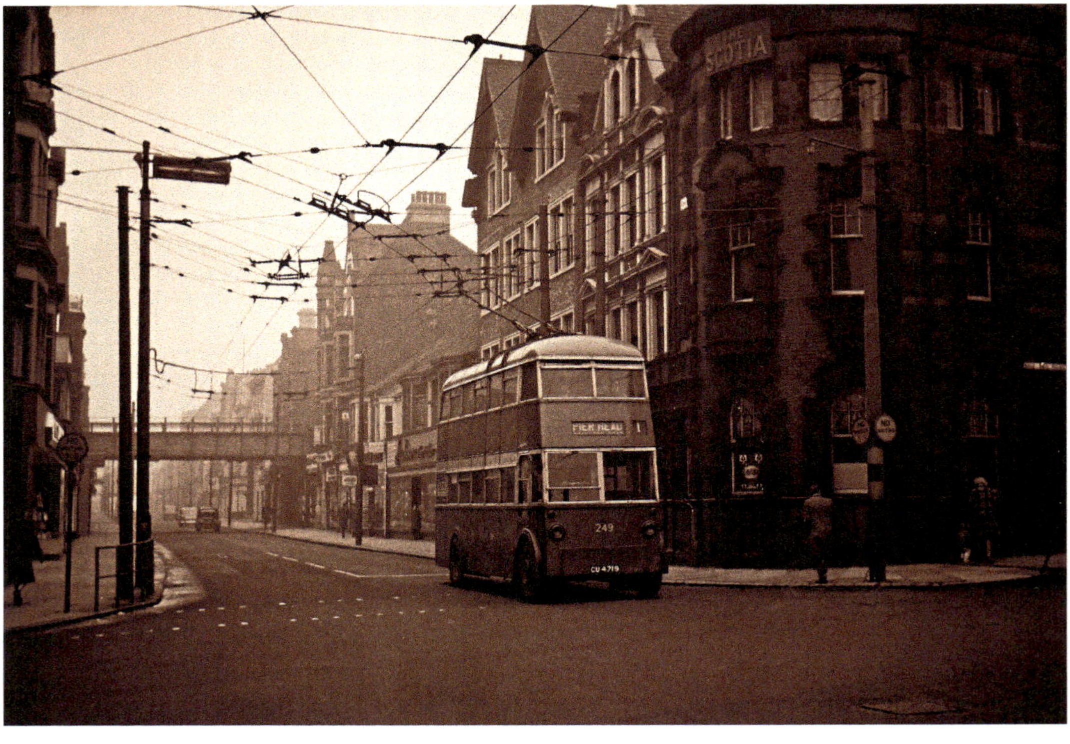

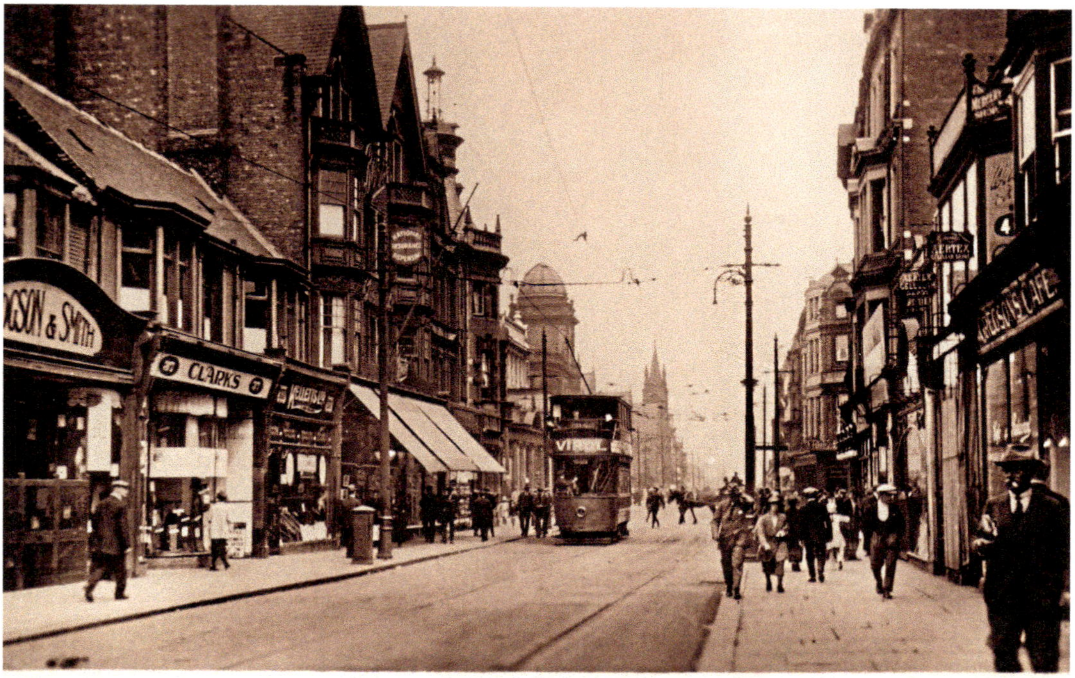

KING STREET, SOUTH SHIELDS.

King Street Towards Ocean Road

King Street looking towards Ocean Road *c.* 1930. The prosperity and importance of King Street during this time can be determined from the quality of the signage and shop displays.

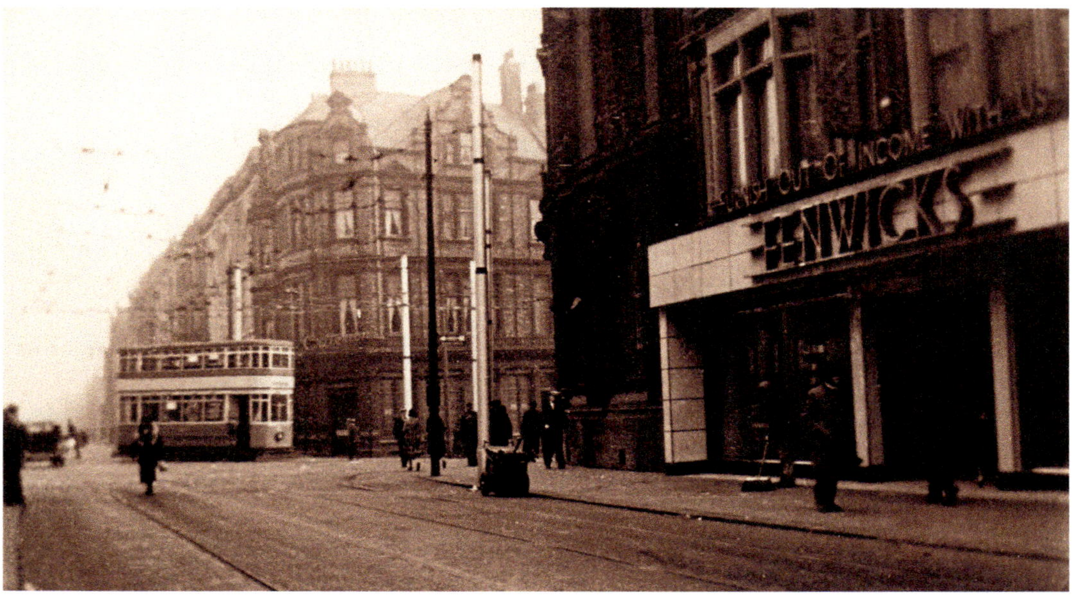

Fenwick's

This image shows what is presumably a branch of Newcastle's Fenwick's in South Shields and its intriguing slogan reads 'Furnish out of income with us'. Is this a discount store selling the people of Shield a 'champagne lifestyle at beer money prices'?

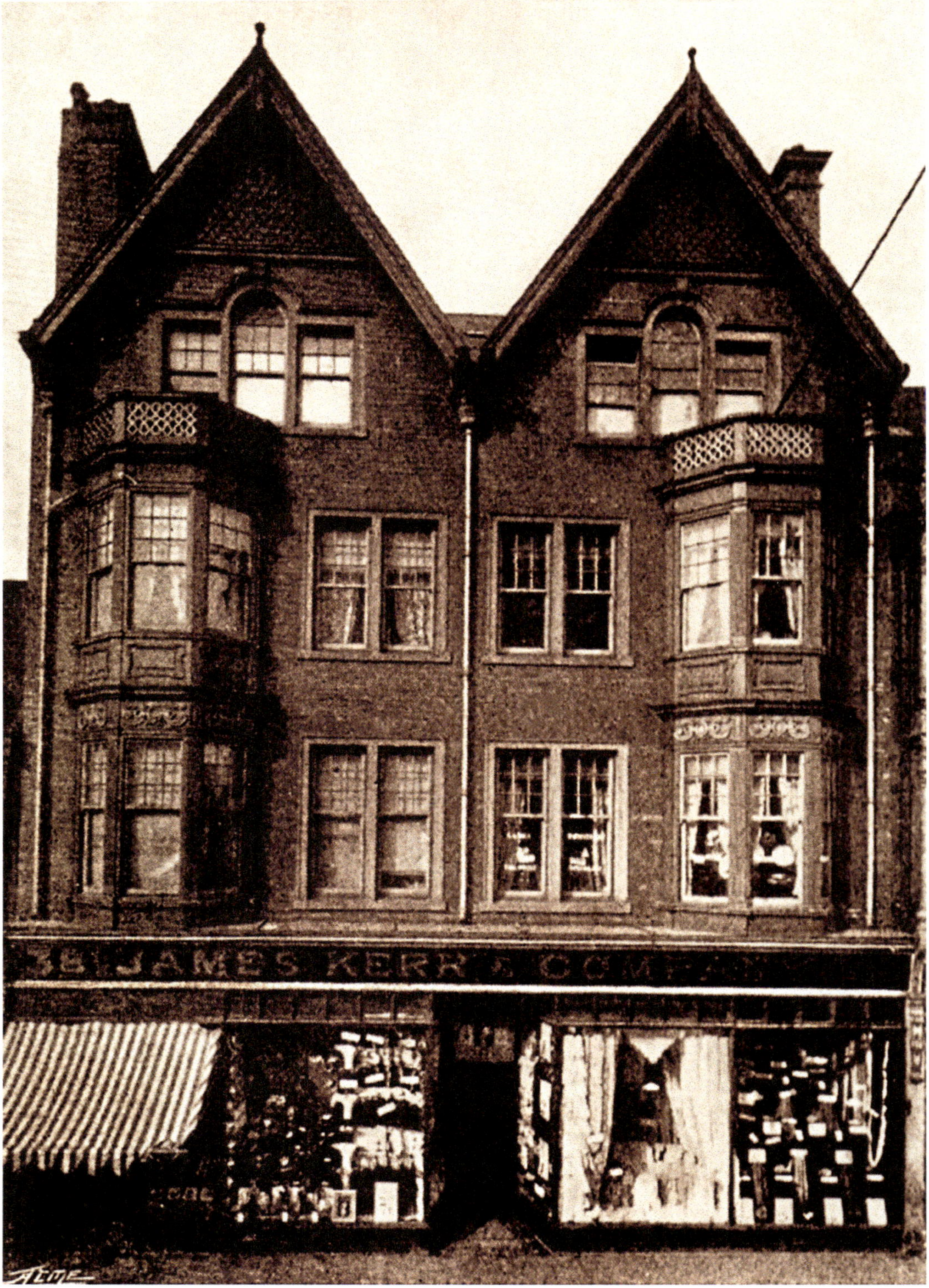

James Kerr & Company
The frontage of James Kerr & Company, King Street.

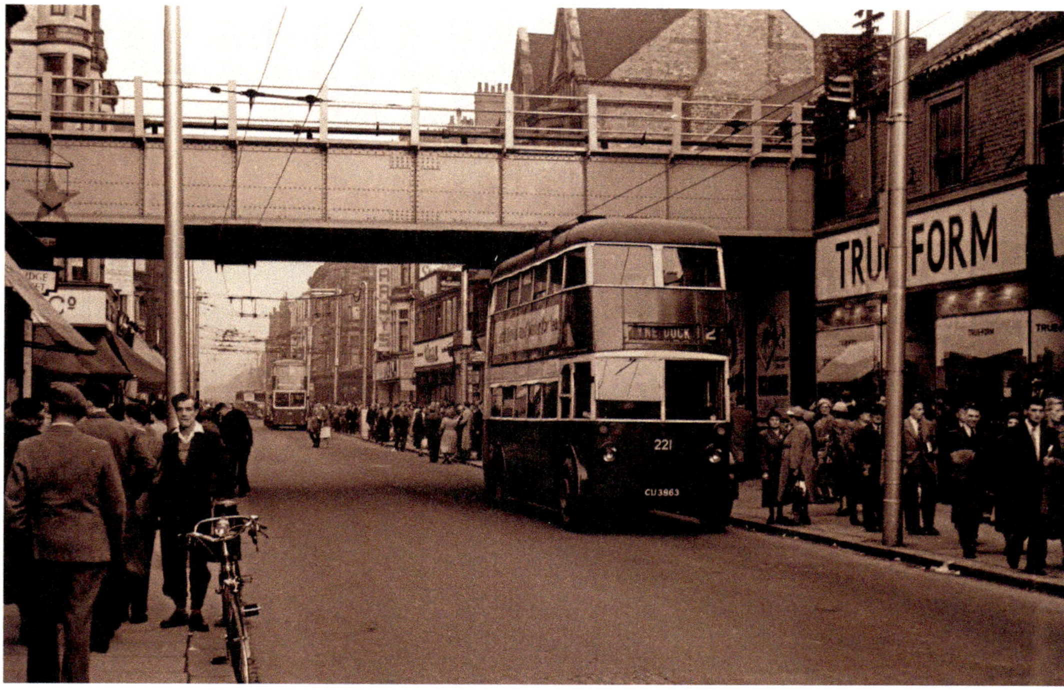

Above and below: King Street, *c*. 1960

A busy view of King Street *c*. 1960. This is another taken by transport photographer David Packer. Below is a 2015 image of what I believe is the same area. Pedestrianisation has long been in place, and King Street is not doing so well.

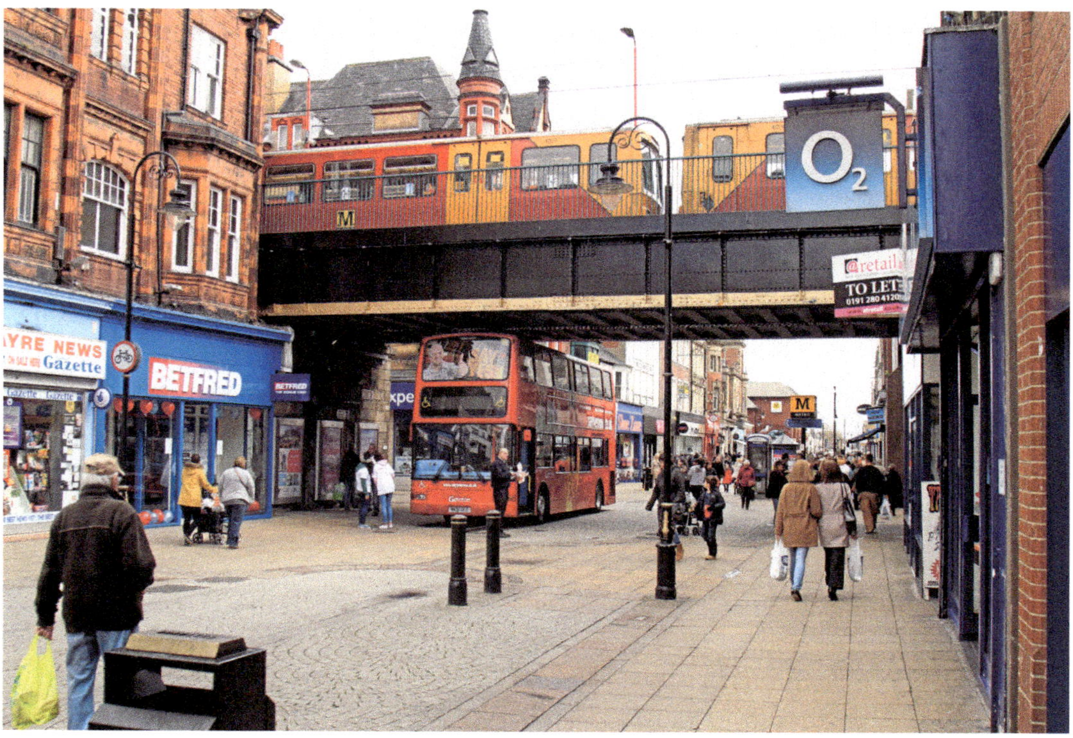

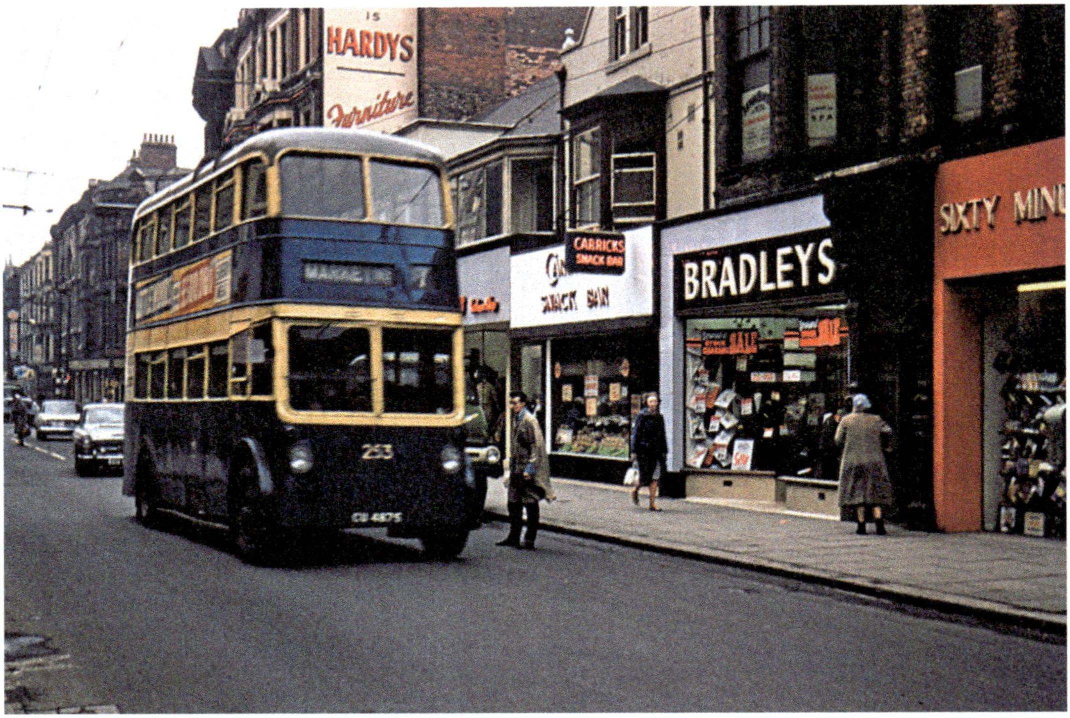

King Street, *c.* 1960
A trolleybus passes along a 'still doing well' King Street *c.* 1960.

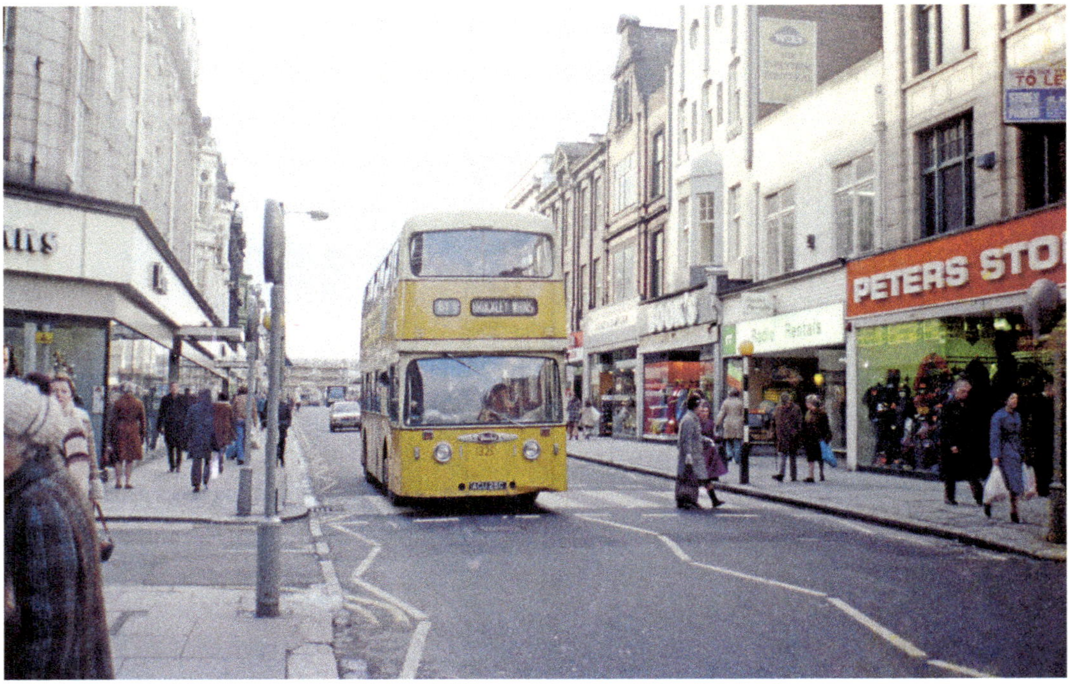

King Street
King Street, now one way and preparing for pedestrianisation. Radio Rentals is to the right.

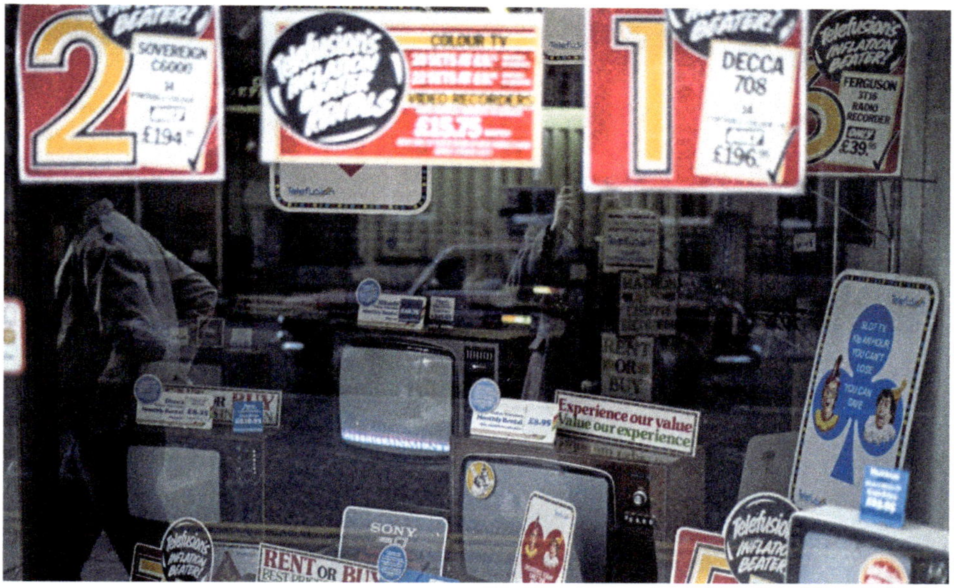

Radio Rentals
The window of Radio Rentals. I believe the shop also did a brisk trade in ex-rental TVs and VCRS.

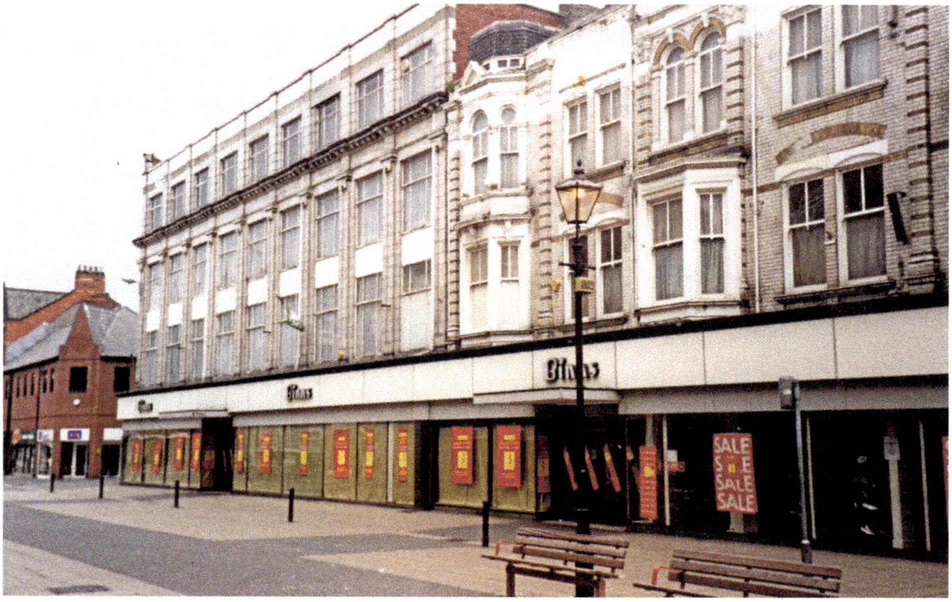

Binns Ltd
The South Shields premises of Binns Ltd shortly before closure. The shop was clearly an amalgamation of several newer and older buildings and could probably tell a few stories today if they had not all been demolished. In Binns, as in other shops, money and receipts were quickly moved around the building by a system of canisters being inserted into vacuum tubes. We suspect you have to be over fifty to remember this and even older to remember how it actually worked. During the demolition of the building parts of the system became visible. A section of it came into the possession of Dennis Boad, formerly a Corporation bus conductor, postman, collector of everything to do with South Shields and one of the people to whom this book is dedicated.

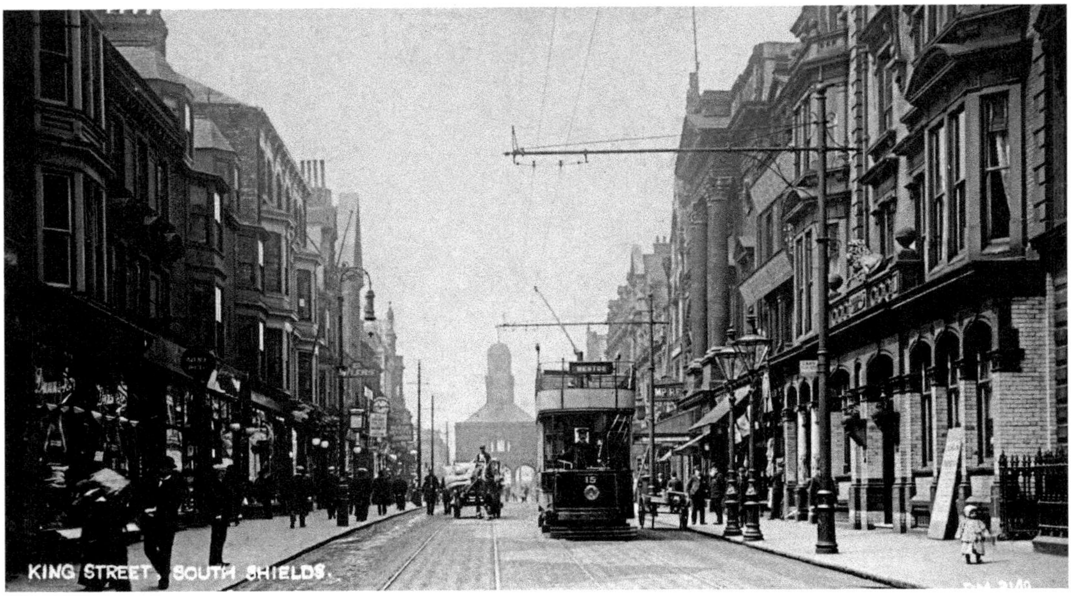

King Street, *c.* 1907

What we believe is a *c.* 1907 view of King Street. Visible to the right is one of the great 'lost' buildings of South Shields: the Golden Lion Hotel. Also visible is the now demolished entrance to what later became the Marks & Spencer building.

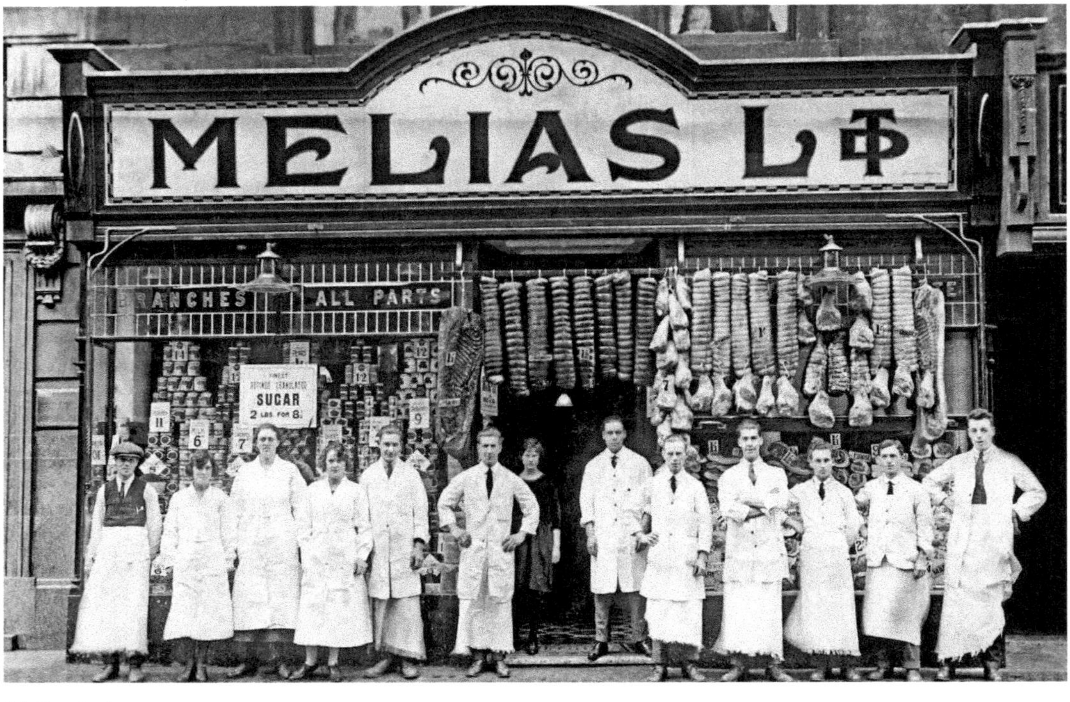

Melias Ltd

The staff and premises of Melias Ltd, located on King Street on the south side near the market. Although the name is no longer familiar, the building is still very much with us, surviving the bombing of the marketplace during the Second World War.

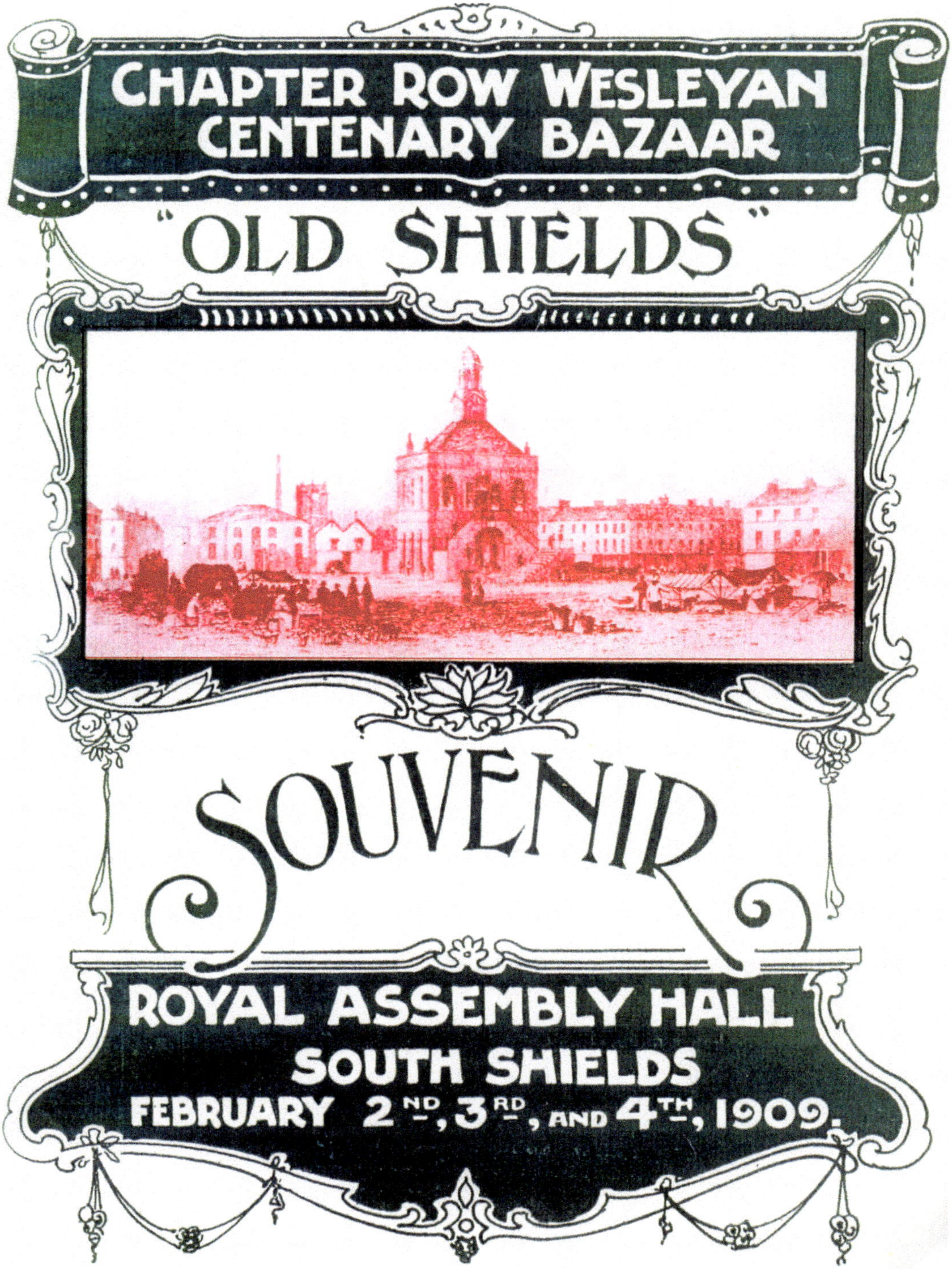

Wesleyan Bazaar

One of the oldest visual representations of South Shields Market presented as nostalgia in 1909 for the brochure of the Wesleyan Bazaar.

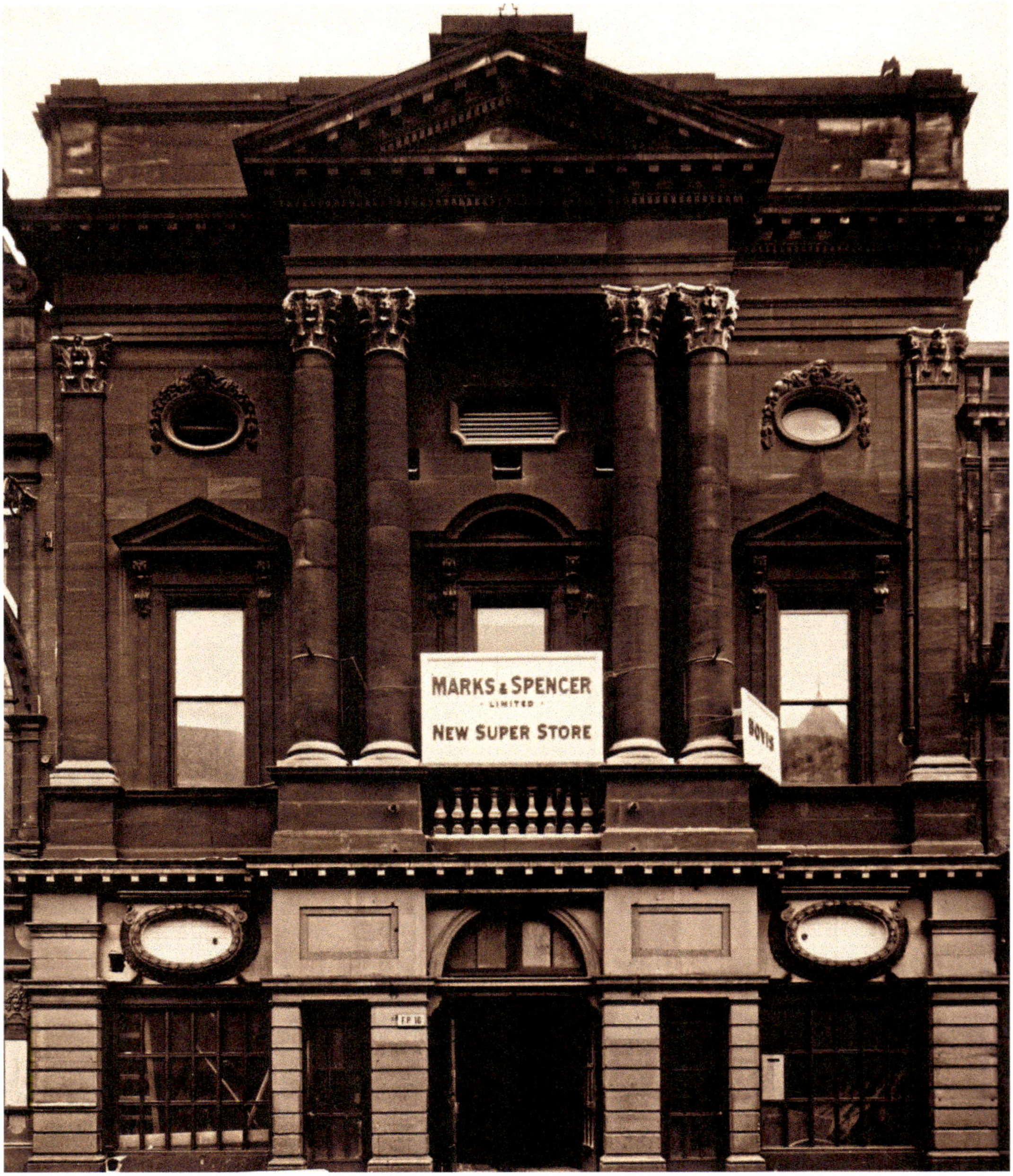

Above and opposite: Marks & Spencer

Marks & Spencer opened their well-known King Street store in 1934. During its conversion from a theatre the rather imposing entrance was removed. The store was very successful and we believe a company policy was to display goods, especially clothing, in as near as possible to daylight conditions so the customer would be aware of what they were getting and the prices would be easily visible. Despite local protest, the store closed its doors in King Street in March 2014.

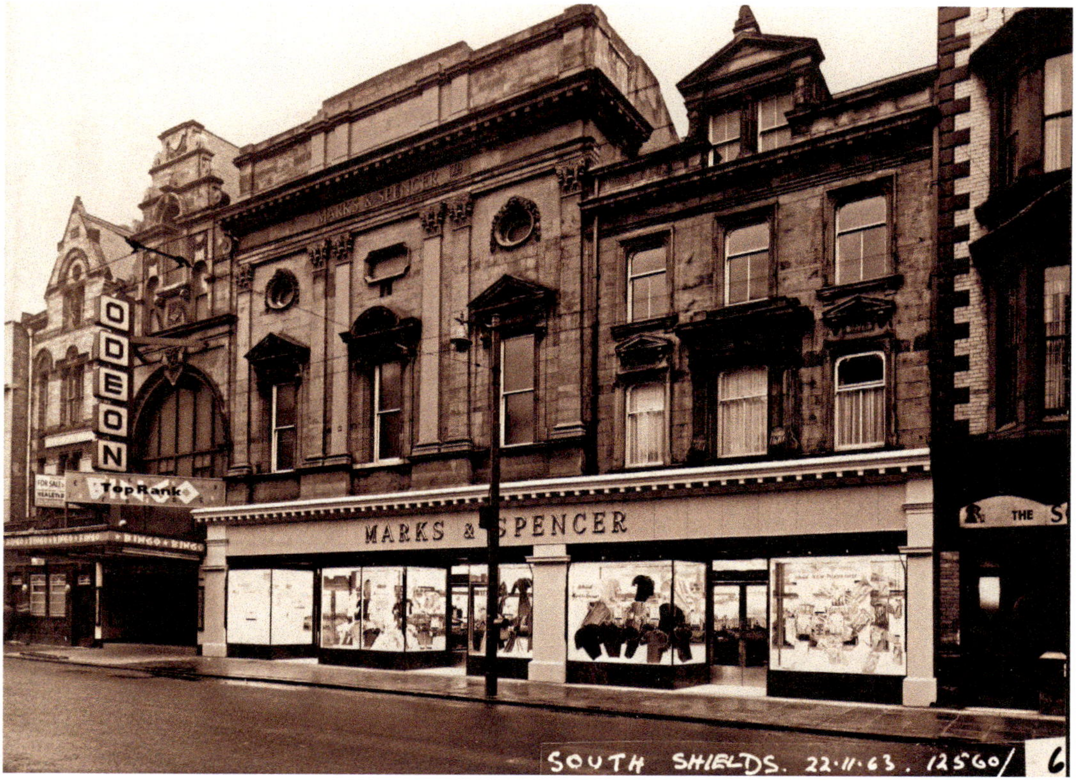
ODEON
TopRank
MARKS & SPENCER
SOUTH SHIELDS. 22·11·63. 12560/ 6

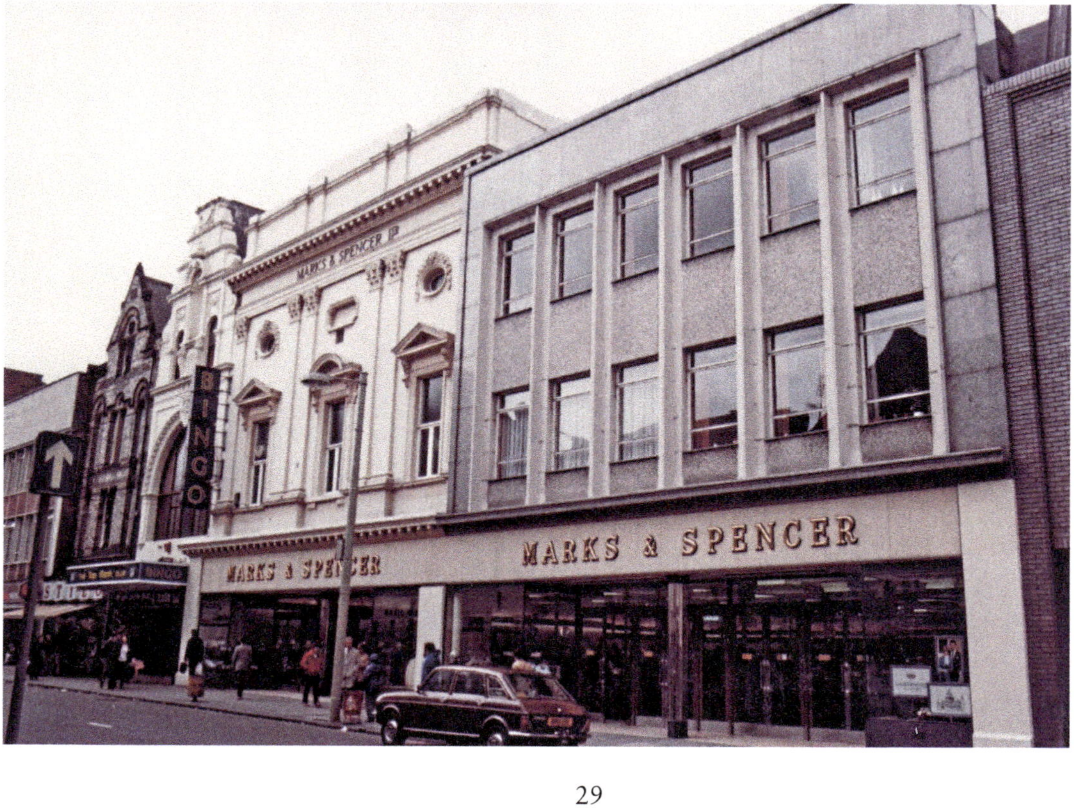
MARKS & SPENCER LTD
BINGO
MARKS & SPENCER

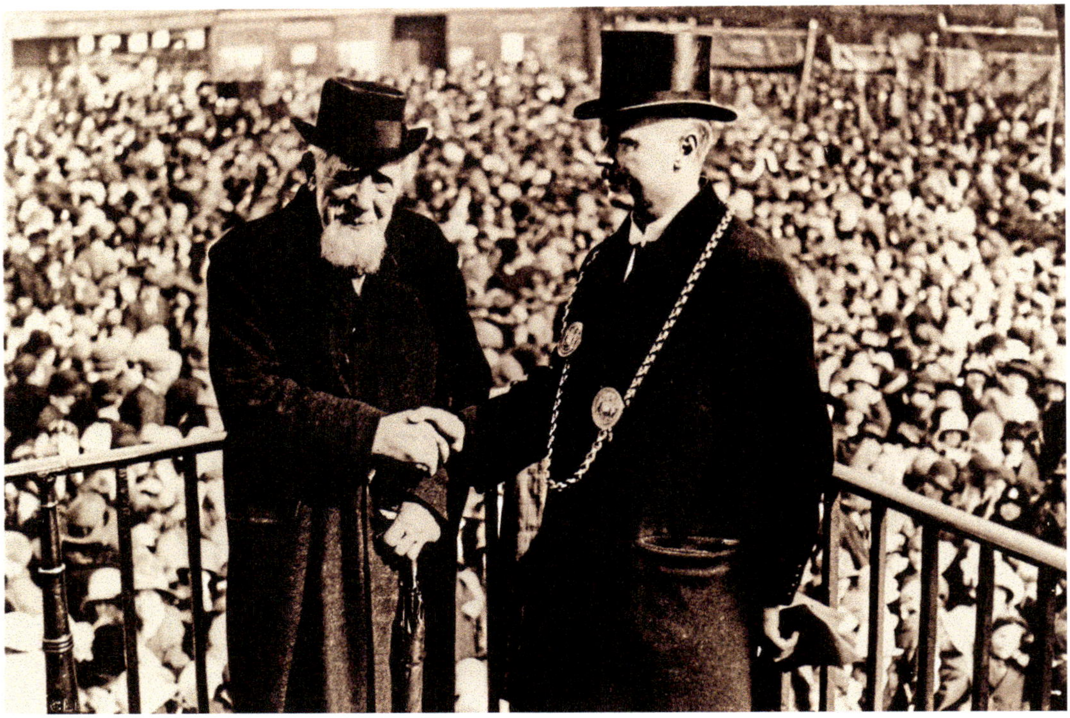

Good Friday at the Market Square, 1925.
Mr W. Owen is being congratulated by the then thoroughly modern-looking mayor for not missing a gathering in seventy years. In his lifetime Mr Owen would have seen the construction of the piers, the arrival of the horse trams and their replacement by electric trams, and all kinds of wonders unique to the town.

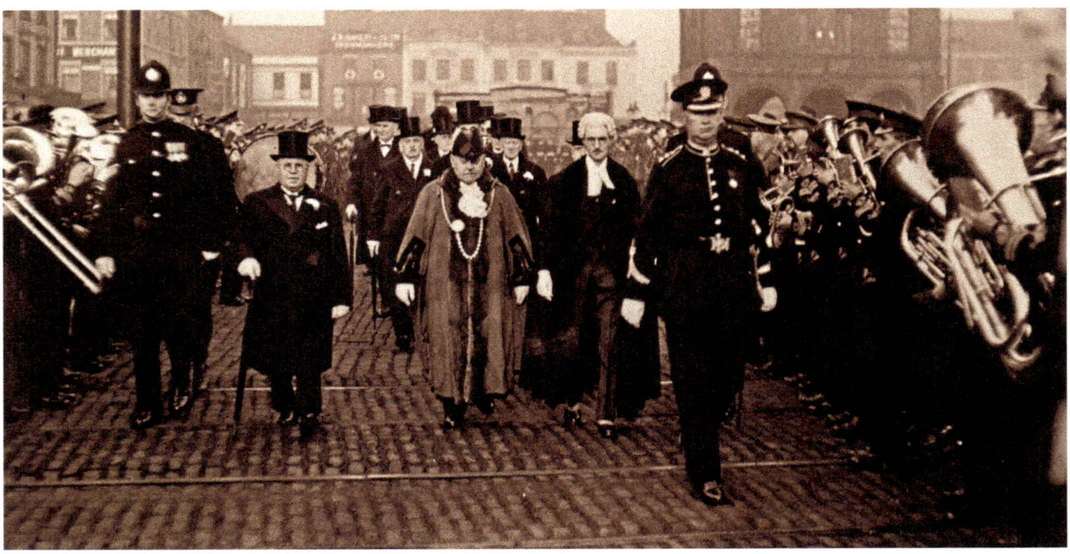

Mayor's Parade
Mayor Samuel Lawman crossing the Market Square during the mayor's Sunday church parade on 12 November 1933.

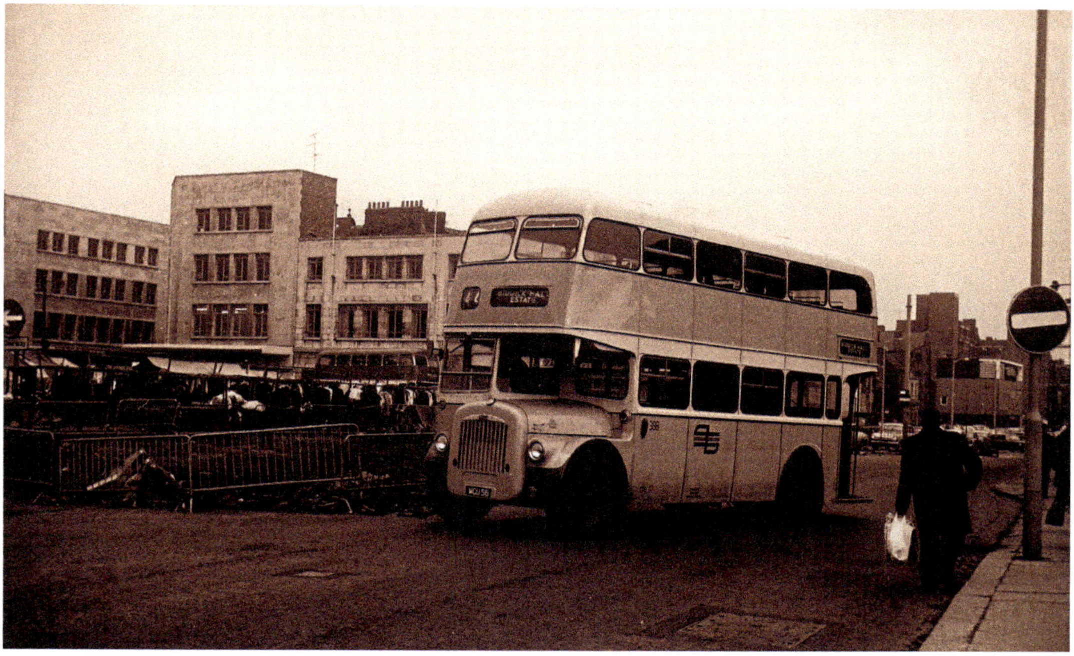

Buses

A bus bound for Biddick Hall pulls away from the market square. This bus is in the livery of the then newly formed Tyneside Passenger Transport executive while the bus behind is still in the colours of South Shields Corporation.

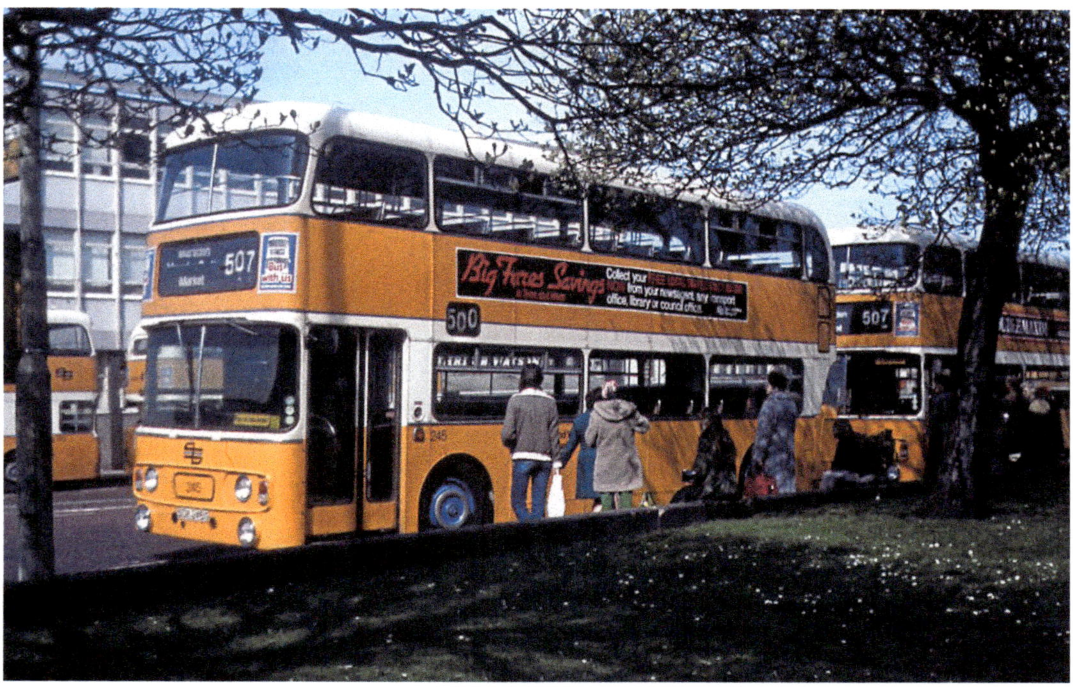

507

Not one but two 507s waiting at the Market Square.

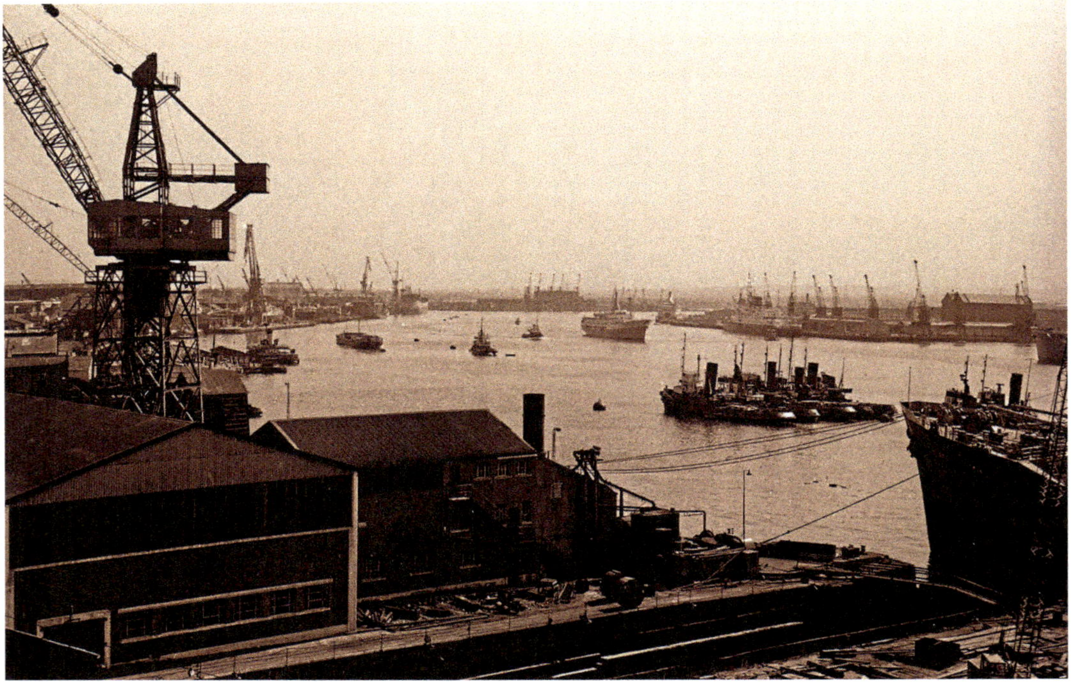

Brigham & Cowan's Yard, *c.* 1963

Brigham & Cowan's Yard seen from River Drive *c.* 1963 The yard was established in 1876 by Thomas Brigham and Malcolm Cowan. At its peak Brigham & Cowan had an extensive ship repair business with three drydocks at South Shields. The company became part of British Shipbuilders in 1977 and closed in 1982. It has now been redeveloped as housing.

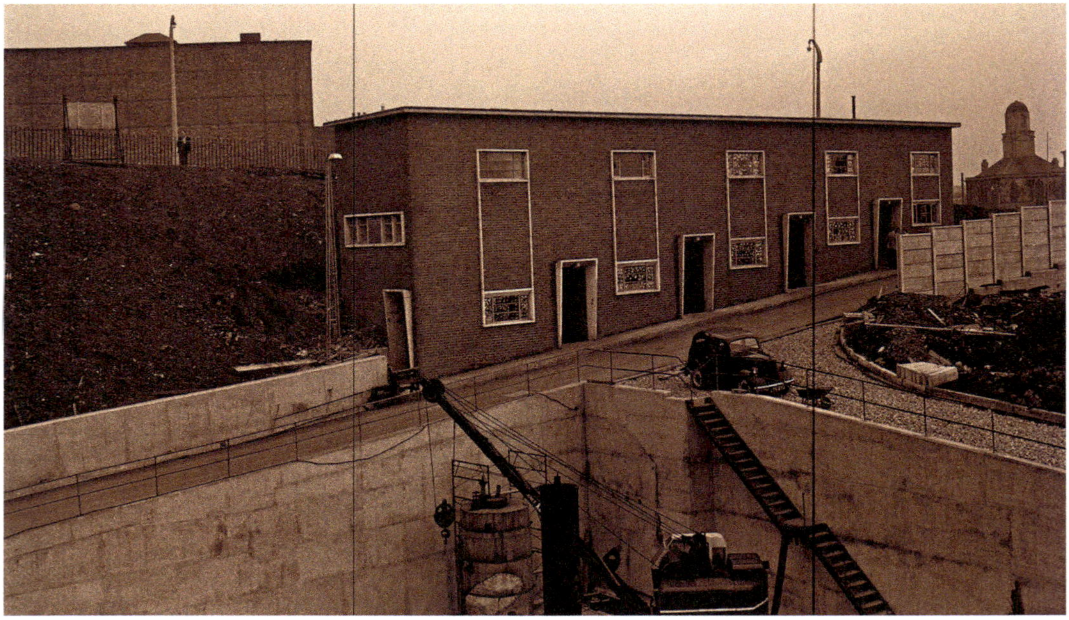

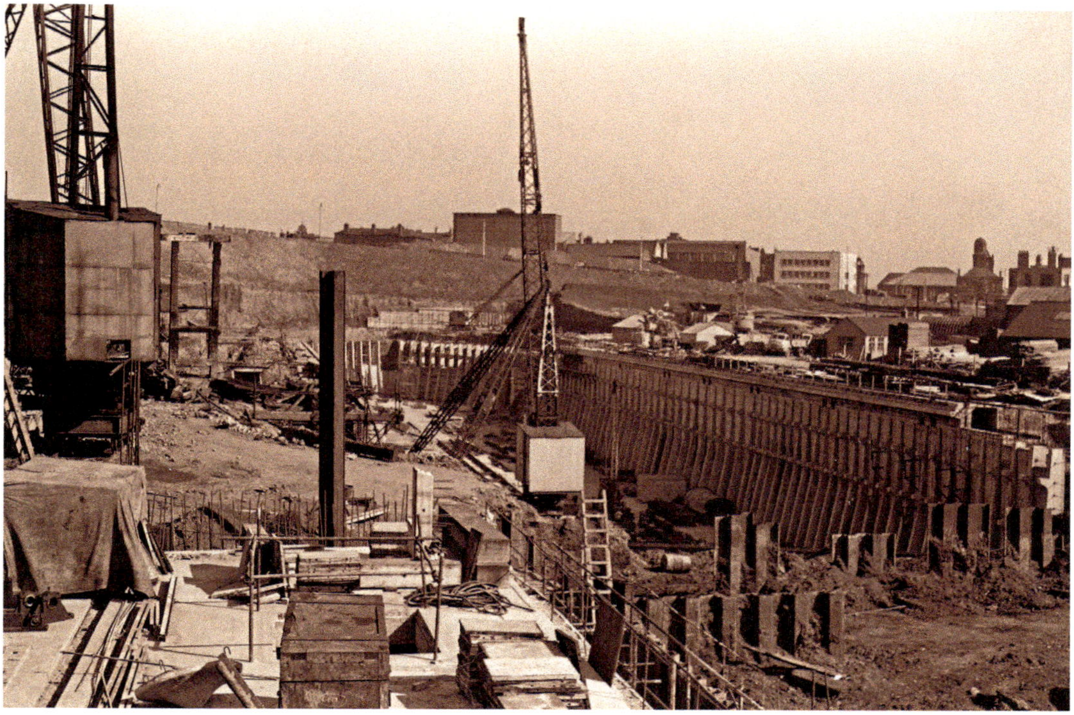

Bingham's Yard

Construction work underway at Brigham's Yard in the mid-1950s. This was taken by 'Rolley' Headley, who worked at the yard as a bricklayer and was commissioned by the owners to take a series of pictures.

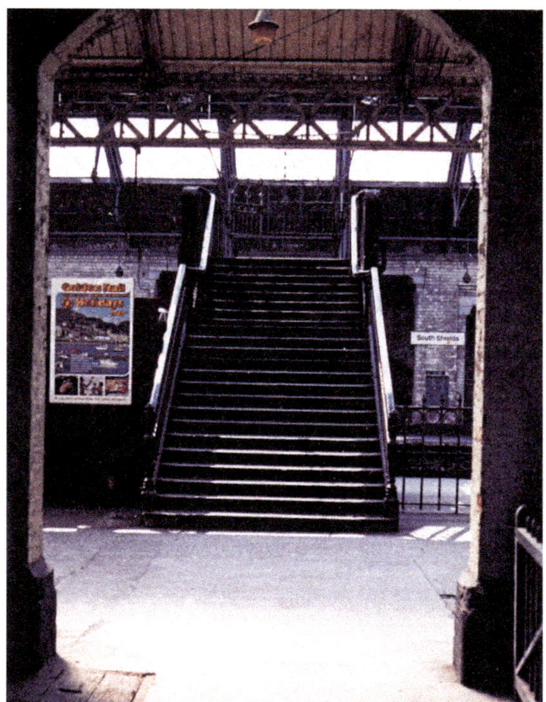

South Shields train station.

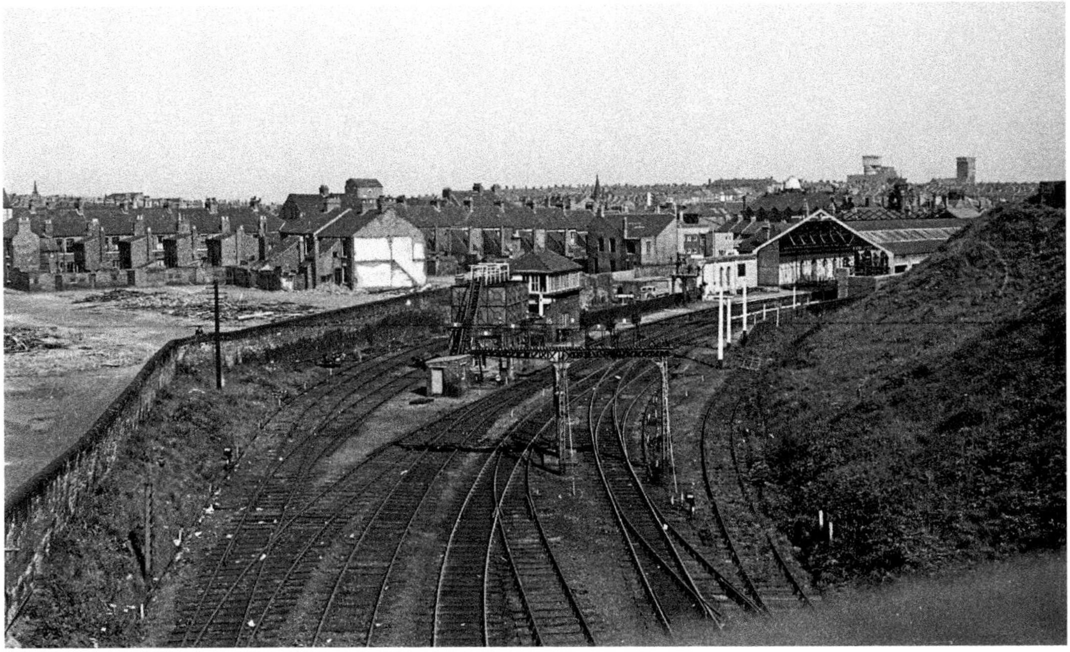

Station Yard
South Shields station yard *c.* 1964. Housing demolition on the left is well underway.

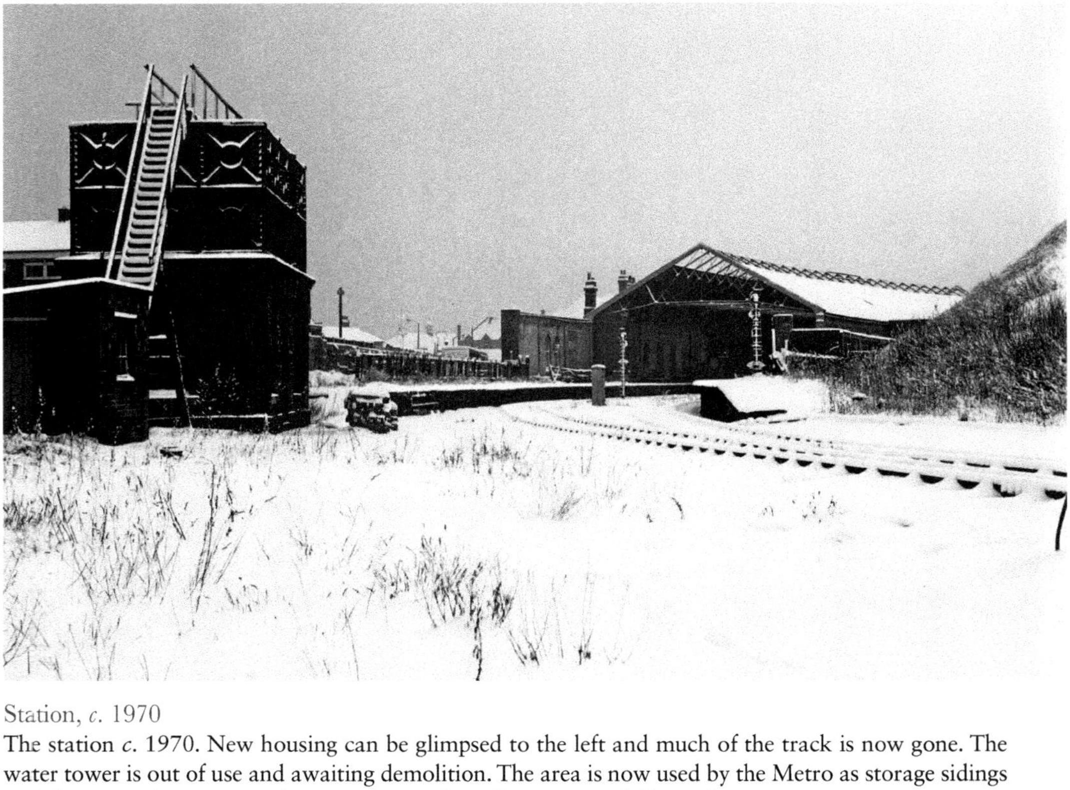

Station, *c.* 1970
The station *c.* 1970. New housing can be glimpsed to the left and much of the track is now gone. The water tower is out of use and awaiting demolition. The area is now used by the Metro as storage sidings and there are plans to turn the area into an £8 million Metro skills academy.

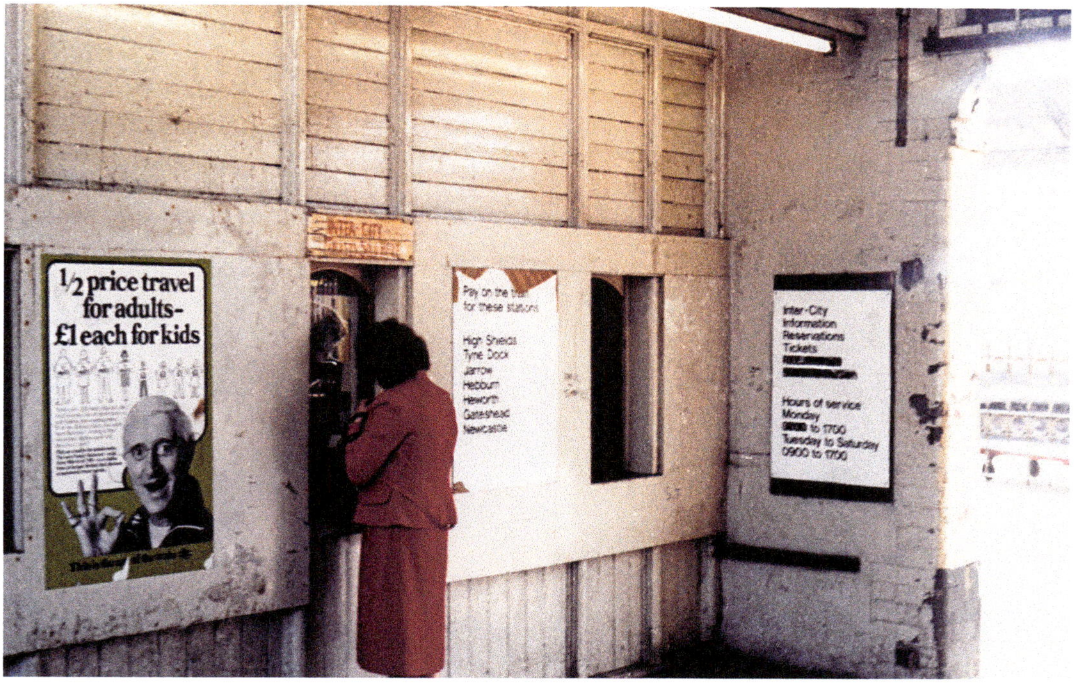

Ticket Office

The rather rundown ticket office at South Shields station.

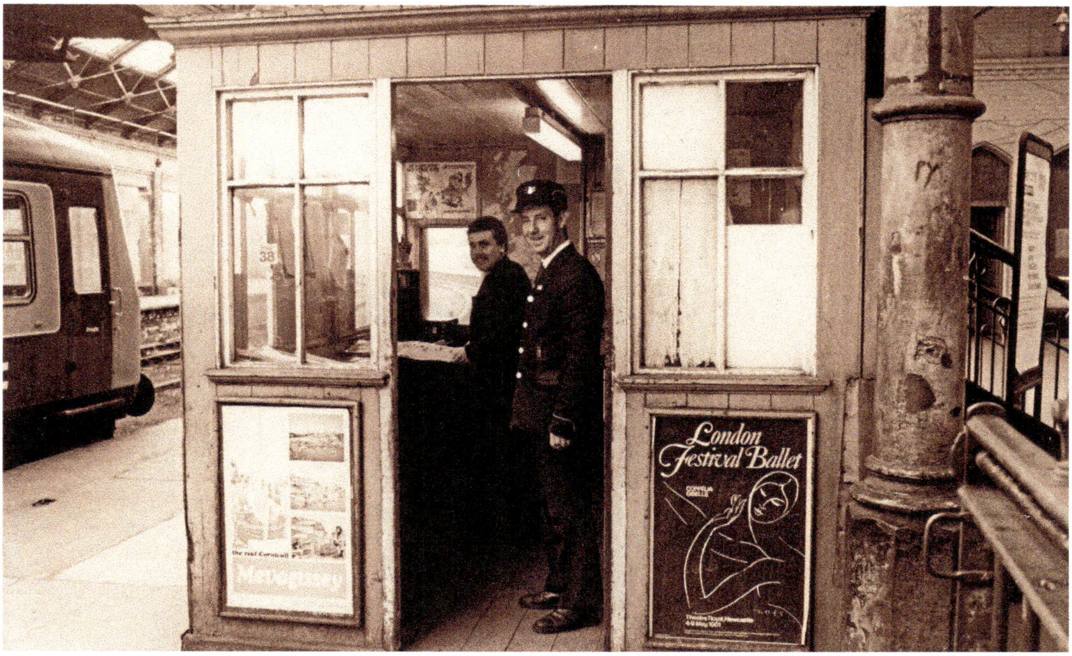

Station Staff

South Shields remained a staffed station long after the other local stations on the line were converted to unstaffed 'Paytrain' stations. The last stationmaster had been a Mr Brimer, who left in 1967. Seen here is chargeman Joseph Gillmartin, who served at the station from 1967 until its closure.

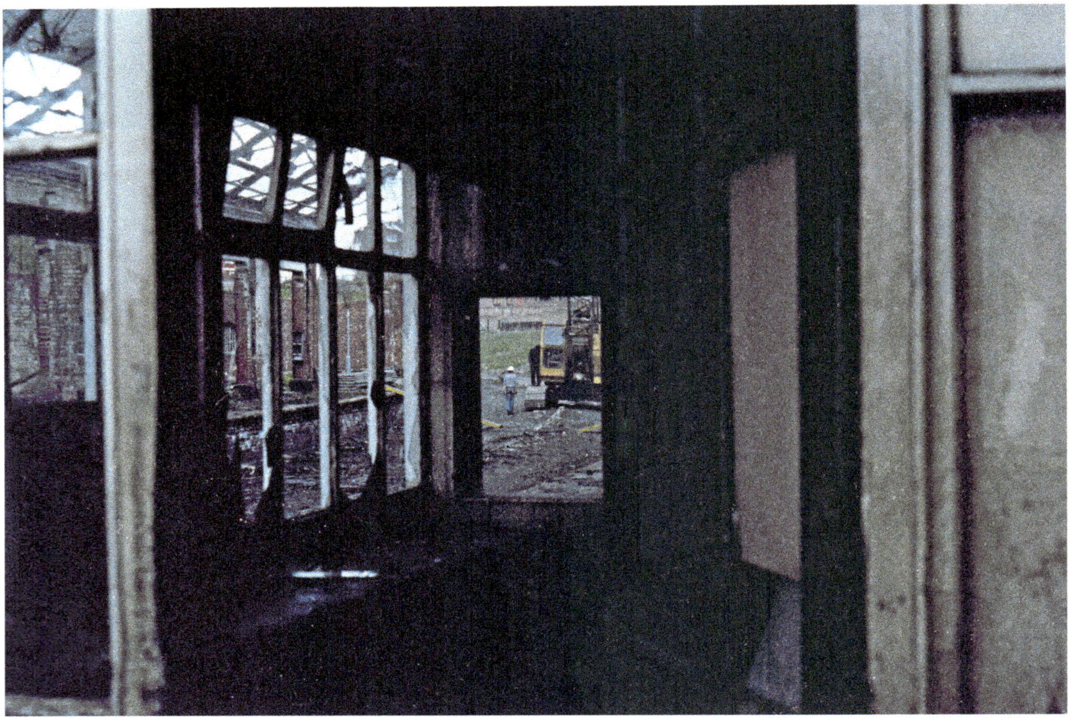

Ticket Office

This image shows the same wooden ticket office after closure. It served staff as a shelter from the wind-tunnel effect of the station and as a bait room for contractors during demolition.

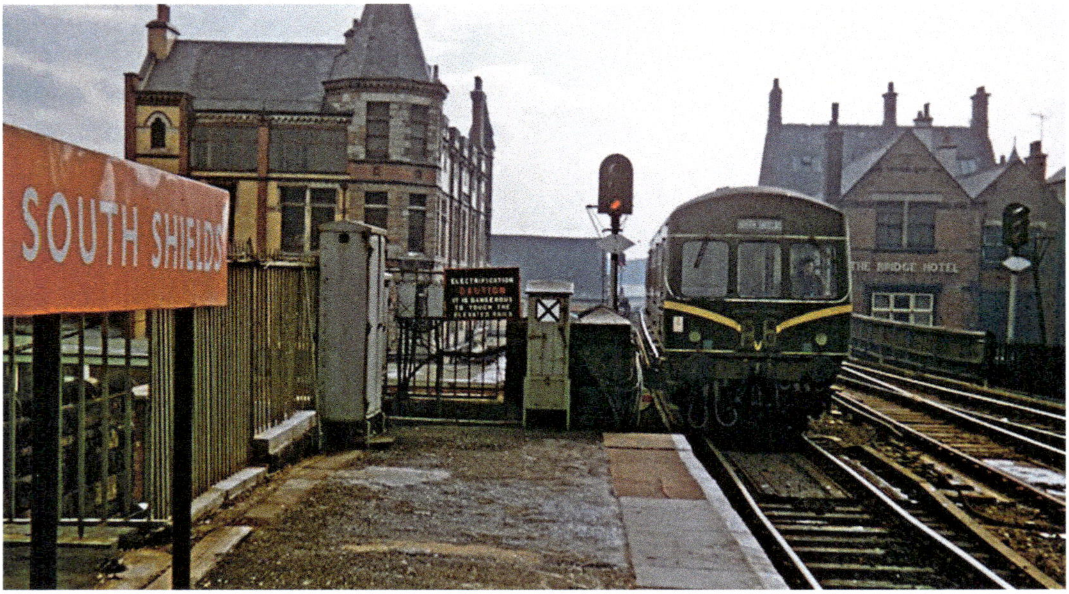

South Shields Station

A South Shields-bound '101' diesel multiple unit heads into the station. The paraphernalia of electrification is still very evident, although the electric trains have gone. This area now leads to South Shields Metro station itself, which is set to be closed and replaced by 2019.

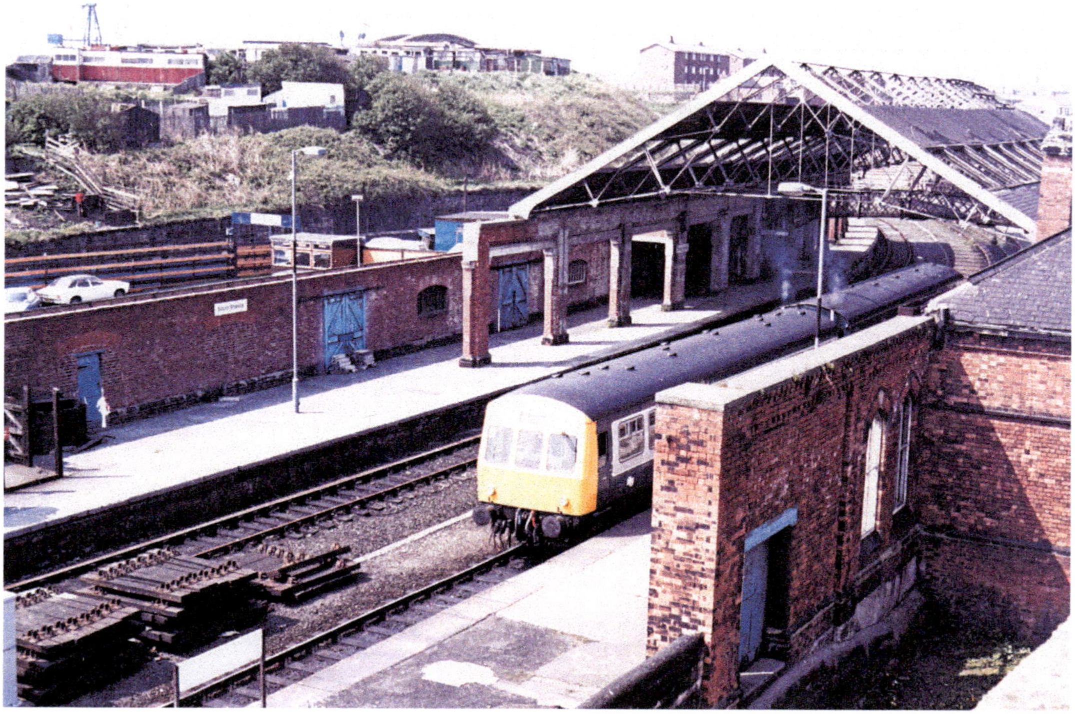

Station Closure

The station shortly before closure. The area behind and to the left has since been redeveloped as offices.

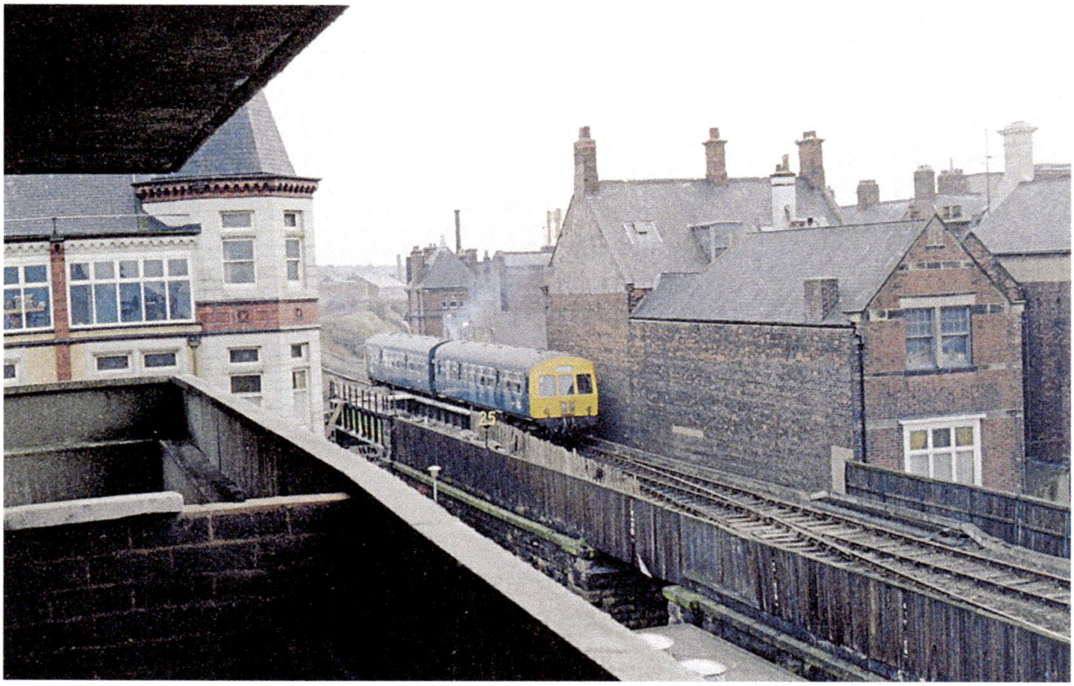

DMU

A DMU runs past building work on South Shields Metro station during the last days of service.

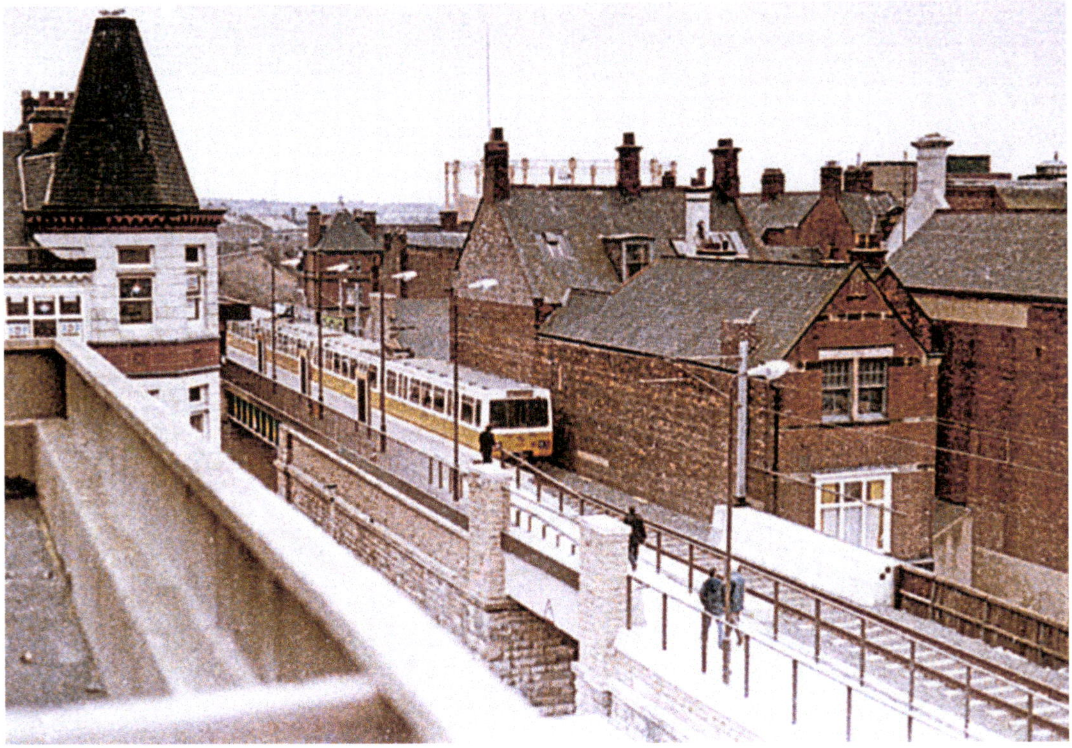

Metro Unit

This image shows a Metro unit at South Shields. This seems to have been a test train before the station opened to passengers on 1 June 1981.

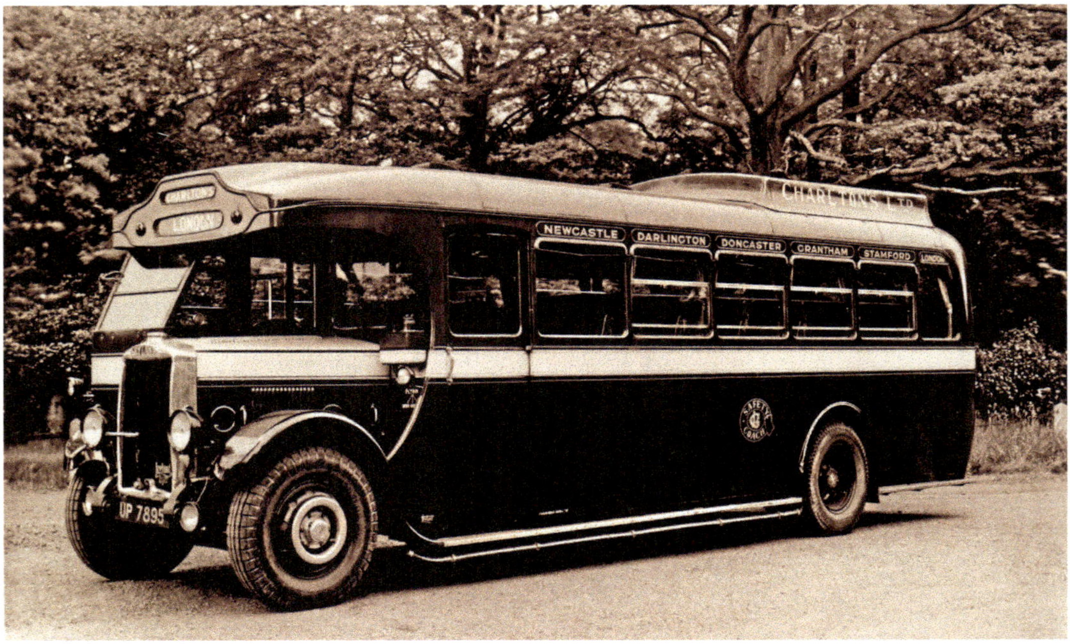

A Charlton's coach.

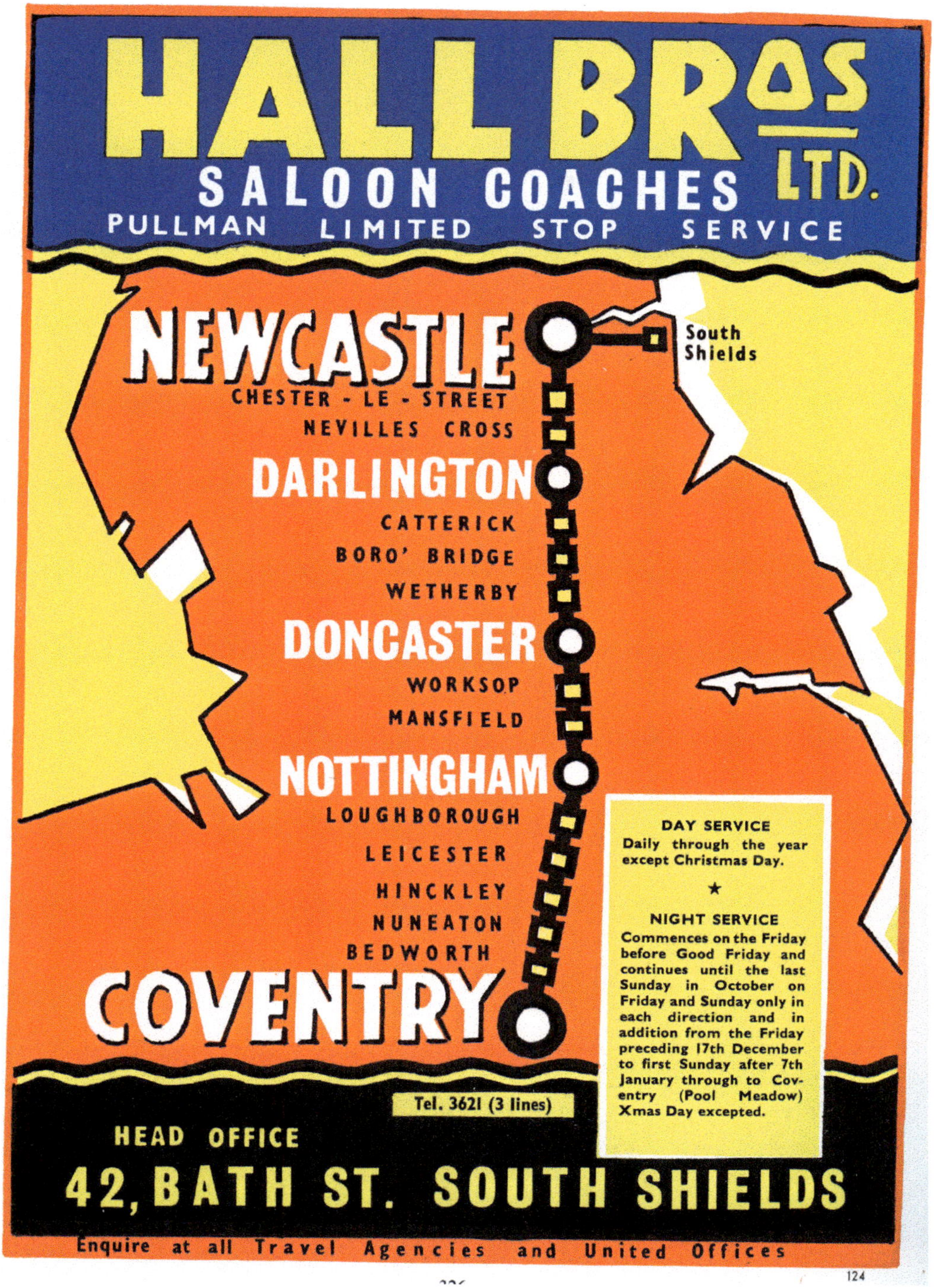

Opposite below, above and overleaf: Mile End Road and Charlton's Coaches

Mile End Road has been a departure point for all kinds of services (including trams and buses) and for all kinds of destinations – near, far, for work or holiday. Seen here is an advertisement for Charlton's coaches, an advertisement for Hall Brothers and the cover of a timetable for the Tynerider Paytrain service.

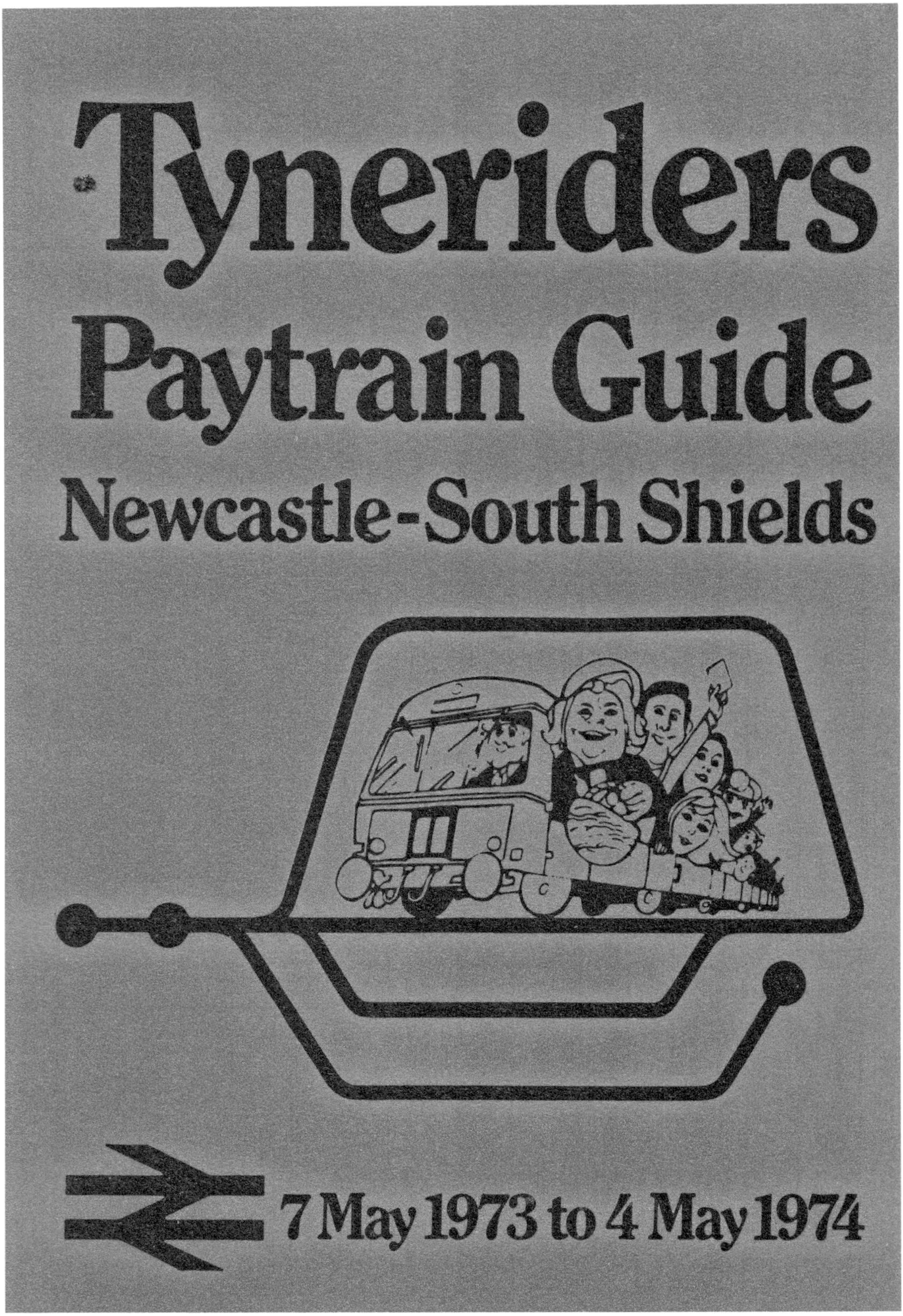
Tyneriders
Paytrain Guide
Newcastle-South Shields
7 May 1973 to 4 May 1974

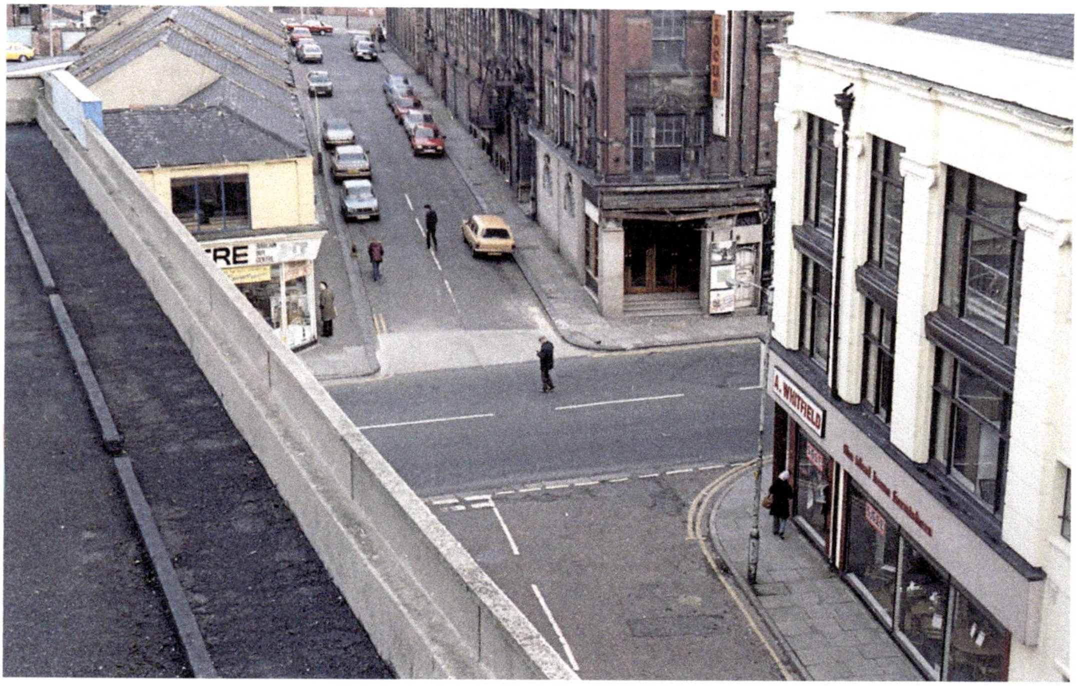

Mile End Road

Looking down on Mile End Road from the multistorey car park.

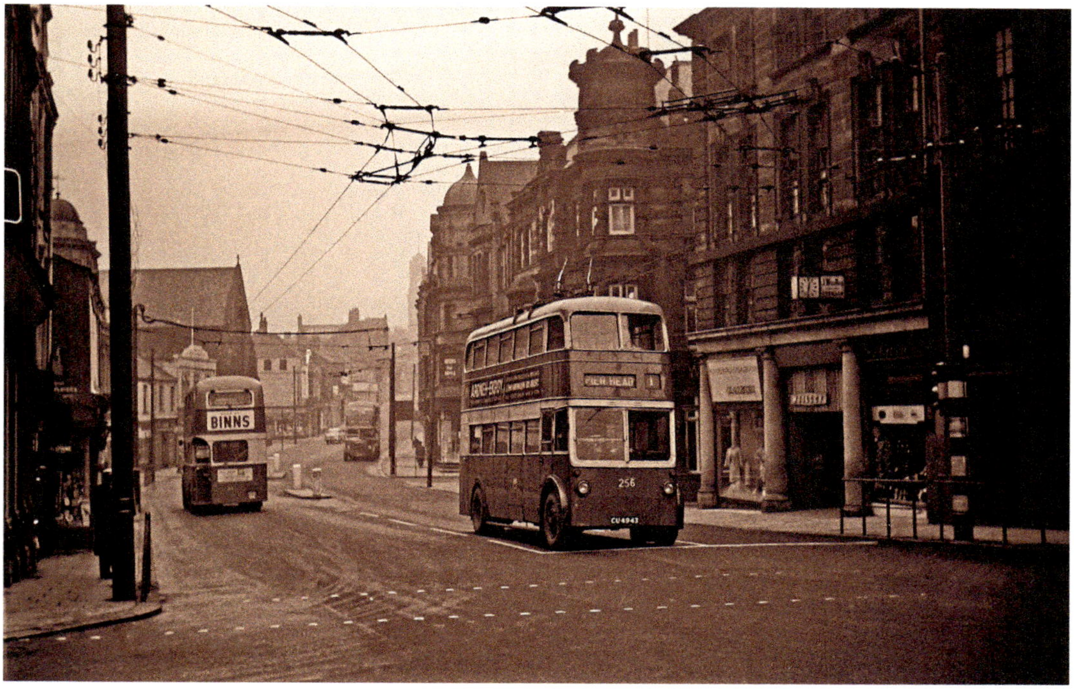

Fowler Street

Fowler Street *c.* 1960. The area to the right has changed with the expansion of Keppel Street into a major thoroughfare through the town.

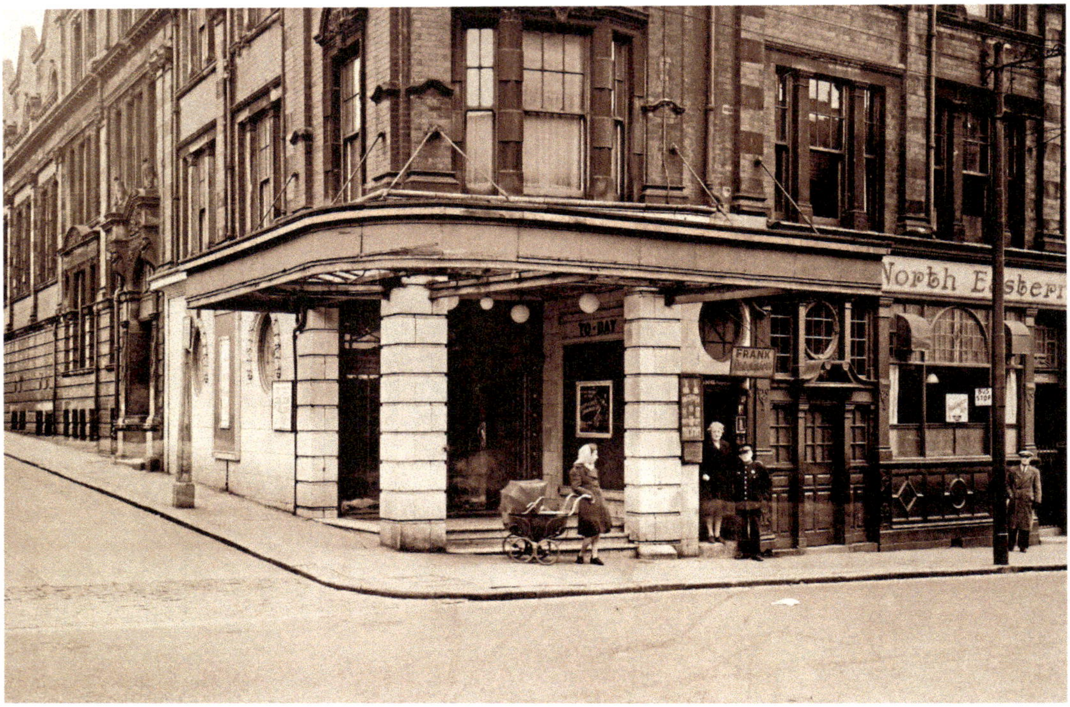

Above and below: Gaumont Cinema

This large building on Mile End Road has served many purposes over the years, from holding dances to becoming a cinema – people of a certain age will remember it as the Gaumont Cinema. At one point it was even adapted into a three-screen cinema by splitting the stalls downstairs into three. In this view the 1949 British film *Once a Jolly Swagman* starring Dirk Bogarde, Bonar Colleano, Bill Owen, Thora Hird and Sid James is showing. The small kiosk to the right is in use by Frank & Sons photographers. The Gaumont Cinema is now a pub.

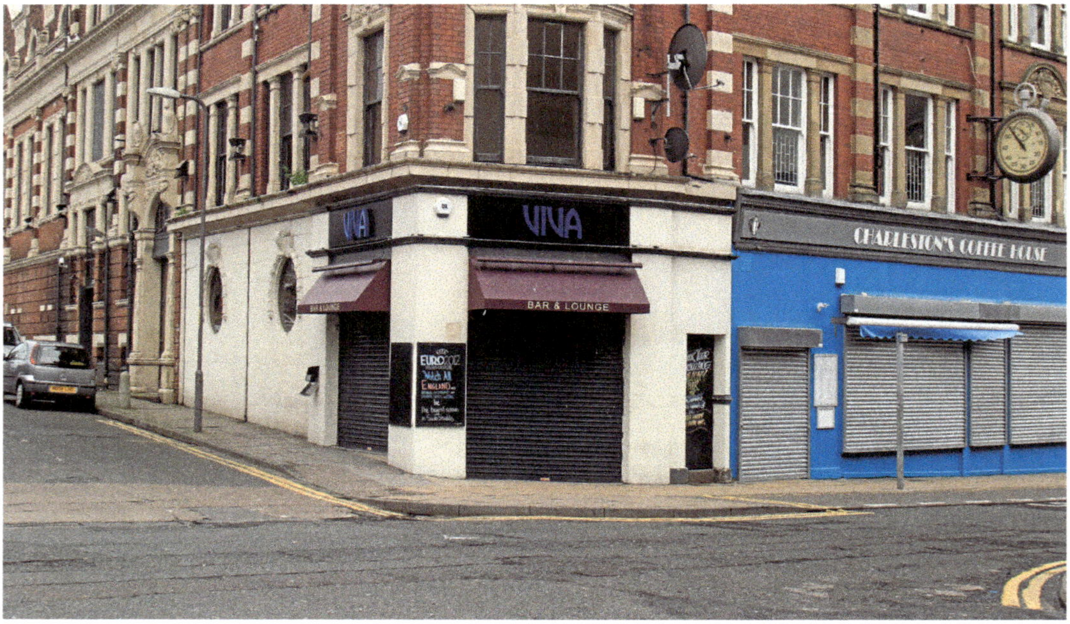

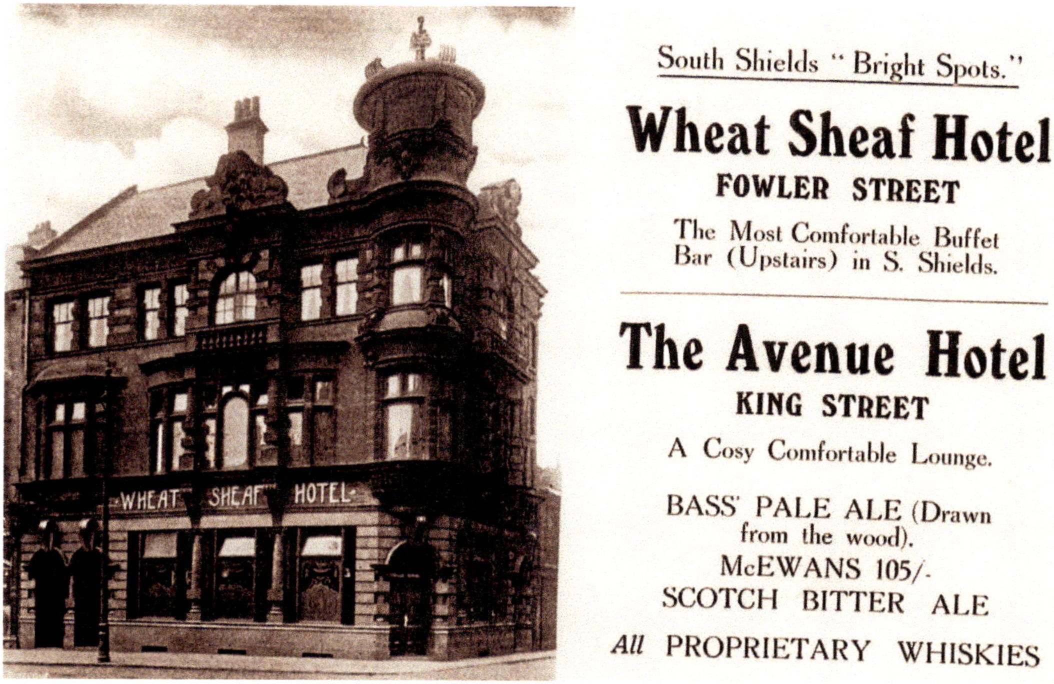

Wheatsheaf Hotel

An advertisement for another of Shields' lost buildings, the Wheatsheaf Hotel. Keppel Street now runs through where the Wheatsheaf once stood.

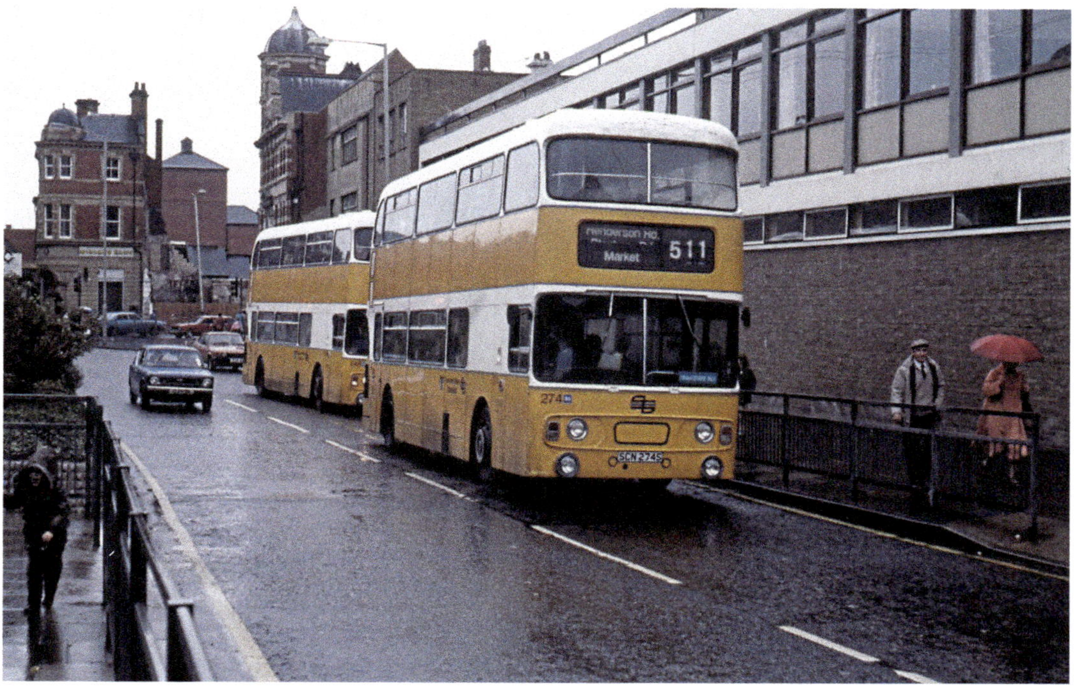

Keppel Street

A rainy day in South Shields. This image shows the No. 511 bus travelling along Keppel Street.

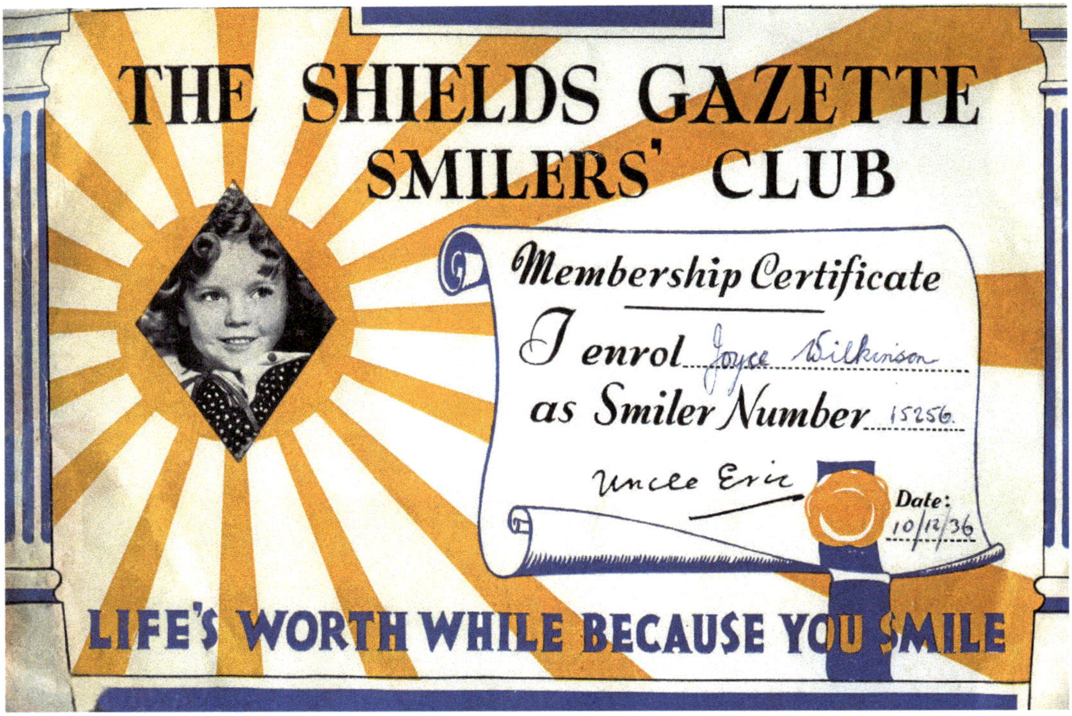

Smilers' Club

A certificate, signed by Uncle Eric, for the *Shields Gazette*'s Smilers' Club.

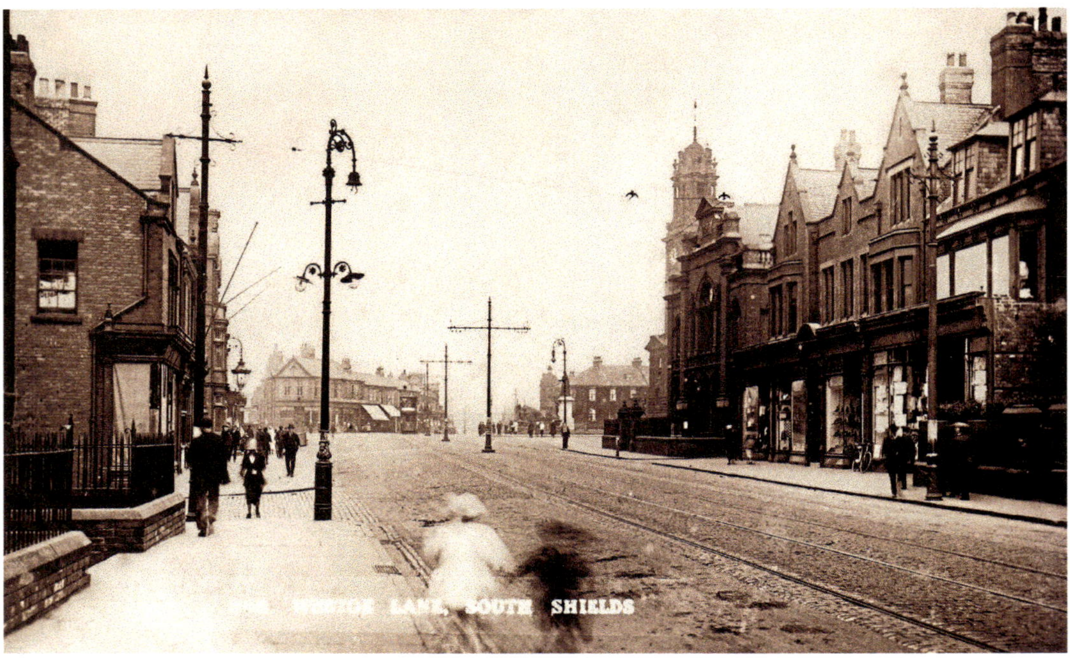

Westoe Lane

Westoe Lane looking towards the top of Fowler Street. The large Co-op building to the right was replaced by a more modern building, which is now South Tyneside House.

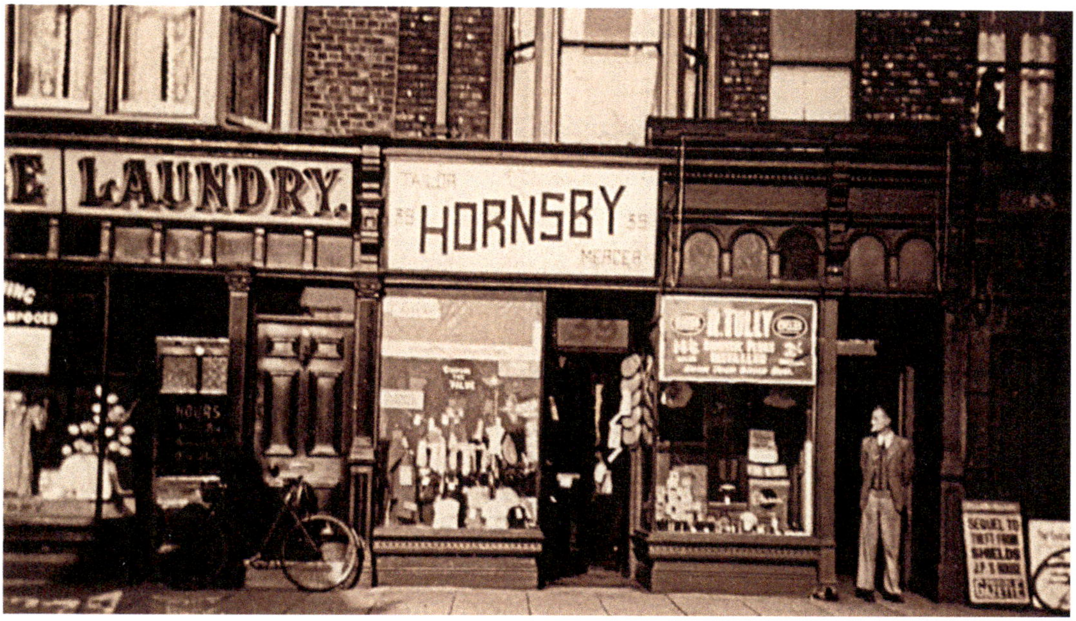

Westoe Lane
Shops on the east side of Westoe Lane.

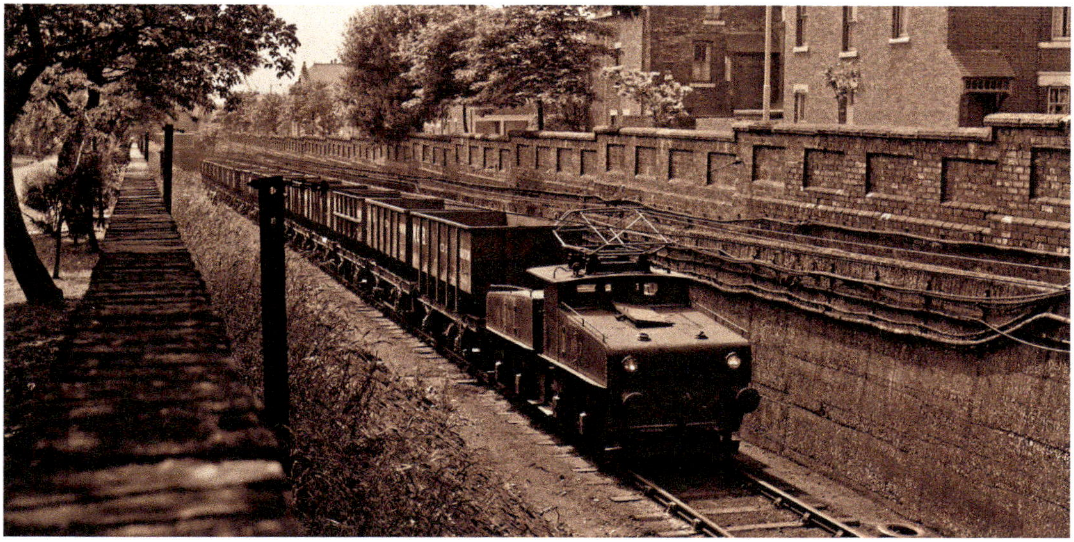

National Coal Board Electric Locomotive
This image shows a National Coal Board electric locomotive pulling a train of empty hopper wagons up Erskine Bank towards Westoe Colliery. This was one of two centre-articulated locomotives designated to get large locomotives around the system's tight bends. They were nicknamed 'crocodiles' by some. Erskine Road is behind the brick wall. Although much noise was be generated by the clanking and screeching train movements, it at least be happened in a walled-off cutting, which gave some shielding for the residents. The railway closed in 1989 and was briefly replaced by a conveyer system that transported stone waste from Westoe Colliery to the Low Staithes, but the writing on the wall for the coal industry. Westoe, along with most of the nation's other surviving pits, closed in 1994. The cutting has since been filled in and grassed over.

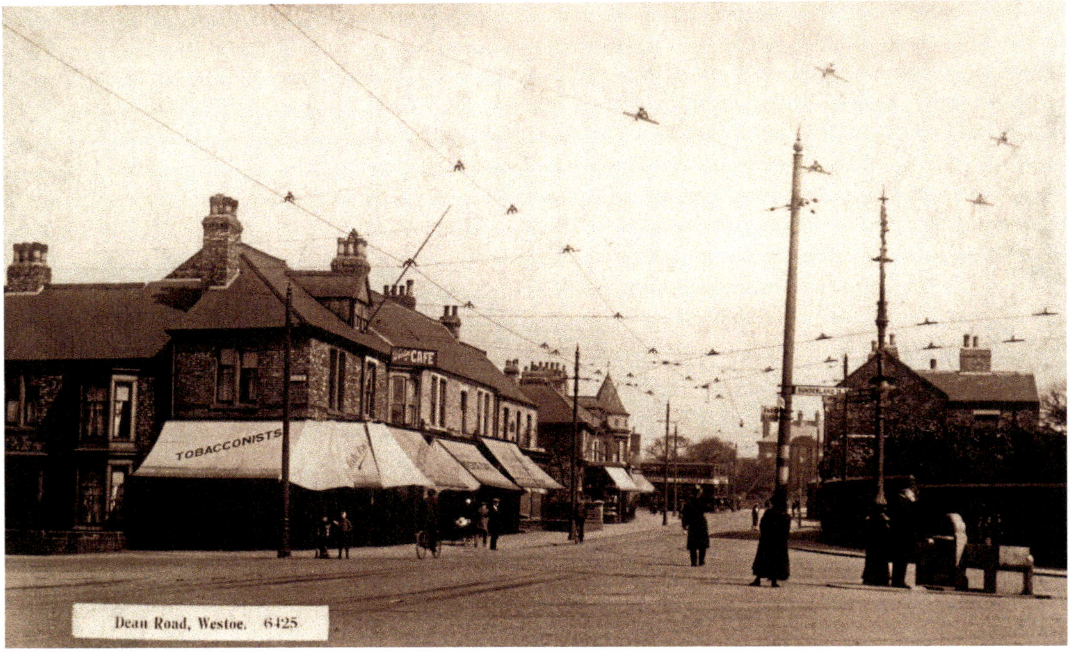

Dean Road at Westoe

This area was once the borough boundary with the then independent Harton. Some signs of the area's rural past remain, but the approaching electric tramcar is a sign that things are firmly marching on.

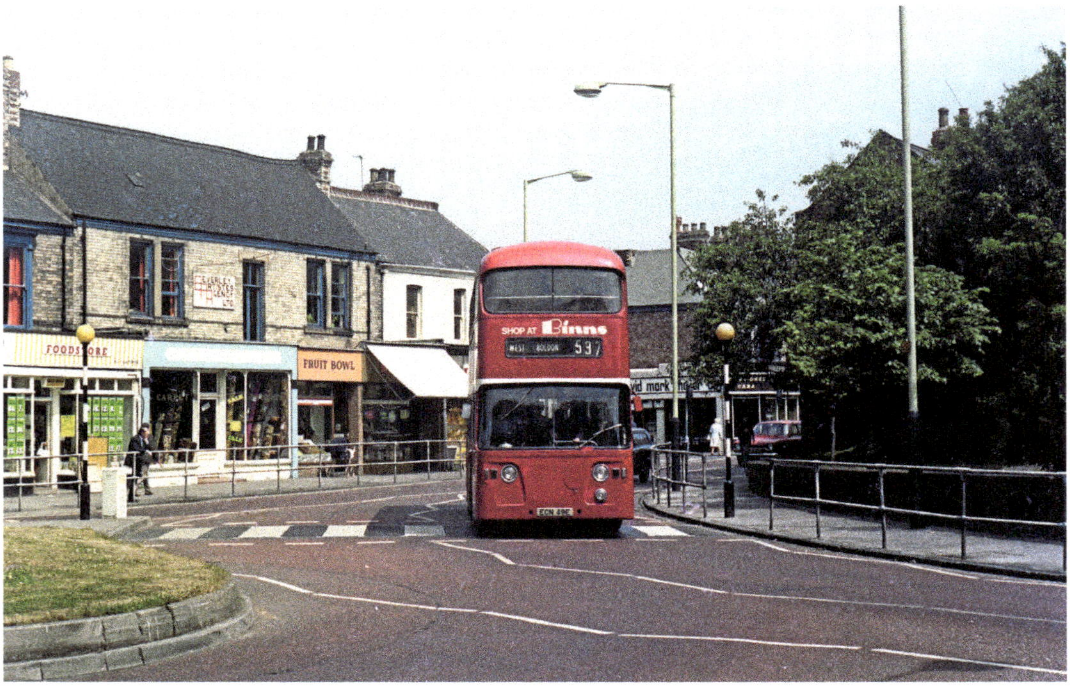

Westoe

Westoe seen from a similar location, but the area is now almost part of an expanded South Shields town centre.

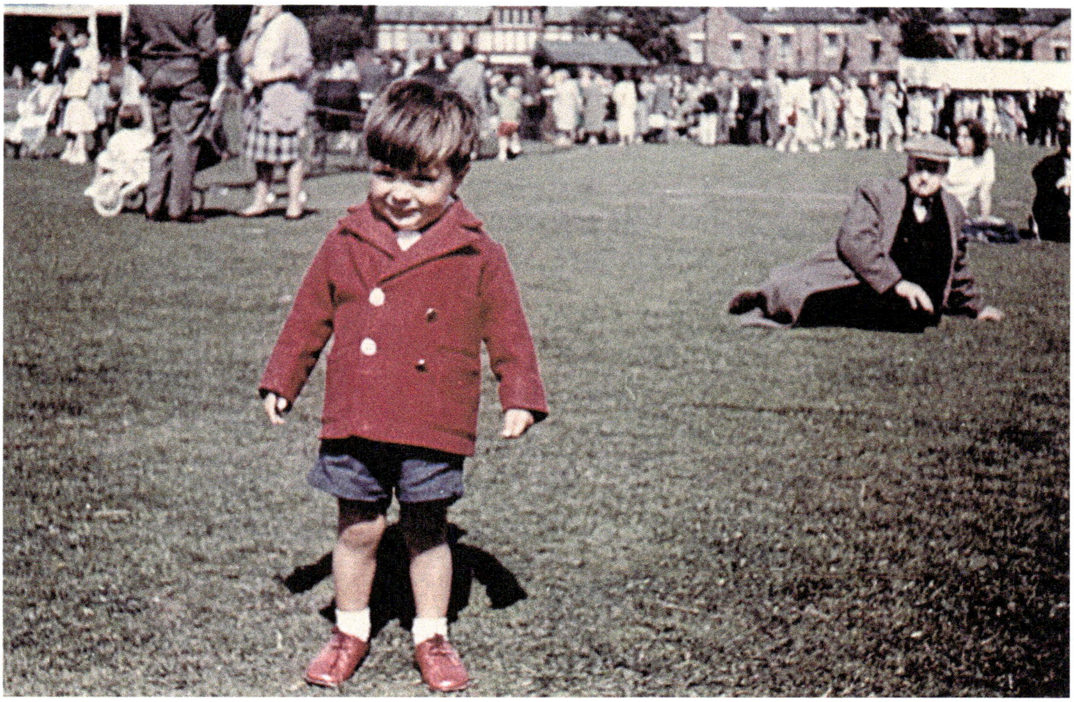

Westoe Cricket Ground

Above: George Foster at Westoe Cricket Ground on August bank holiday Monday, 1962. *Below*: George with his parents Jim and Irene Foster.

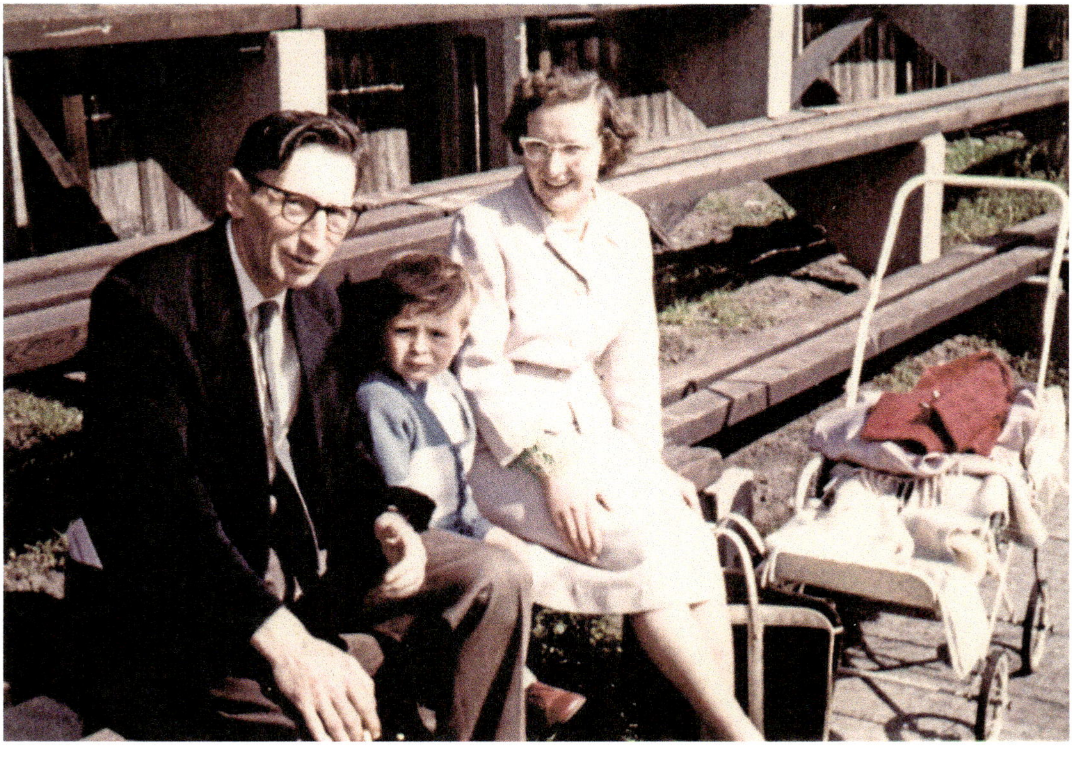

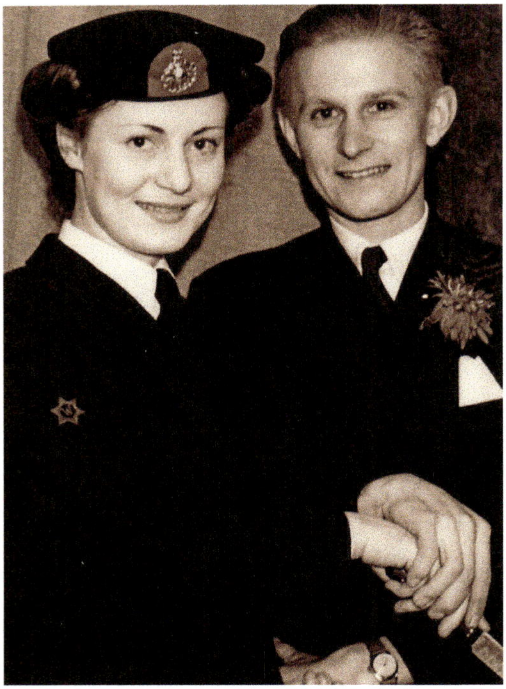

Left: Wartime Wedding
Albert and Catherine Wilkinson at their wartime wedding in 1944. Albert served in the merchant navy and was torpedoed while at sea.

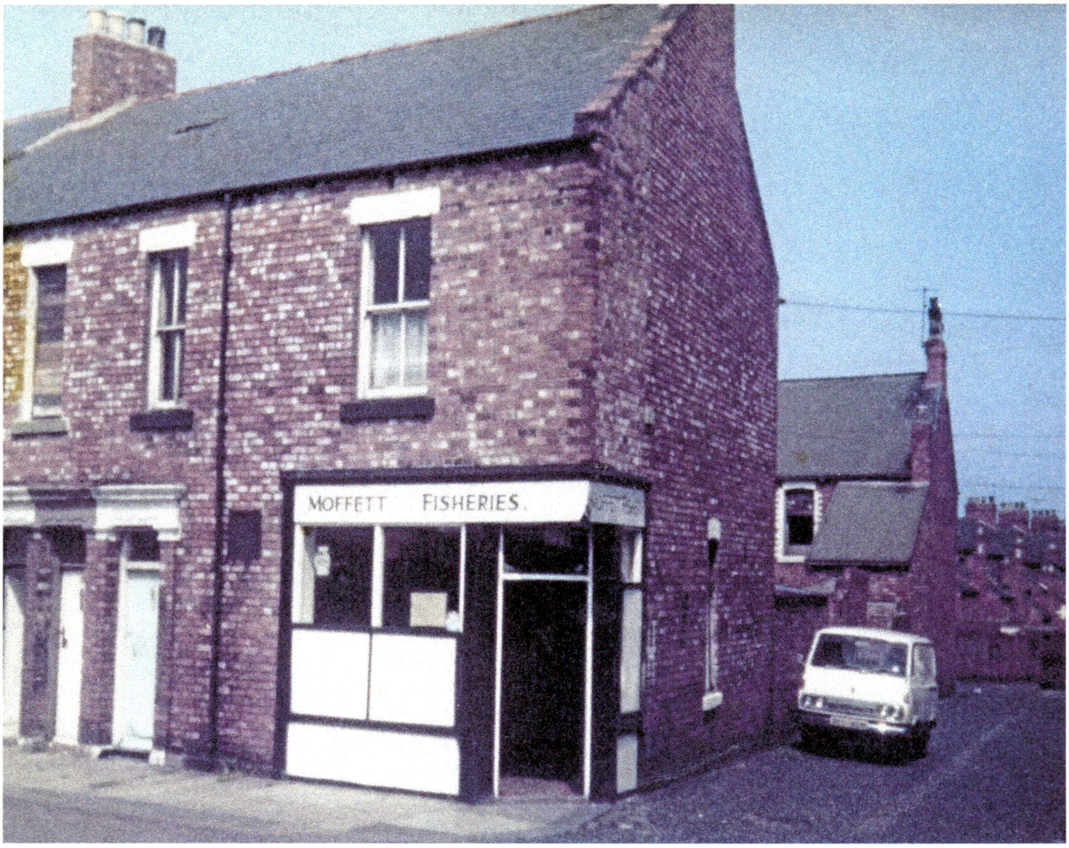

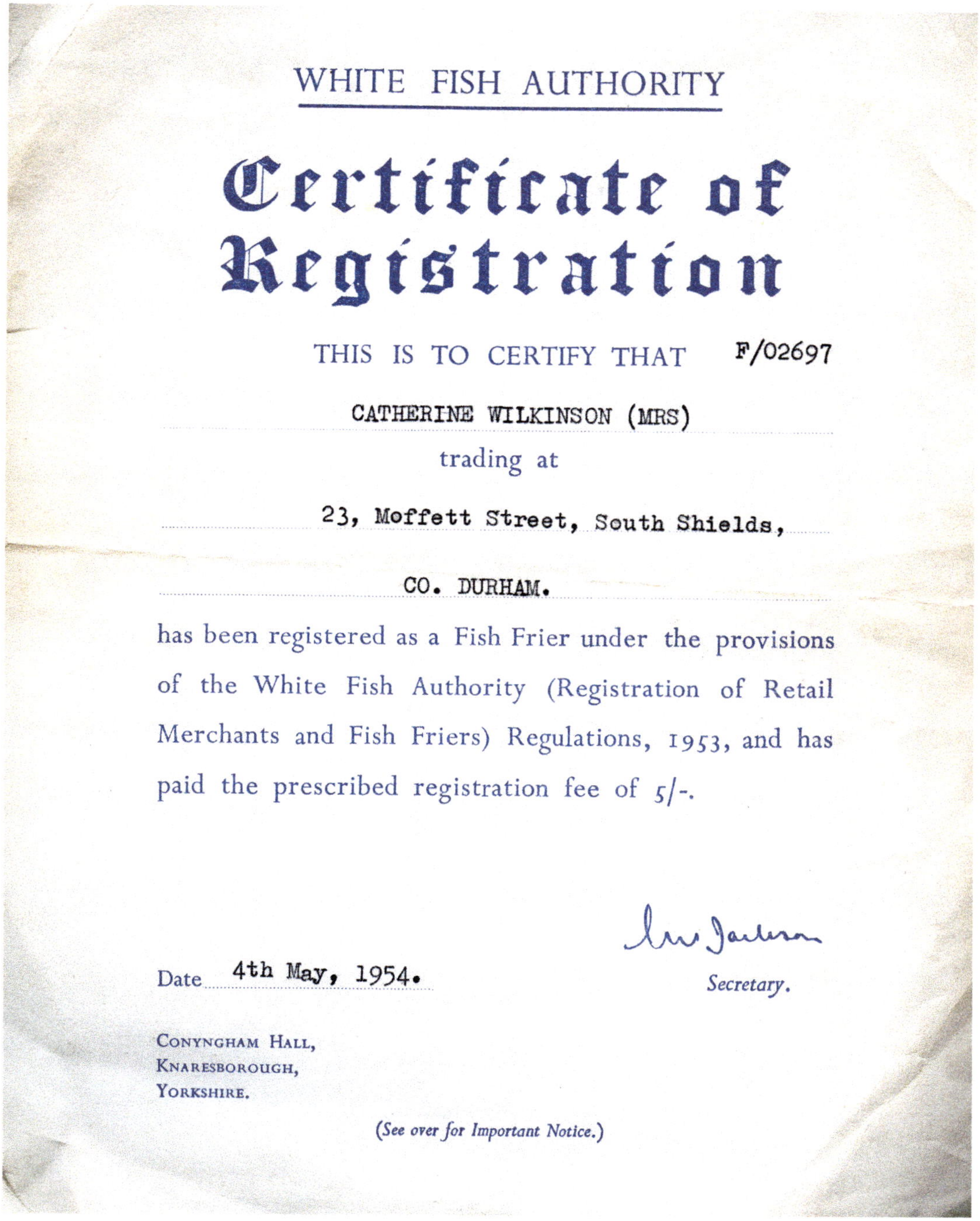
WHITE FISH AUTHORITY

Certificate of Registration

THIS IS TO CERTIFY THAT F/02697

CATHERINE WILKINSON (MRS)

trading at

23, Moffett Street, South Shields,

CO. DURHAM.

has been registered as a Fish Frier under the provisions of the White Fish Authority (Registration of Retail Merchants and Fish Friers) Regulations, 1953, and has paid the prescribed registration fee of 5/-.

Date 4th May, 1954.

[signature]

Secretary.

CONYNGHAM HALL,
KNARESBOROUGH,
YORKSHIRE.

(See over for Important Notice.)

Above and opposite below: Moffett Fisheries

For many years Albert and Catherine Wilkinson ran Moffett Fisheries in Moffett Street. The high quality of the couple's fish and chips was well known and the subject still pops up occasionally on internet discussion forums. We believe the recipe was obtained by Albert during his wartime service. It is believed people occasionally attempted to prize the recipe out of him, but never succeeded. During council redevelopment of the area the shop was compulsorily purchased and, due to age troubling the war wound in his leg, on closure Albert opted instead for a post office in the then developing Washington area.

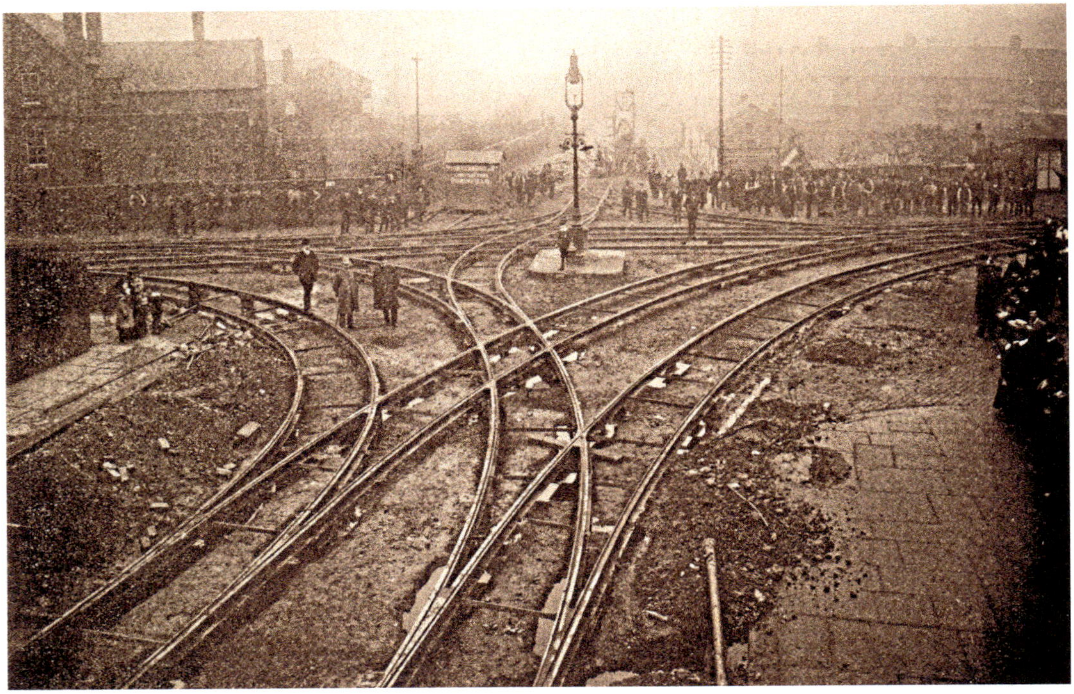

Chichester Crossing

Chichester Crossing during the construction of the tram system *c.* 1905. I have never been able to find any earlier images of this area, which seems strange. Chichester Metro station is now to the right of the picture.

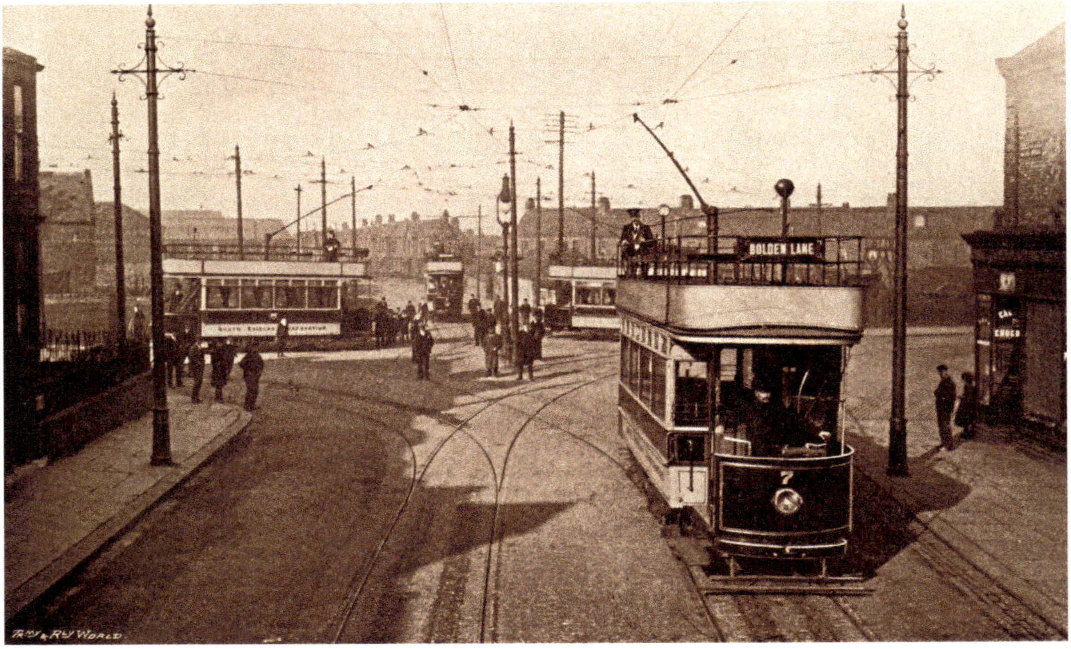

Trams

Testing taking place on the tram system in 1906.

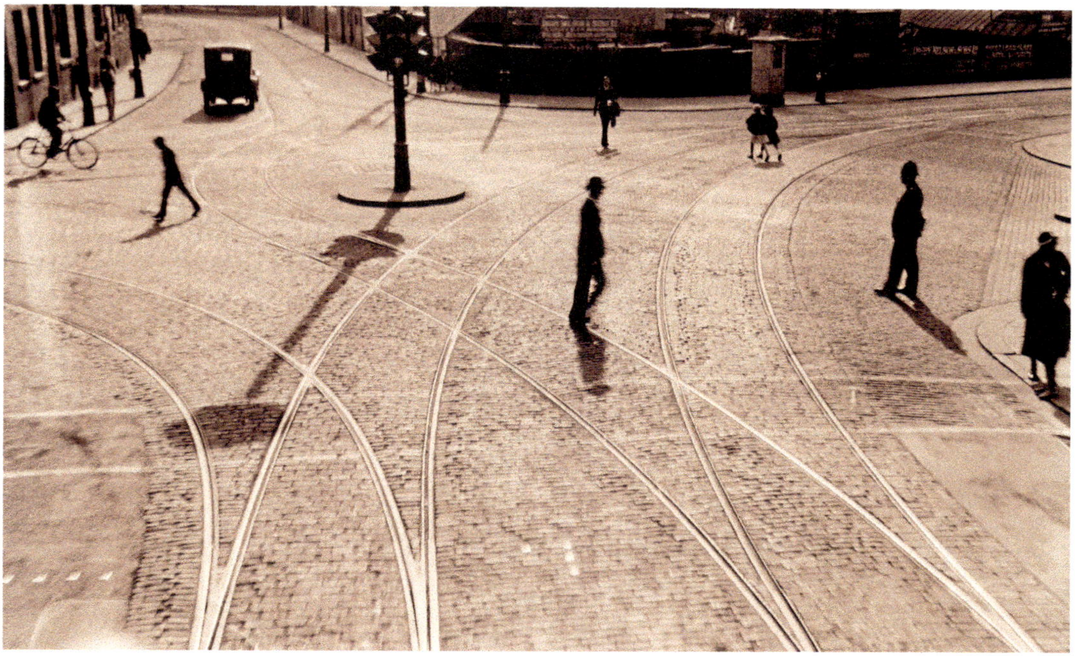

Chichester Junction

A view of Chichester Junction taken from the top deck or balcony of a corporation tram. The photographer was probably a visiting enthusiast looking for a simple record shot of the junction, but shooting into the sunlight gave this slightly impressionistic view.

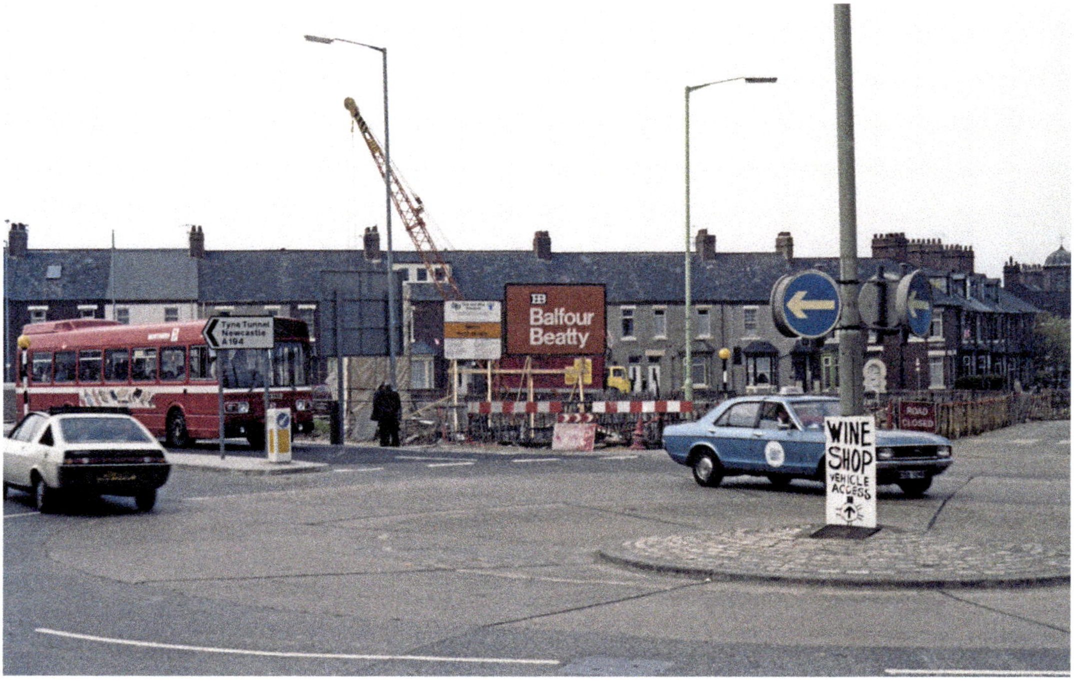

Chichester Metro Station

Construction underway on Chichester Metro station *c.* 1981.

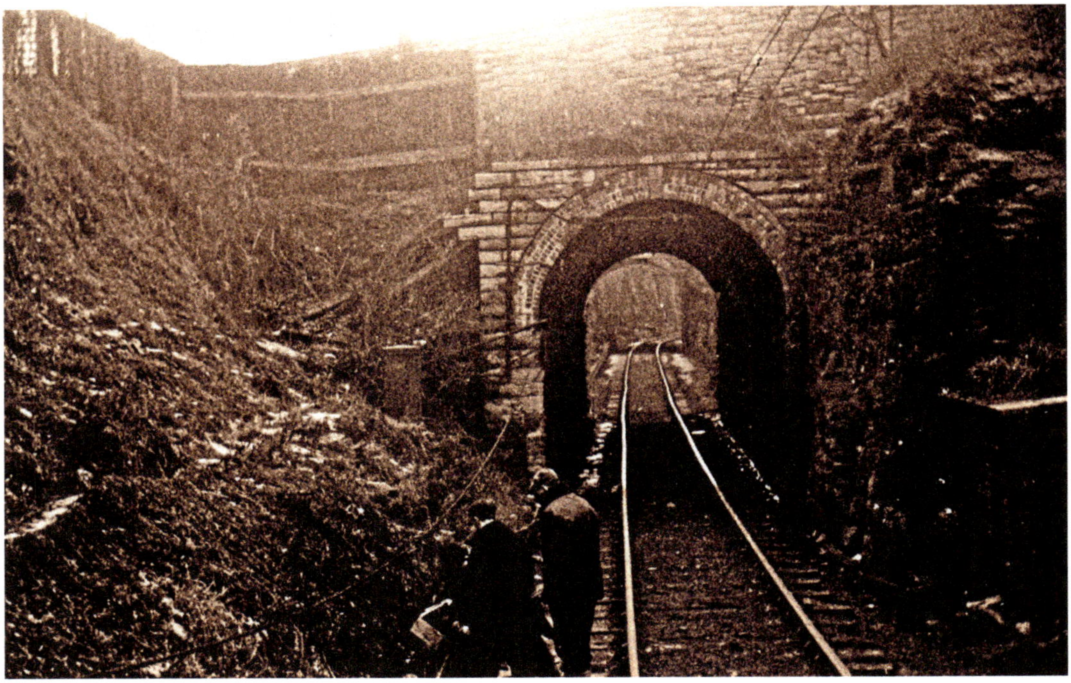

Checking trackside,1950s.

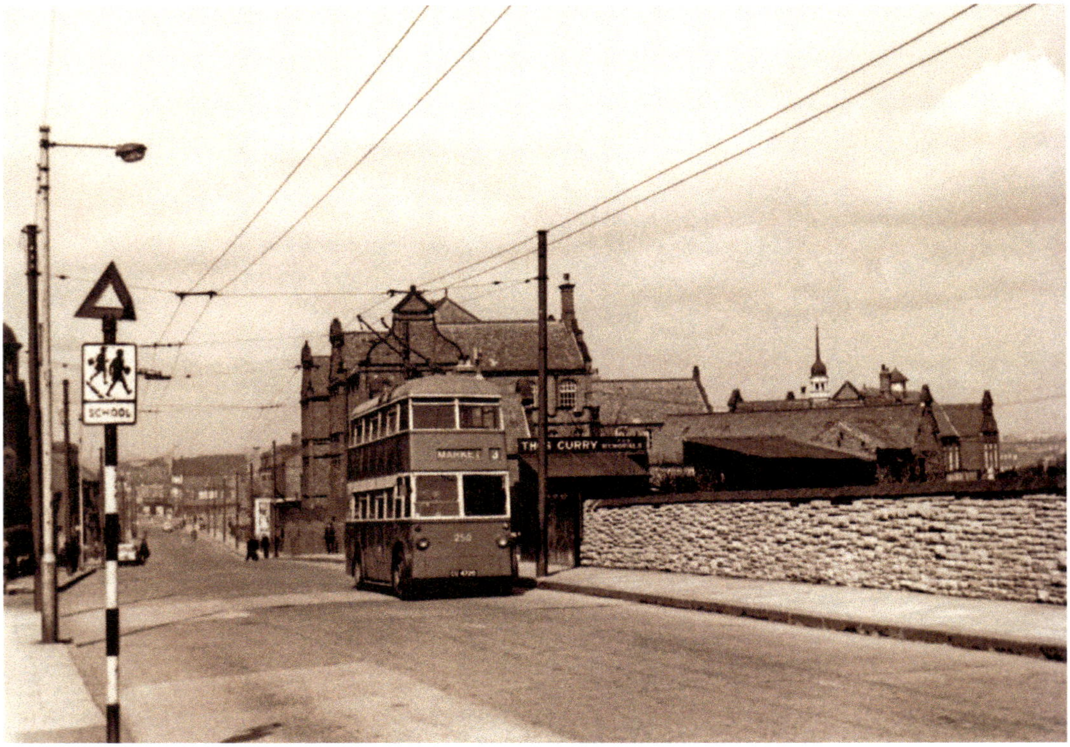

Corporation Trolleybus

This image shows a Corporation trolleybus running up Laygate towards Chichester *c*. 1960.

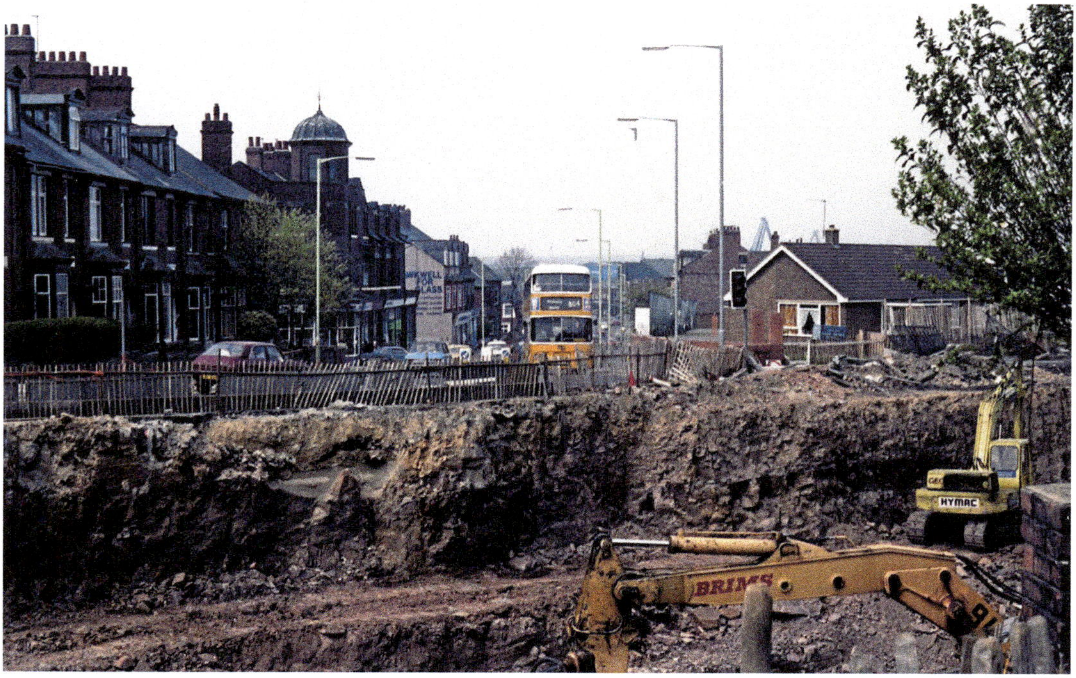

Metro
This image shows a view of the same location as that on the previous page after Metro construction work has started, *c.* 1981.

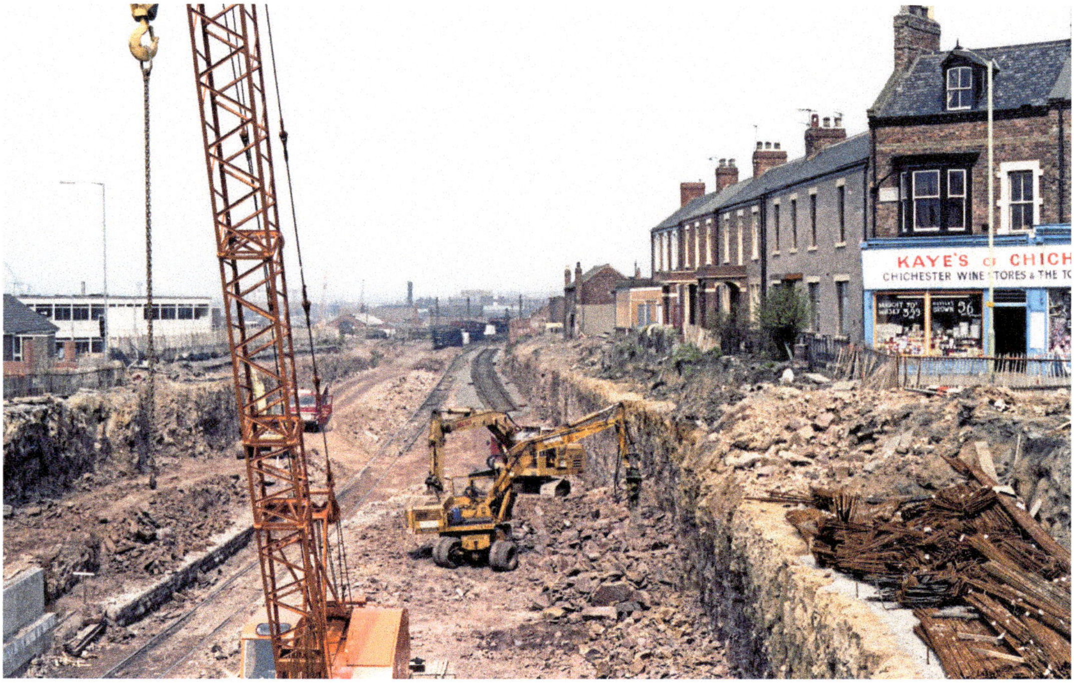

Metro
Metro construction *c.* 1981, looking from Chichester towards South Shields.

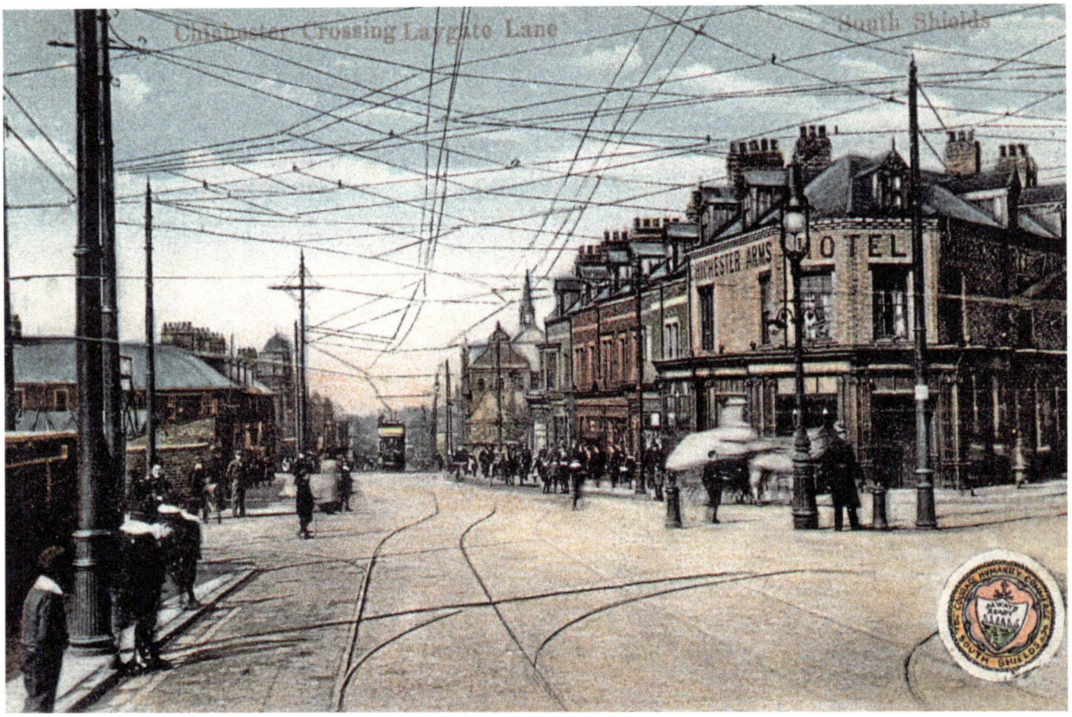

Chichester
This is a colourised image of Chichester *c.* 1906.

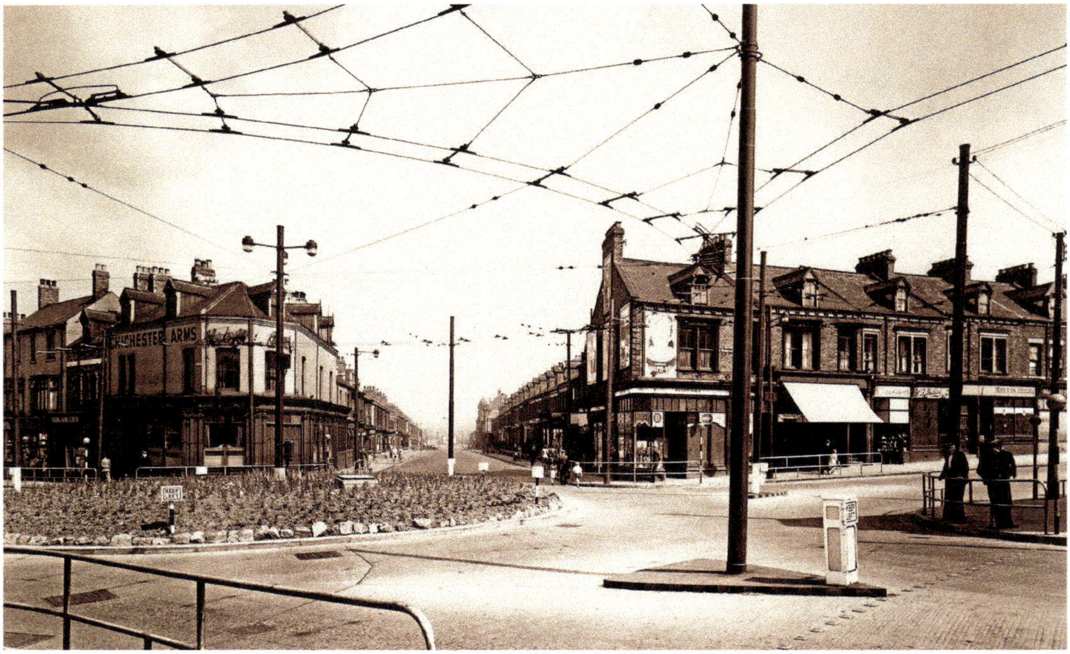

Trolleybus Overhead Power Lines
An image of the area *c.* 1950. This wide-angle shot was probably taken to illustrate the instillation of new trolleybus overhead power lines and a roundabout after the tram system had gone.

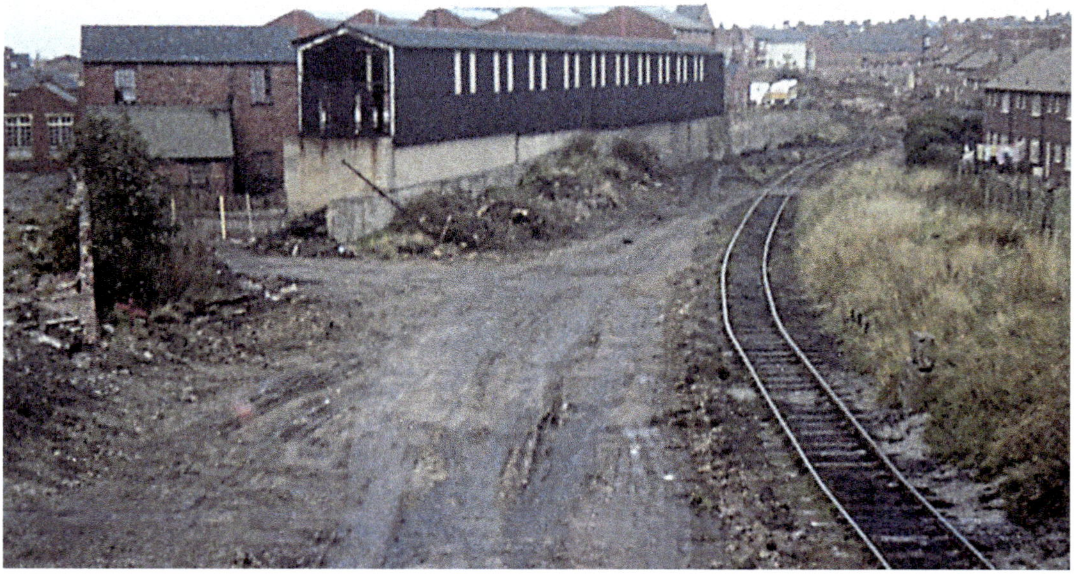

Metro Construction Seen from West Park Road Bridge

The beginning of Metro construction seen from West Park Road Bridge *c.* 1981. The track to the right was at that time the NCB link between Westoe Colliery and the national rail system. The coal staithes, which served Dean Road coal depot to the left, are about to be demolished.

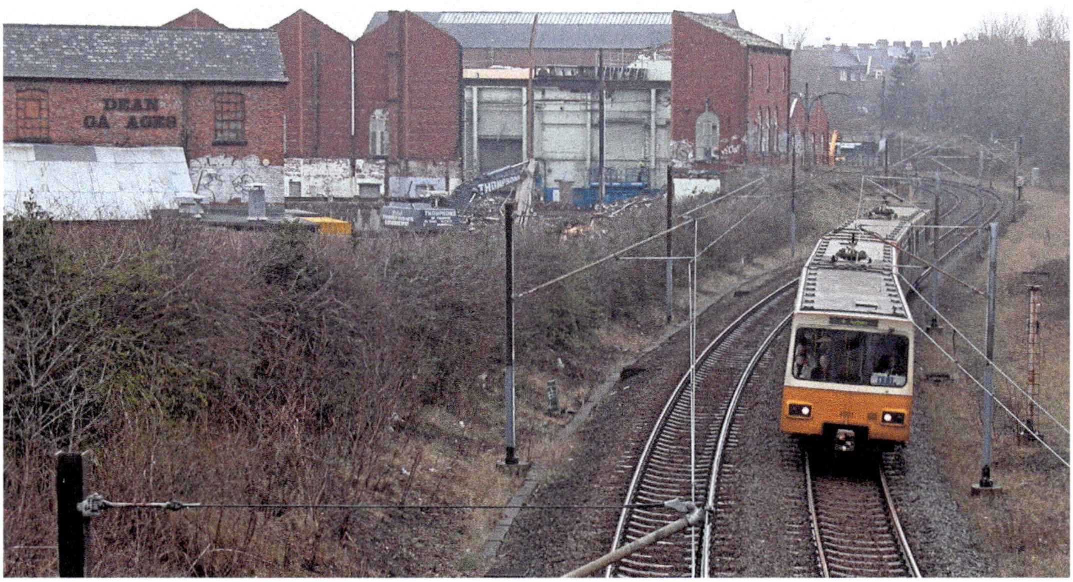

Dean Road Coal Depot, Now Garage

The same view in 2006 with demolition of part of the former tram depot underway. The remains of Dean Road coal depot had been converted into a garage, but were themselves about to be part of housing development.

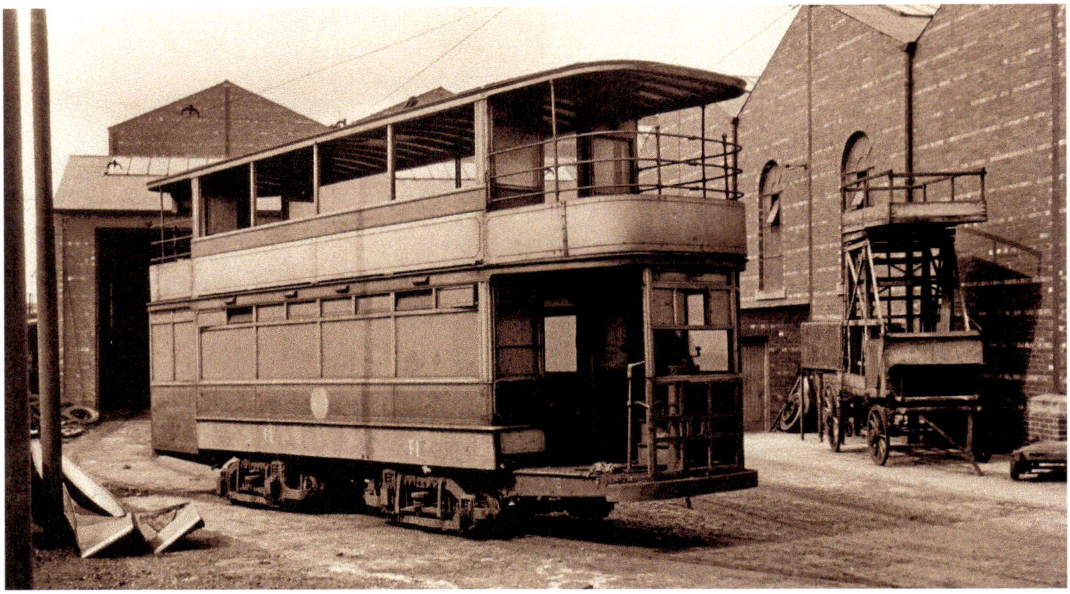

Above and below: Converting Trams

South Shields Corporation was a dab hand at converting other systems' old trams into luxury cars for its own system. Shown above is a tramcar body bought from Wigan Corporation at Chichester Depot and below is a finished example of the same type of car running smartly out of the depot on a test run.

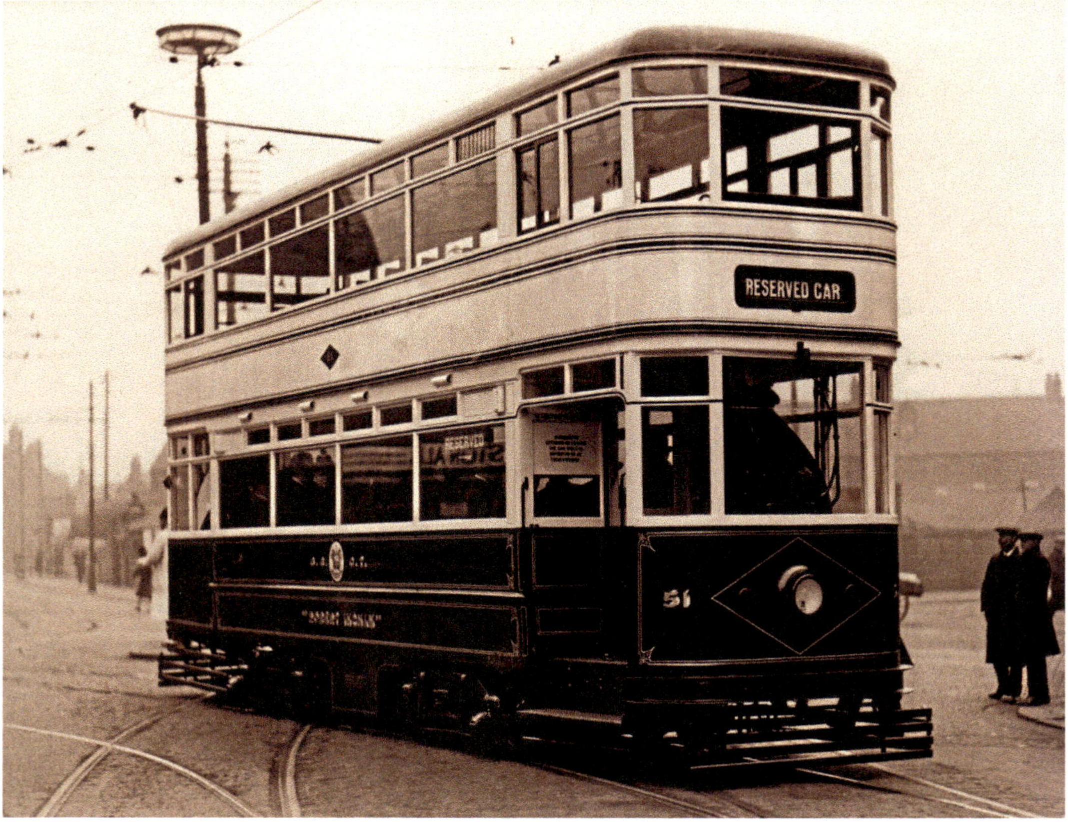

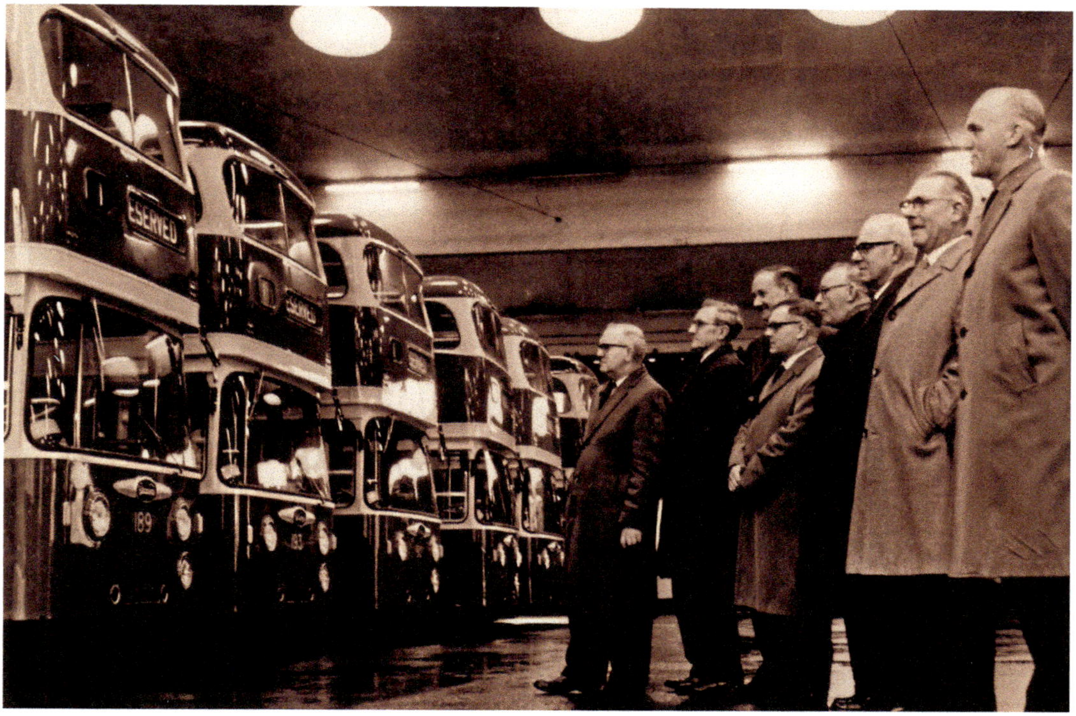

Inspection
This images shows officials inspecting new South Shields Corporation buses in Chichester Depot.

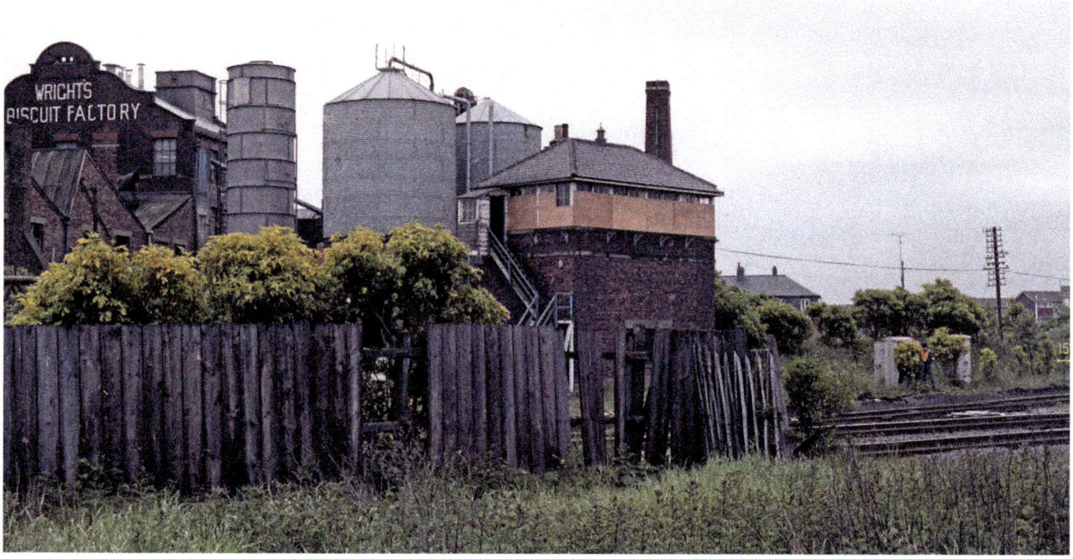

Signal Box after Closure
This image shows the signal box after closure of the line in 1981. It was the last surviving operating box on the South Shields line when the rote switched from semaphore signalling to electronically coloured lights. The Wright's Biscuits factory still seen behind did not survive for much longer either. In October 1972 the company had been put into administration and the factory closed in 1973. It then reopened in 1975 for the production of dog biscuits. It finally closed and was then demolished in 1983.

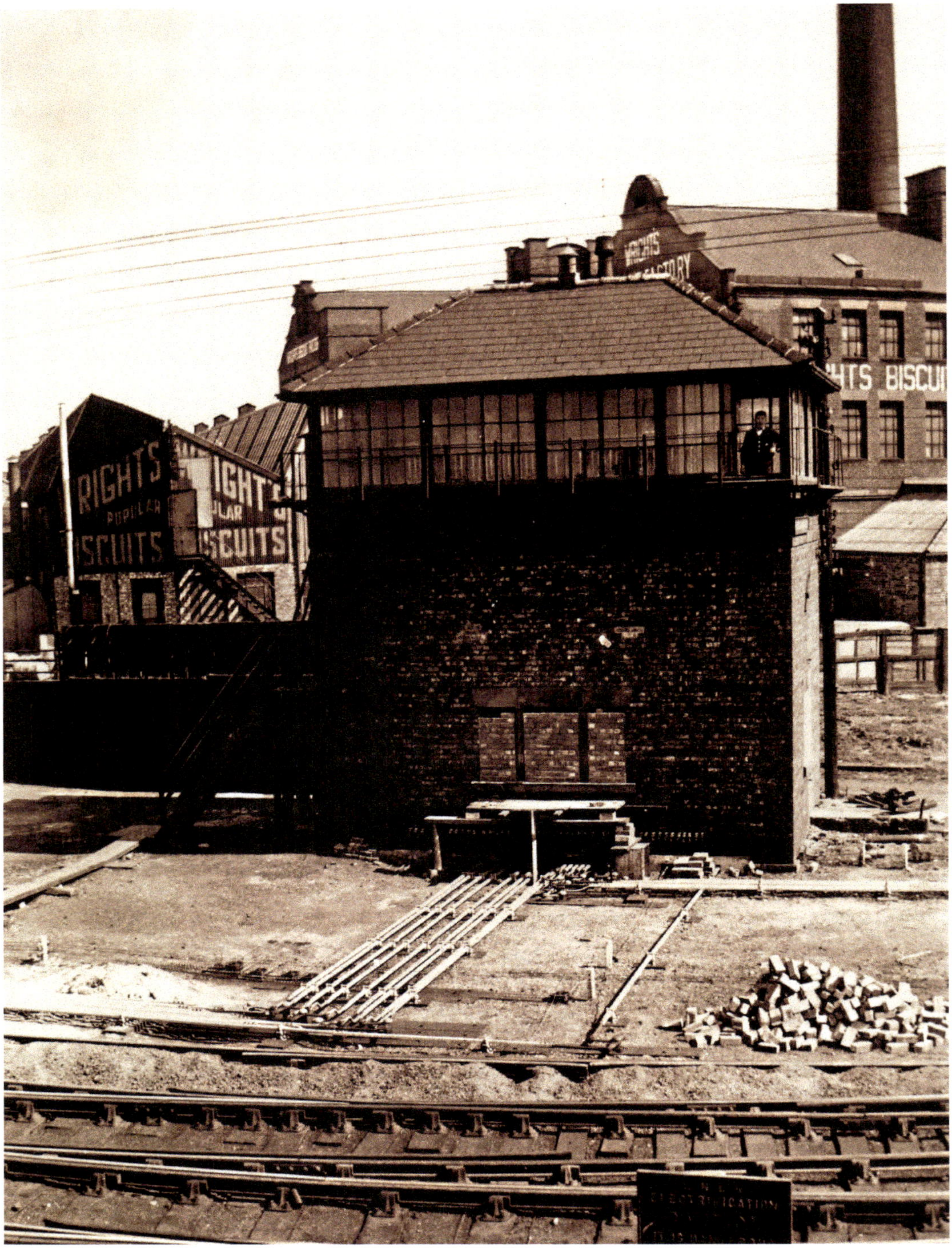

Harton Signal Box

This box controlled many of the busy lines in the Tyne Dock area. Wright's Biscuits factory is behind the Malcom G. Charlton collection in 1972. Wright's Biscuits was began at Holborn in South Shields in 1790 producing ships' biscuits. After a fire in 1898, the company moved to this completely new building at Tyne Dock.

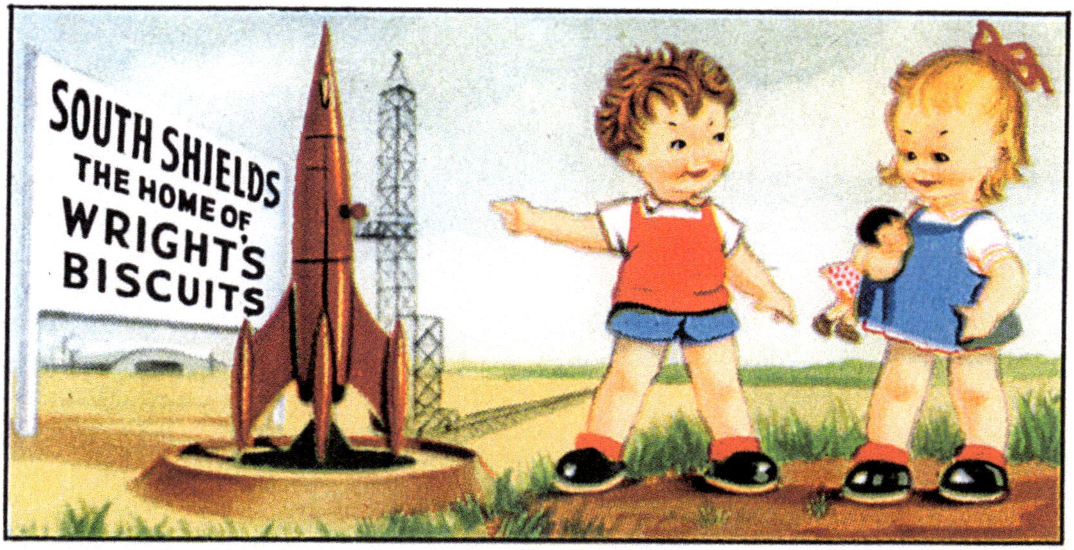

Above: Mischief Goes to Mars

One piece of ephemera that does survive in many people's collections is the colourful series of Wrights' Biscuits 'Mischief goes to Mars' cards. Mischief was designed by children's illustrator Mabel Lucie Attwell, although I don't think she had much to do with the cards themselves. Many cards were garnered from a skip when the factory closed down.

Right: Wright's Biscuits

Wright's Biscuits seen from Tyne Dock station.

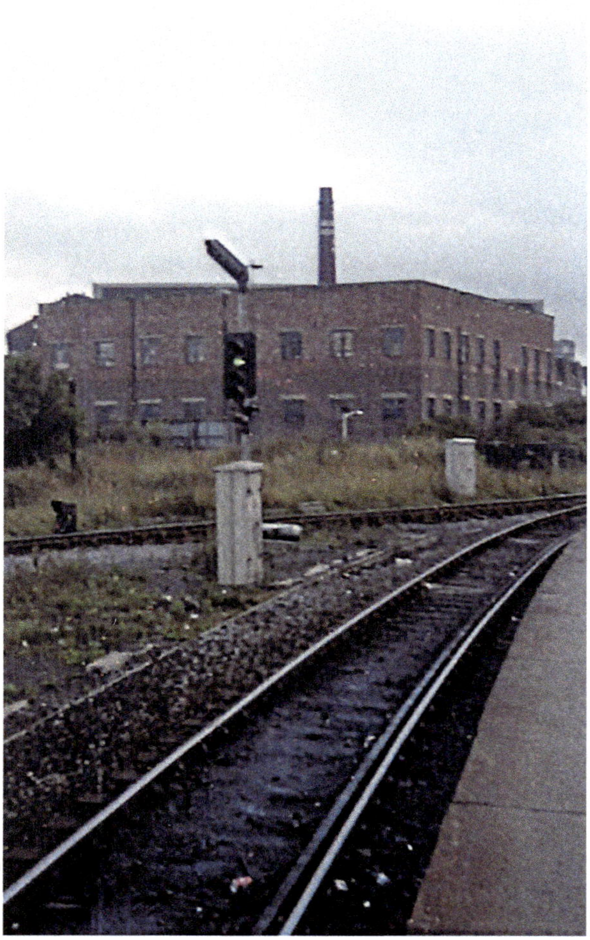

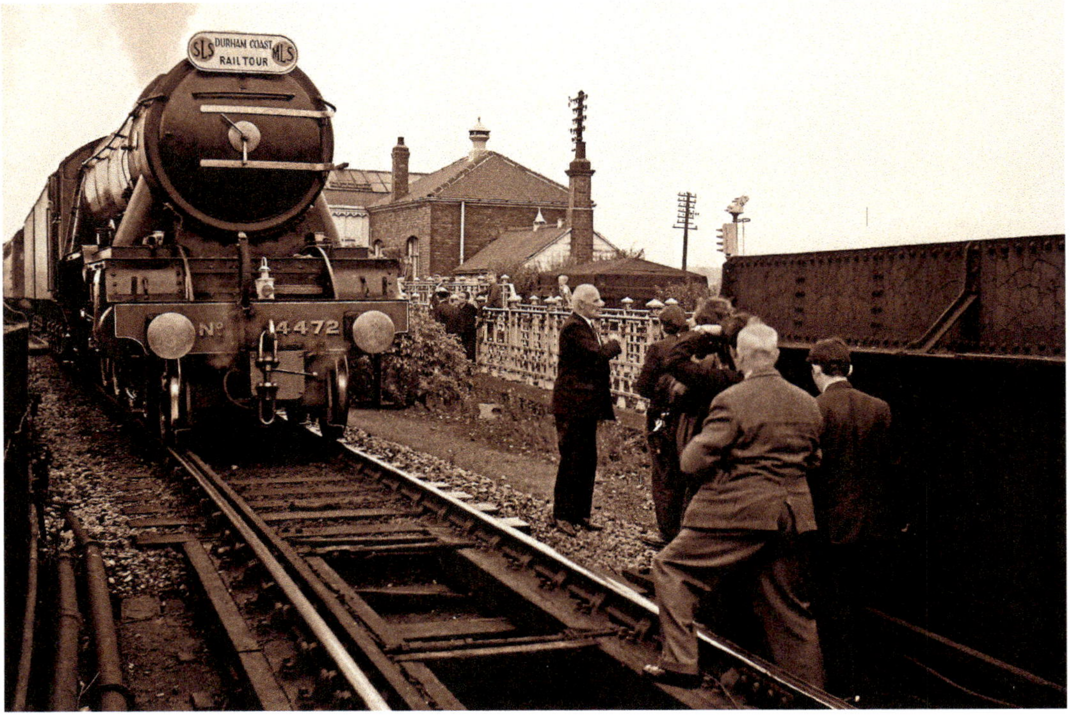

The Flying Scotsman

London & North Eastern Railway locomotive No. 4472 forever to be known as *The Flying Scotsman* at Tyne Dock. It was pulling the Durham Coast rail tour of 1968. Members of the tour also visited the Westoe system and photographs of this are seen later in this book.

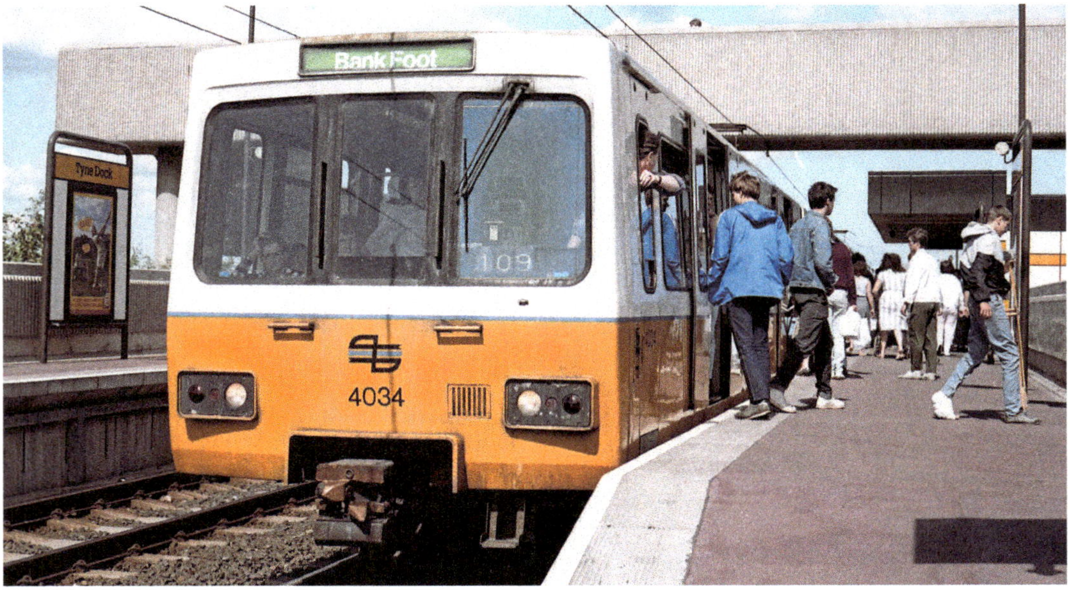

Tyne and Wear Metro

A reasonably shiny and new Tyne and Wear Metro train or 'unit' at Tyne Dock bound for Newcastle on what I believe might be the first day of public service.

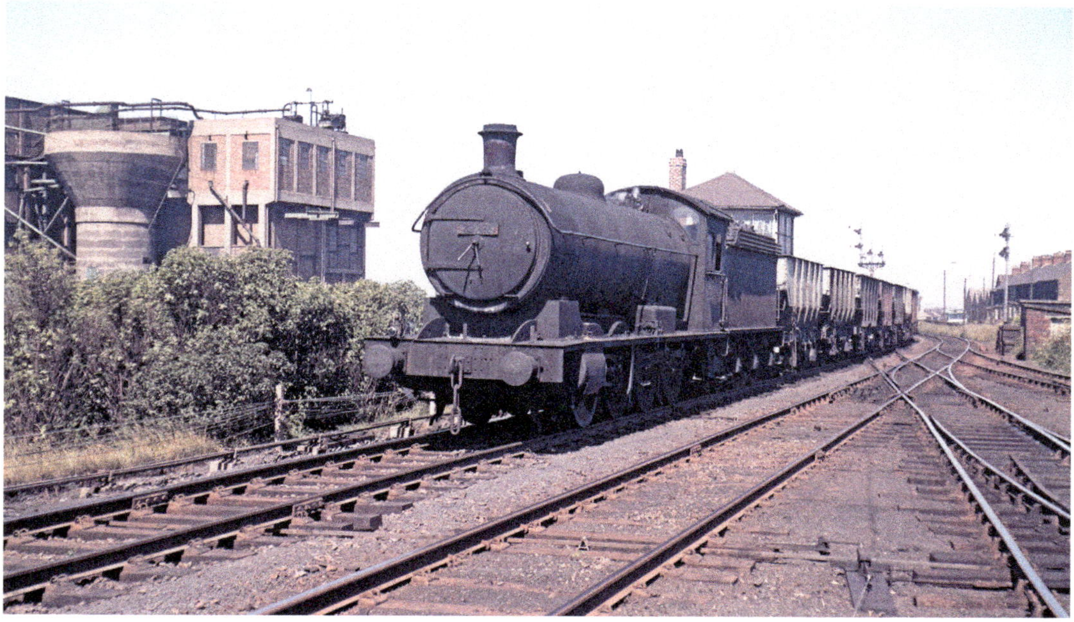

British Railways Locomotive

This image shows a British Rail locomotive running past Wright's Biscuits factory. (Date and photographer unknown.)

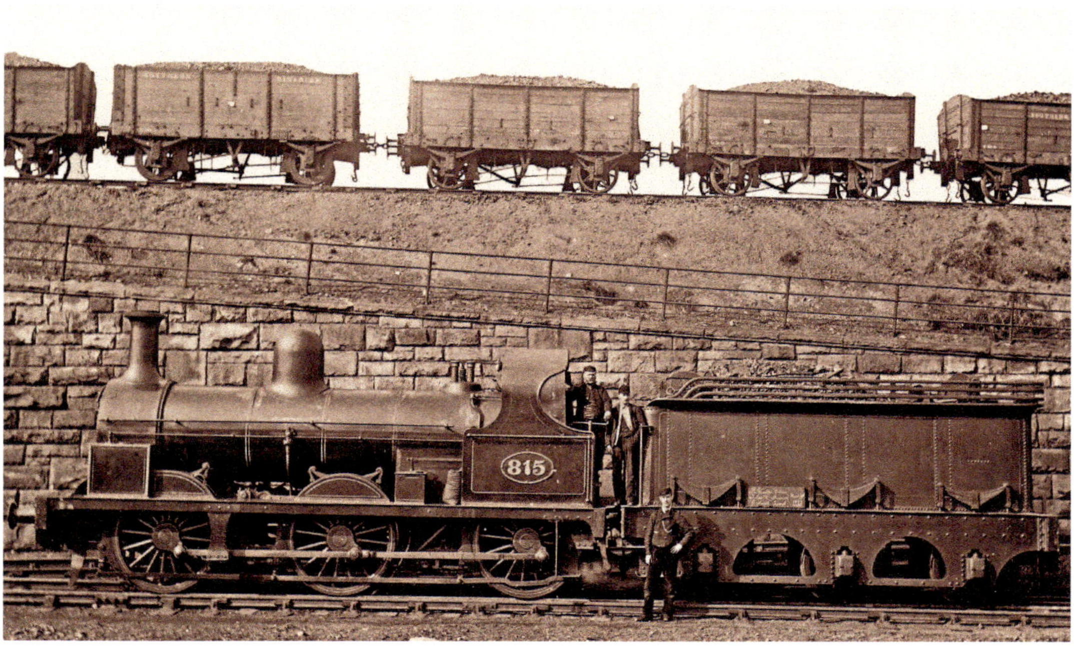

Locomotive and Crew

This image shows one of the locomotives and crews that worked coal trains into Tyne Dock for unloading. This would be in the area of what is now Middlefields Industrial Estate. The locomotive is a Fletcher Class No. 398 standing at No. 1 Hole Tyne Dock. The driver is Ralph James Charlton, the fireman T. Ewin and guard G. Smith. (Photo: Malcolm G. Charlton collection)

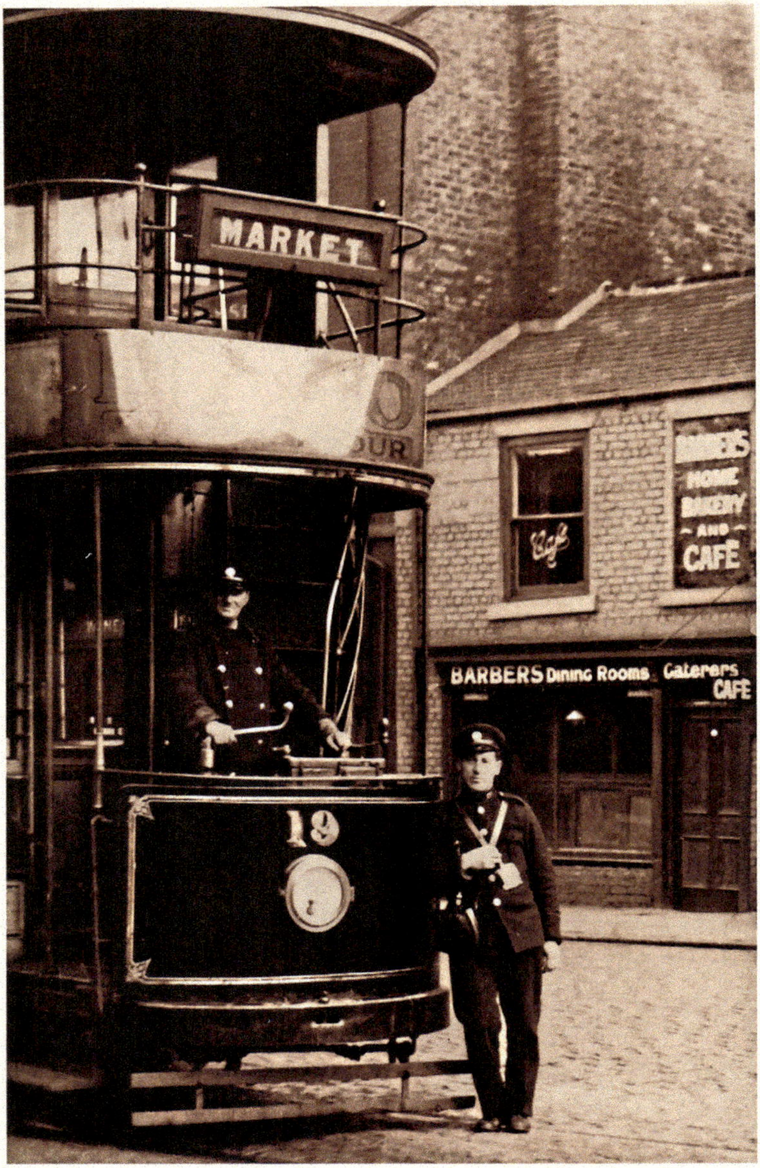

Tram Crew

Tram crew at Tyne Dock. This area has now changed beyond recognition. This were supplied to me by the now sadly deceased South Shields collector Dennis Boad.

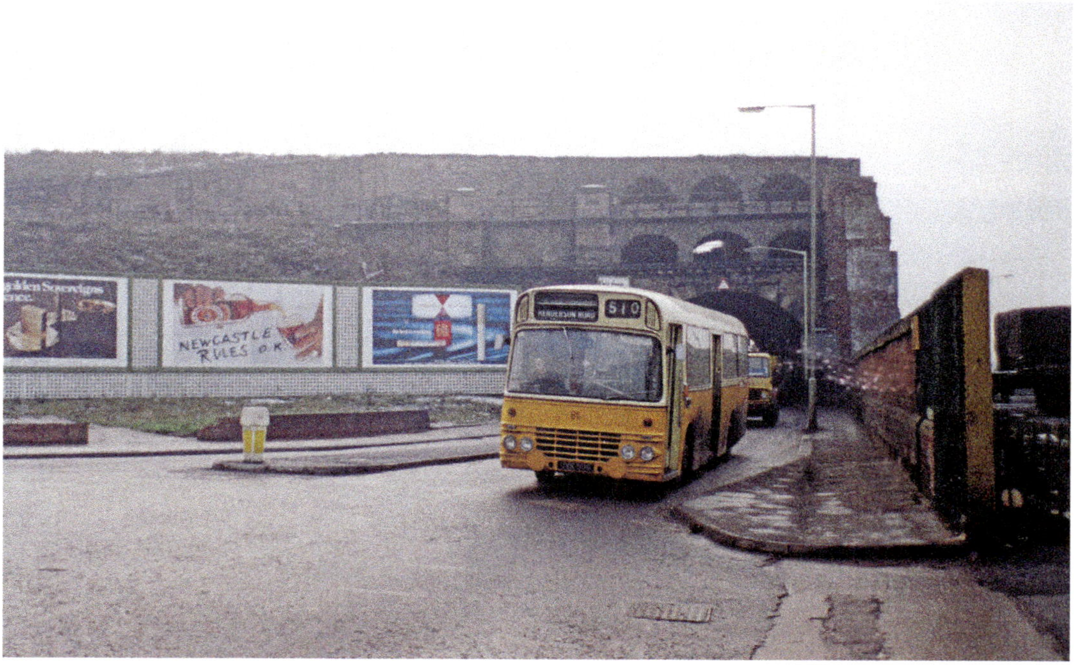

Tyne Dock Arches

The remains of Tyne Dock Arches, now also demolished.

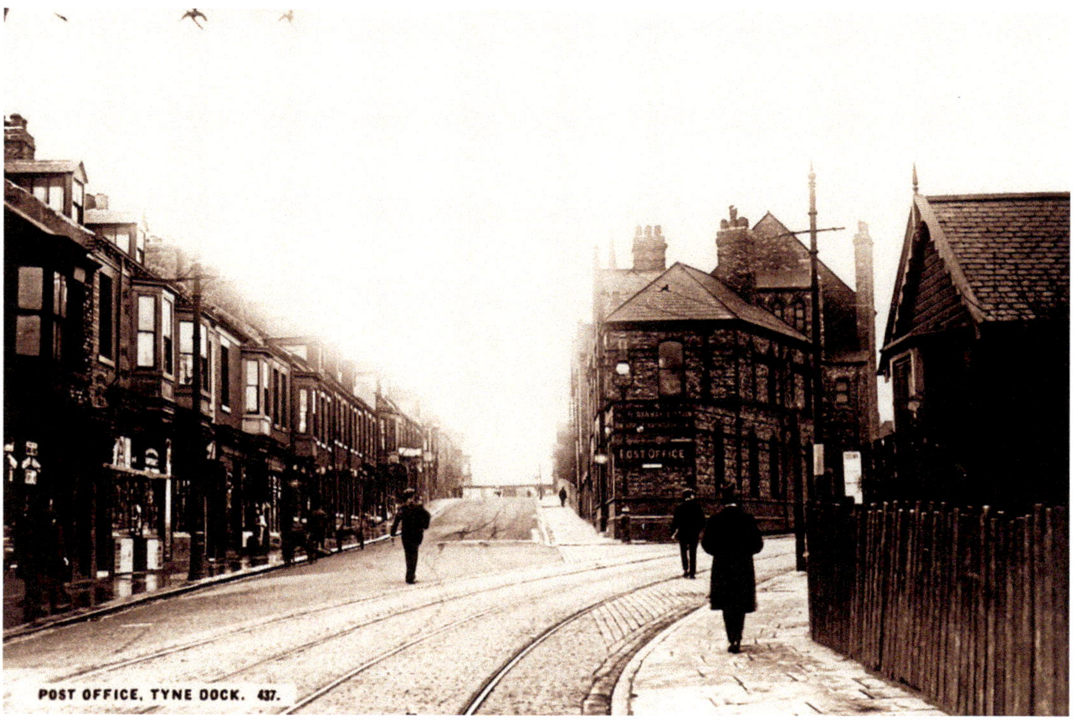

Post Office

This image shows the former post office at Tyne Dock.

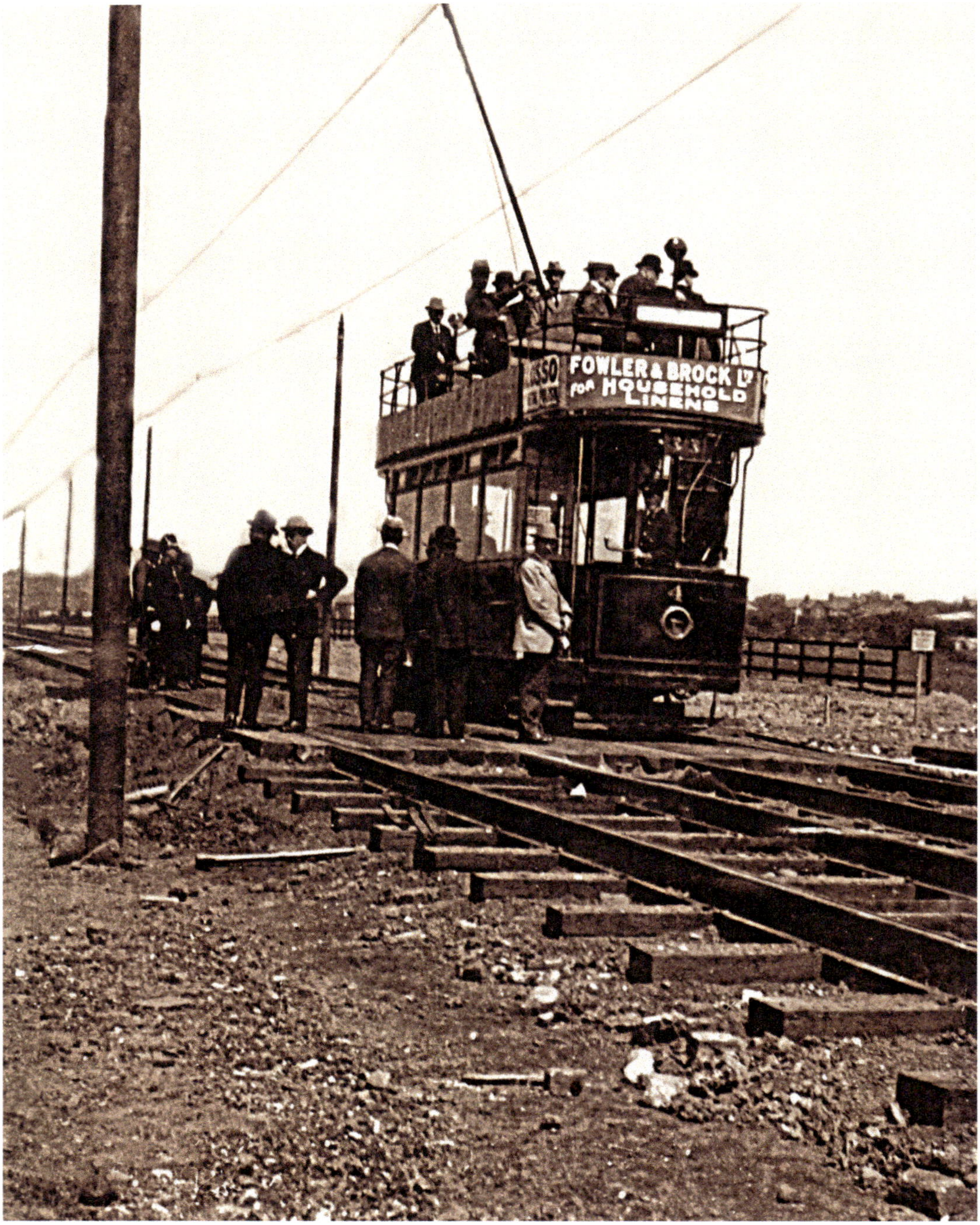

King George Road

A tramcar running along what became the central reservation of King George Road *c.* 1921. I suspect the car might be a party of 'officials' viewing the work and having a bit of a day out. The car was actually one of the oldest on the system at that time and when the service started the trams used were far bigger and much more modern.

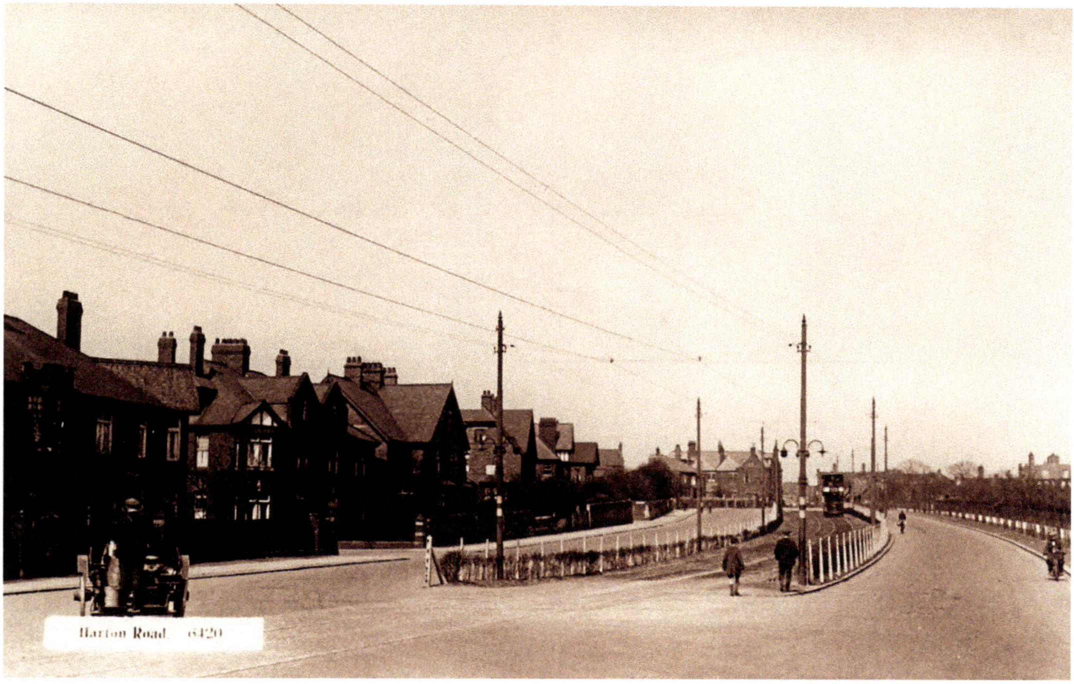

Harton Road

Harton Road (now Sunderland Road) *c.* 1924. The County Pub is in the centre of the picture and the Readhead Park is to the right.

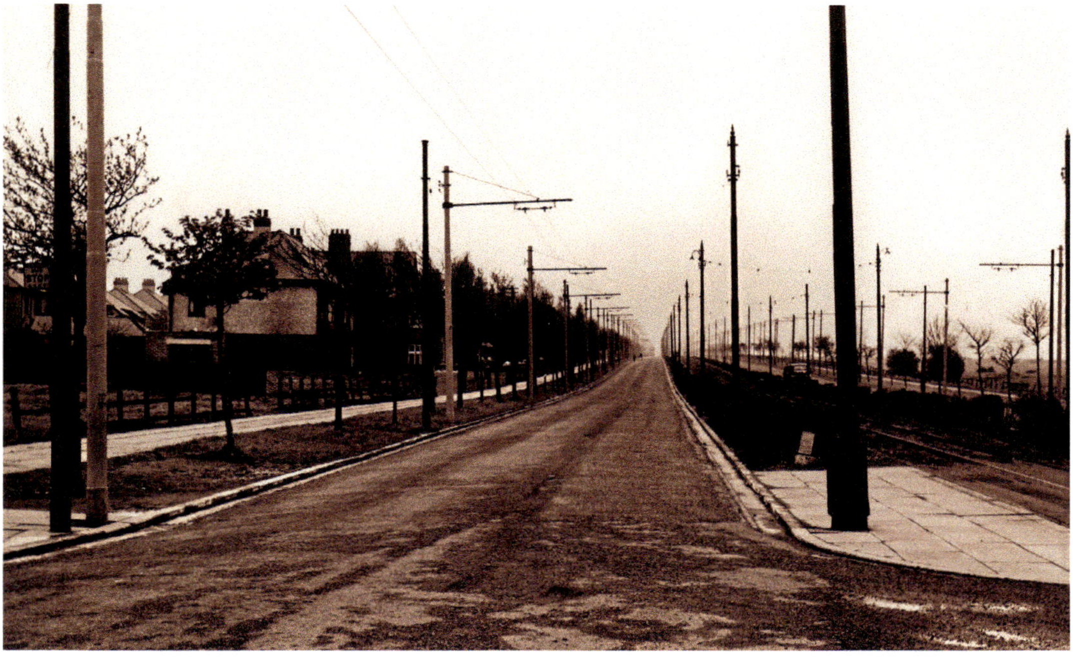

King George Road Trolleybus

May 1946 and the trolleybus wiring is now fully in place on King George Road and the trams have gone. The last tramcar ran on 31 March 1946.

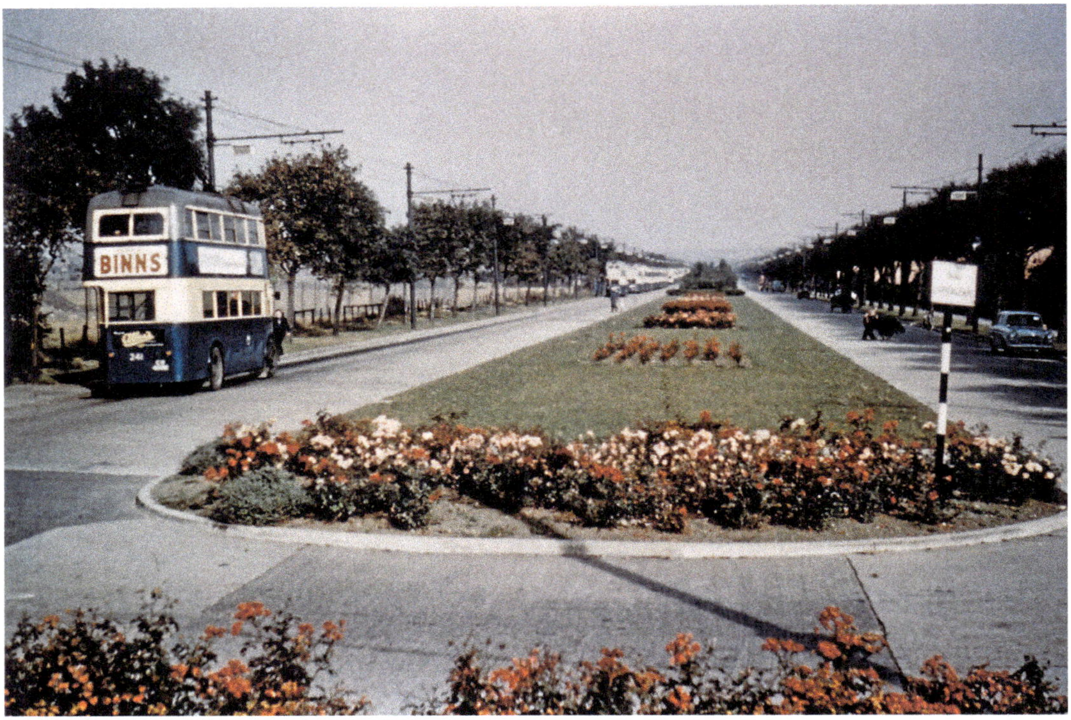

Trams and Trolleybuses

Grass and flowers have replaced the tram tracks and the trolleybuses themselves will soon be a part of history.

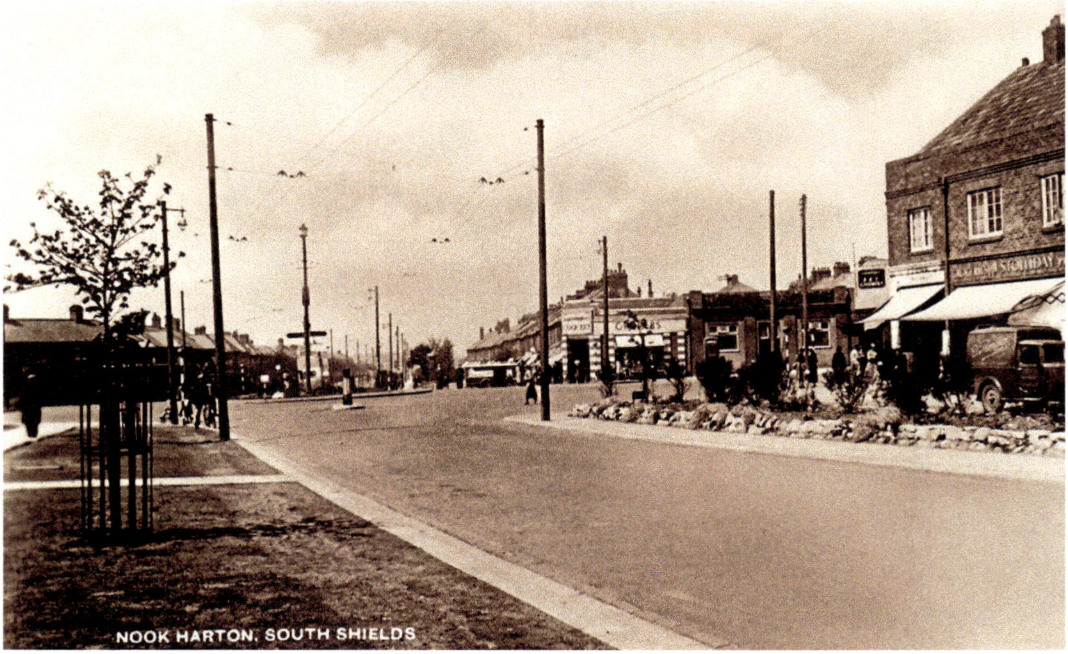

Harton Nook

A postcard view of Harton Nook.

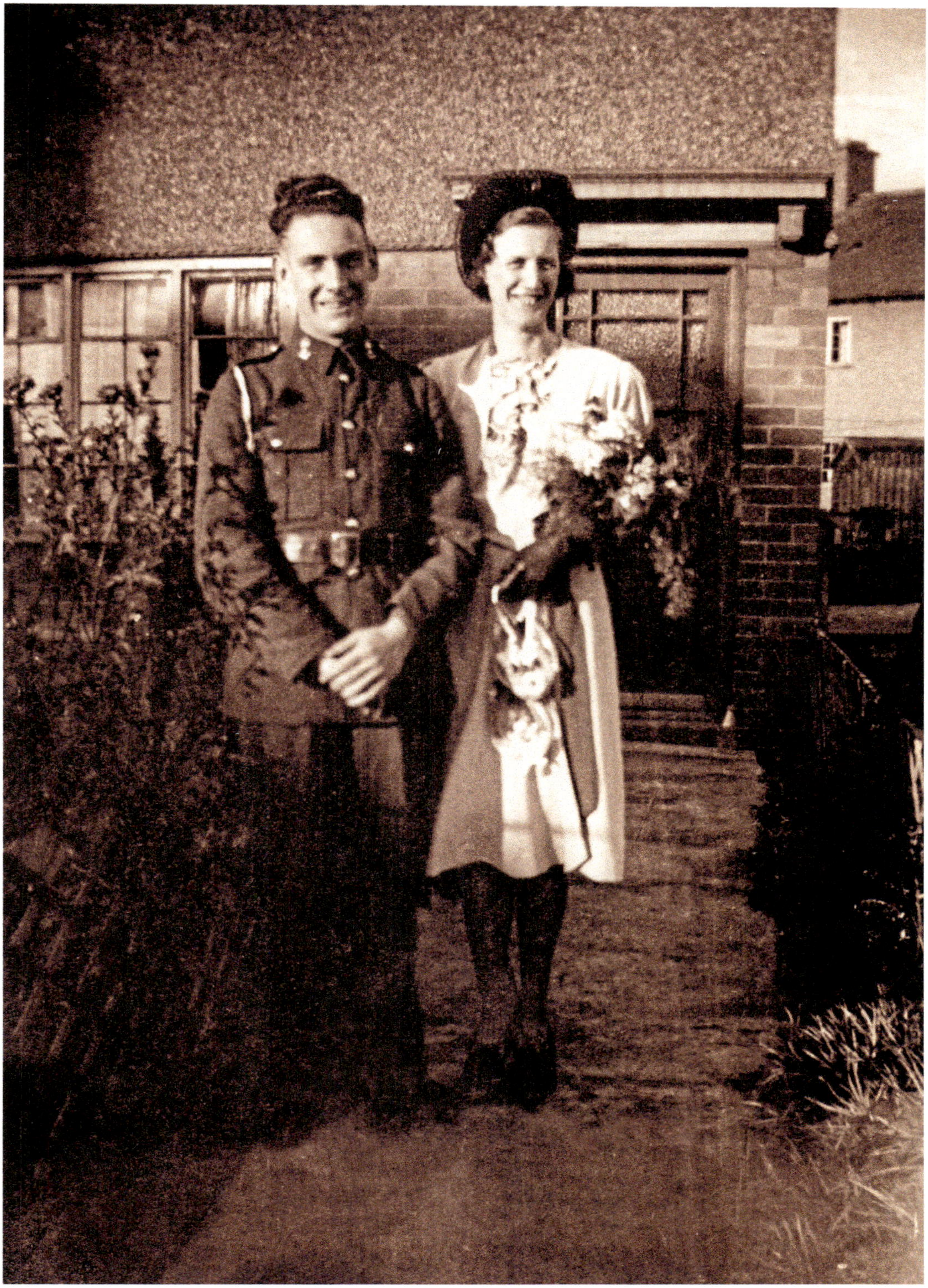

Cleadon Park
Newly-weds Bob Hanrahan and Jenny Wilkinson outside their new Cleadon Park home *c.* 1941.

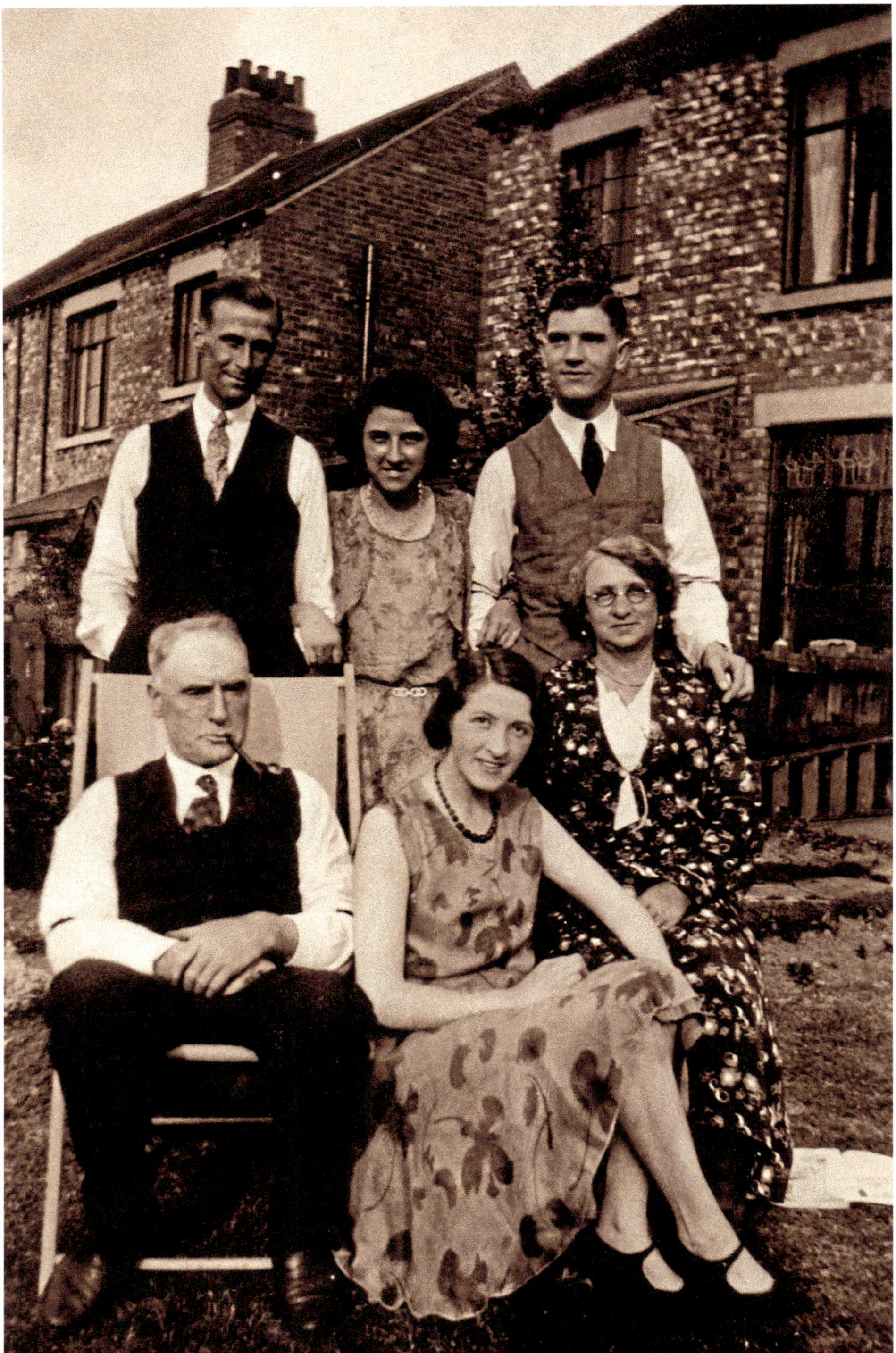

Harton Lane
Joe Tyndale, Kathleen and Cuthbert Nicholson and Madge Hunter with other family members in their back garden on Harton Lane in 1932.

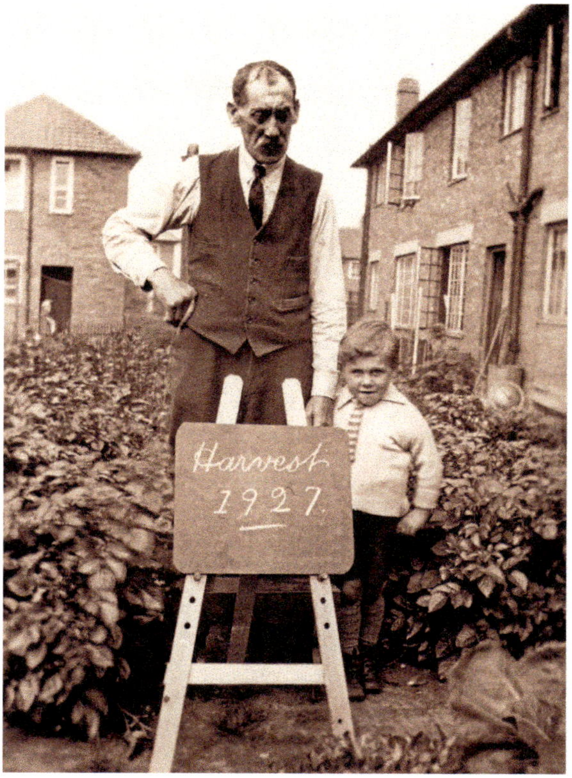

Park Avenue
George Branch and his son Ernie in Park Avenue, 1927.

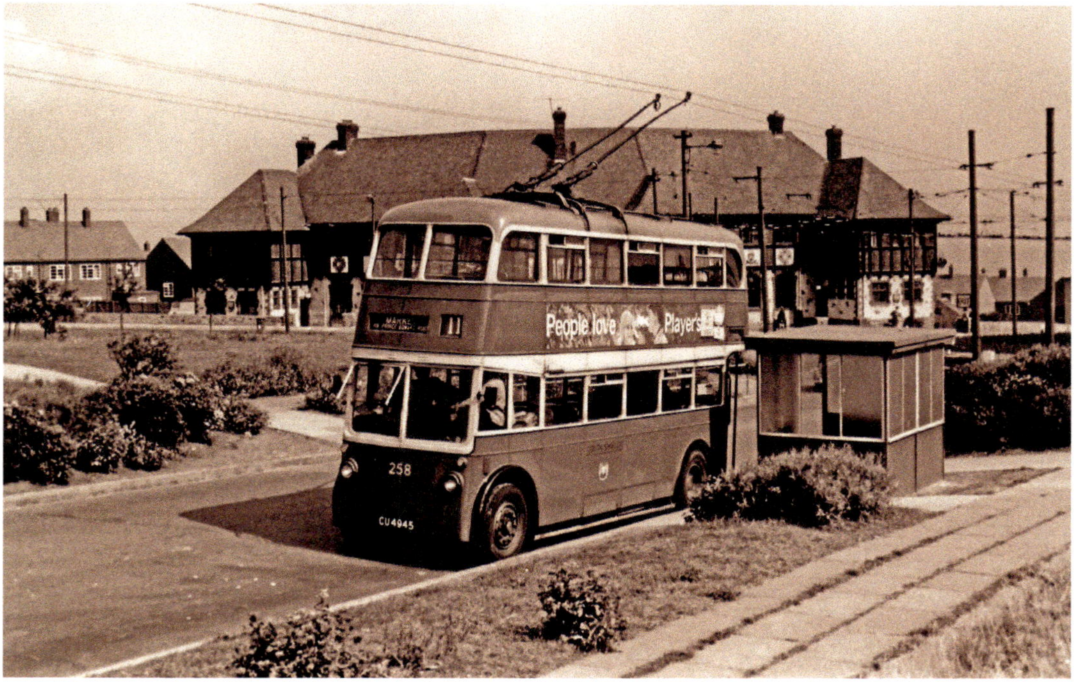

Marsden Inn
This image shows a Corporation trolleybus outside the Marsden Inn *c.* 1960.

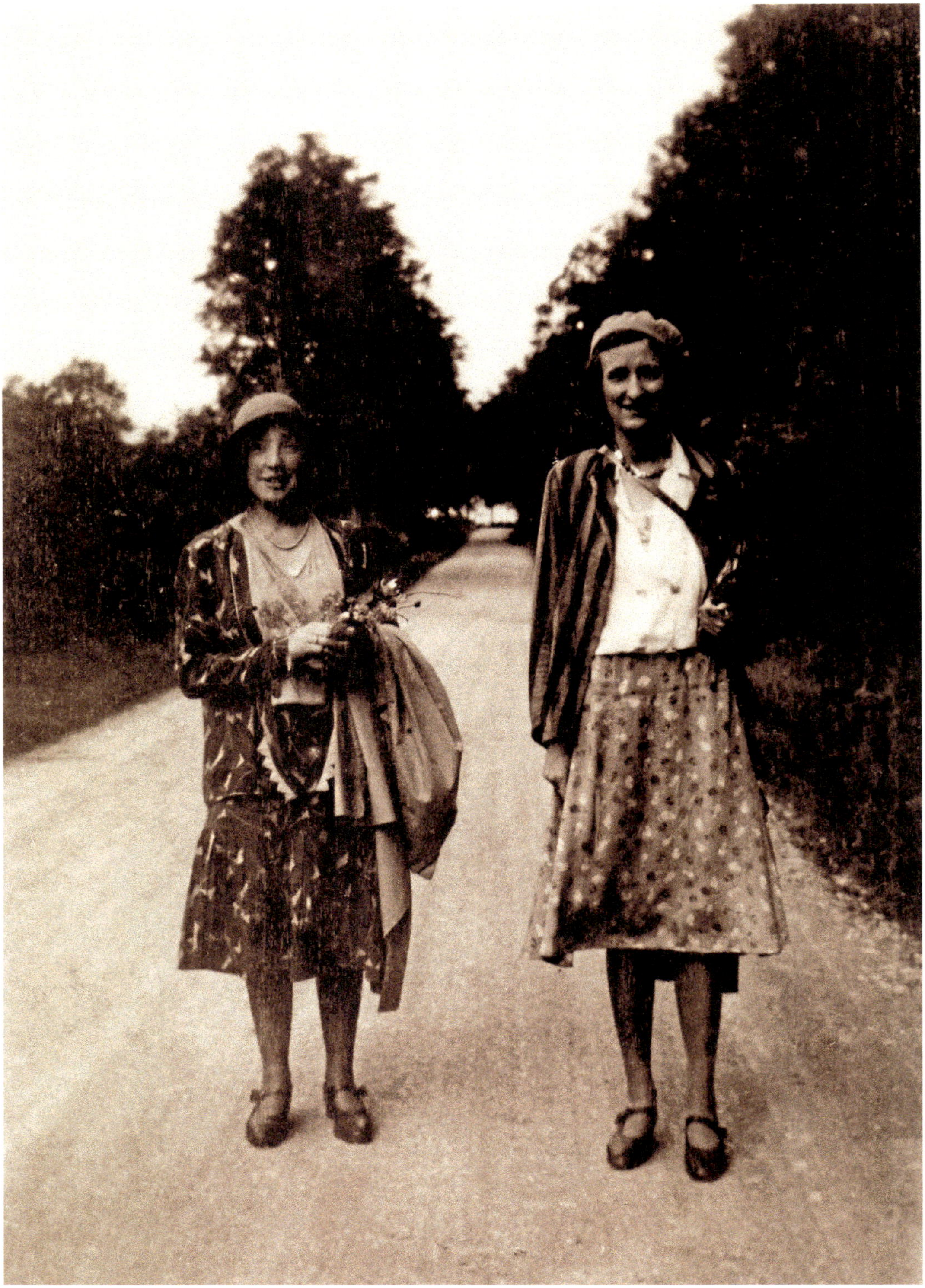

Marsden Lane
A couple out for a walk along what is now Marsden Lane.

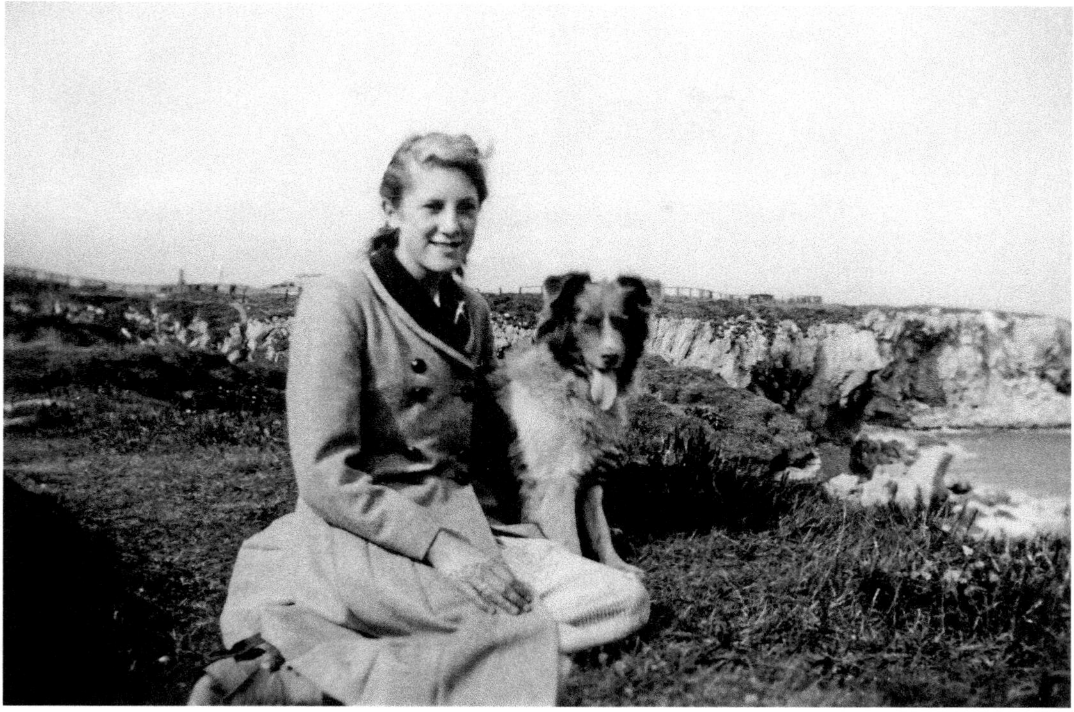

Marsden Bay
Joan Wilkinson with the family dog, Rance, at Marsden Bay.

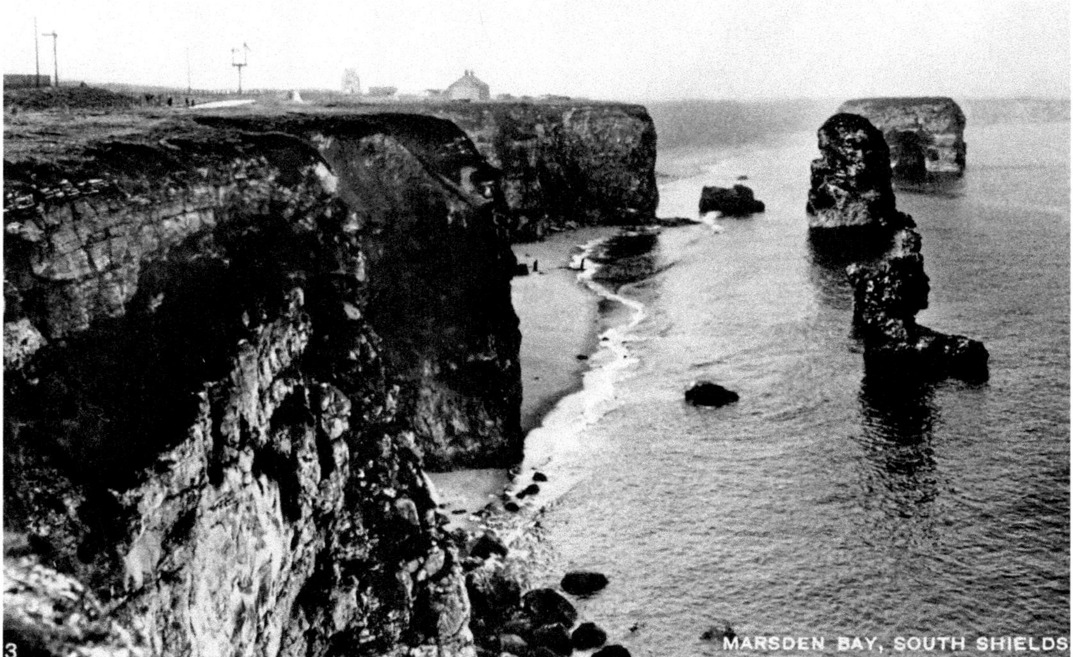

Marsden Bay
A postcard view of the Masden Bay area.

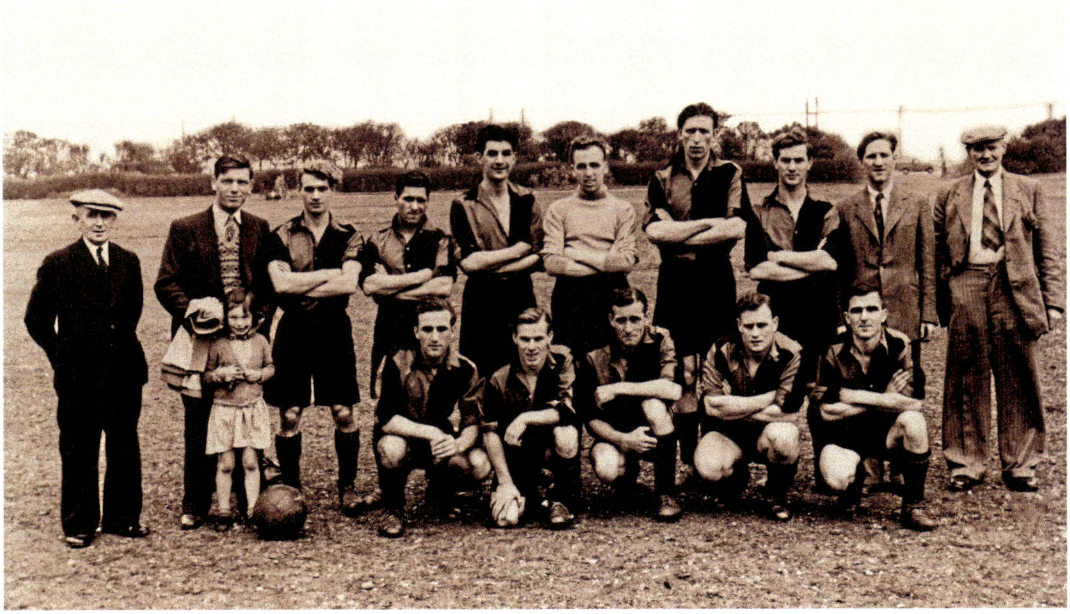

Westoe Colliery Football Team

Westoe Colliery football team at the Bents Park, 1952–53. Charles Carlson is in the back row on the middle left.

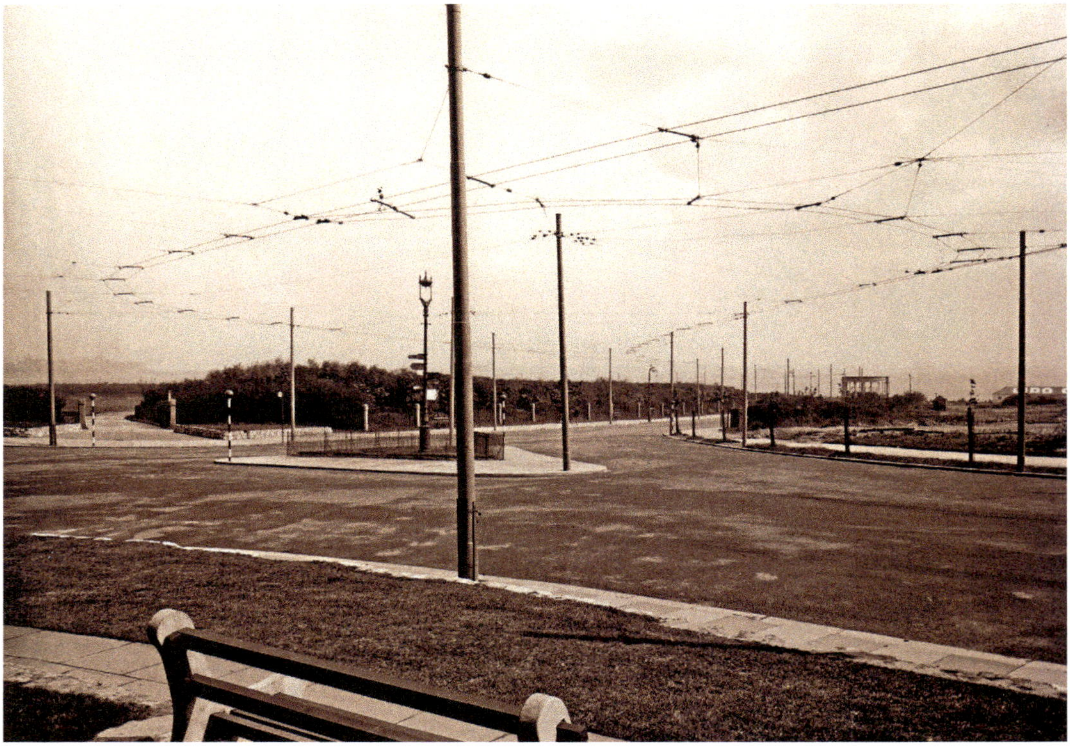

Bents Park

A view of the Bents Park area *c.* 1950. This is one of a number taken to illustrate trolleybus wiring.

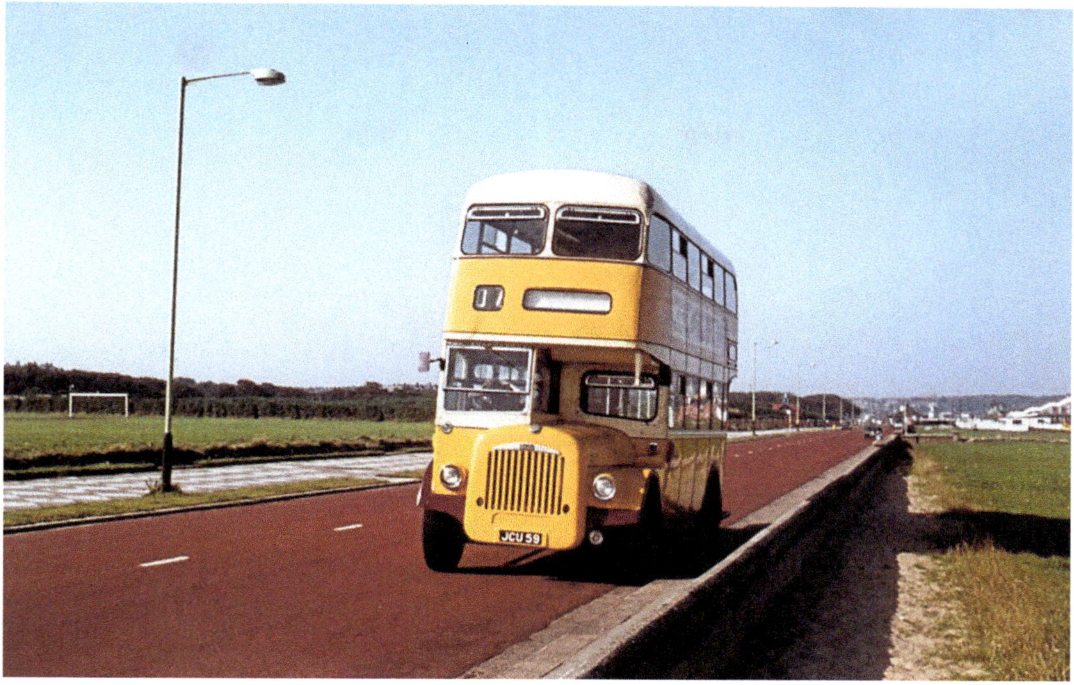

South Shields Corporation Bus

A former South Shields Corporation bus, now in yellow Passenger Transport executive livery, running past the Bents Park.

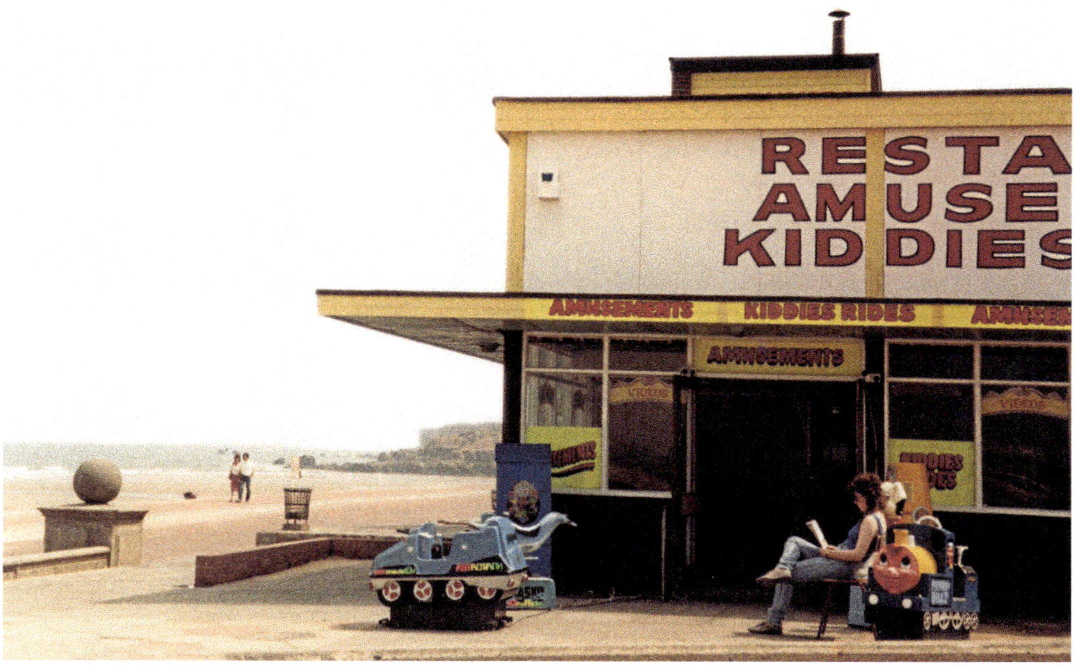

Frankies Café

The former Frankies café on the foreshore.

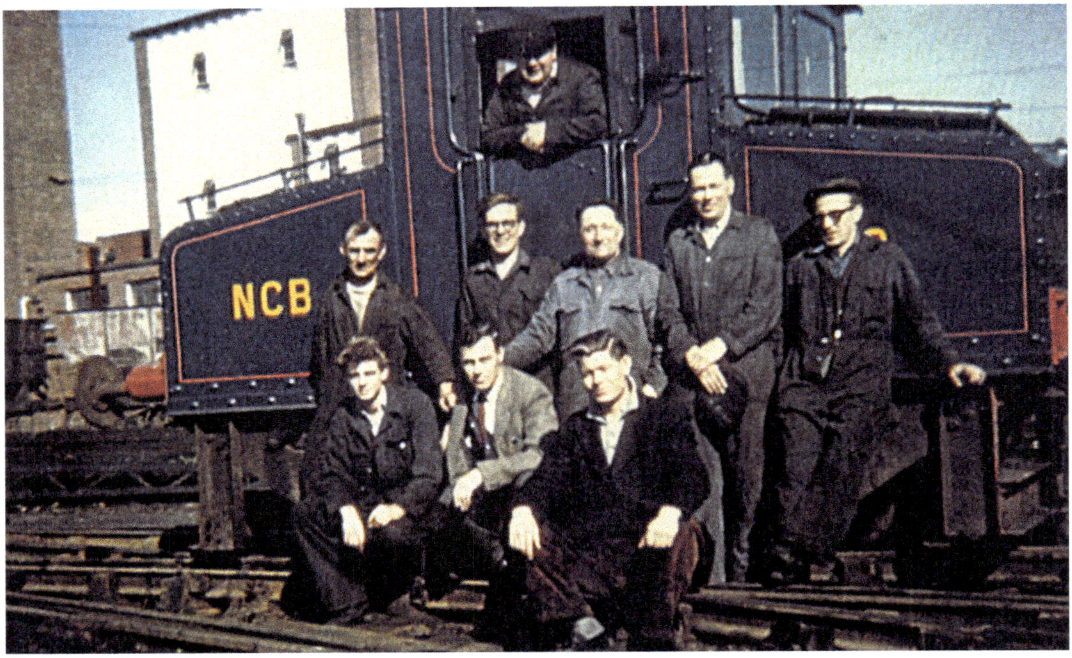

National Coal Board Electric Railway Staff

Staff of the National Coal Board electric railway at the Westoe Colliery site. This photo was taken by staff member Bill Henderson.

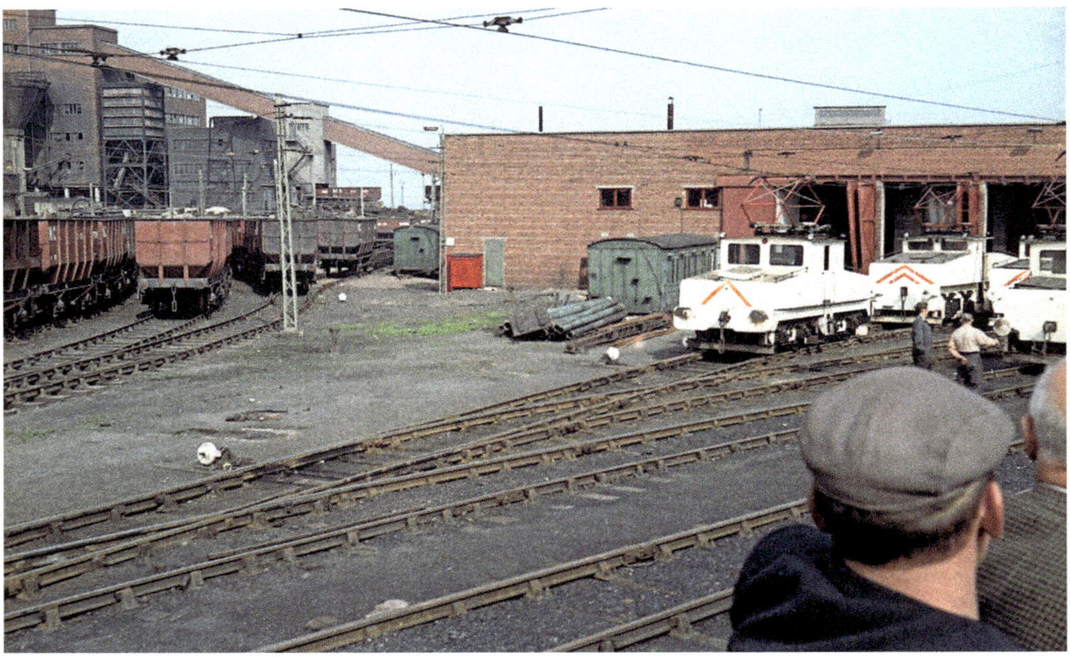

Westoe Colliery Electric Railway

Railway enthusiasts visiting the Westoe Colliery electric railway as part of the Durham Coast rail tour referred to previously in this book. This whole area is now unrecognisable as it is now covered by the Westoe Crown Estate.

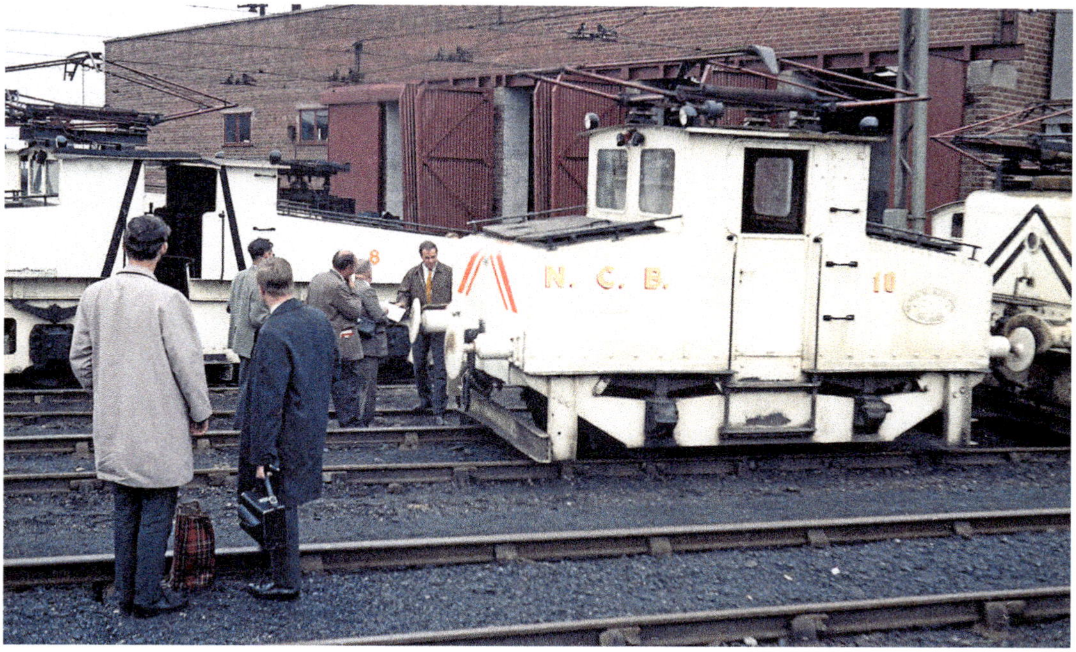

Painting Locomotives
Following a fatal accident on the line, the locomotives were painted a brilliant white livery intended to increase visibility.

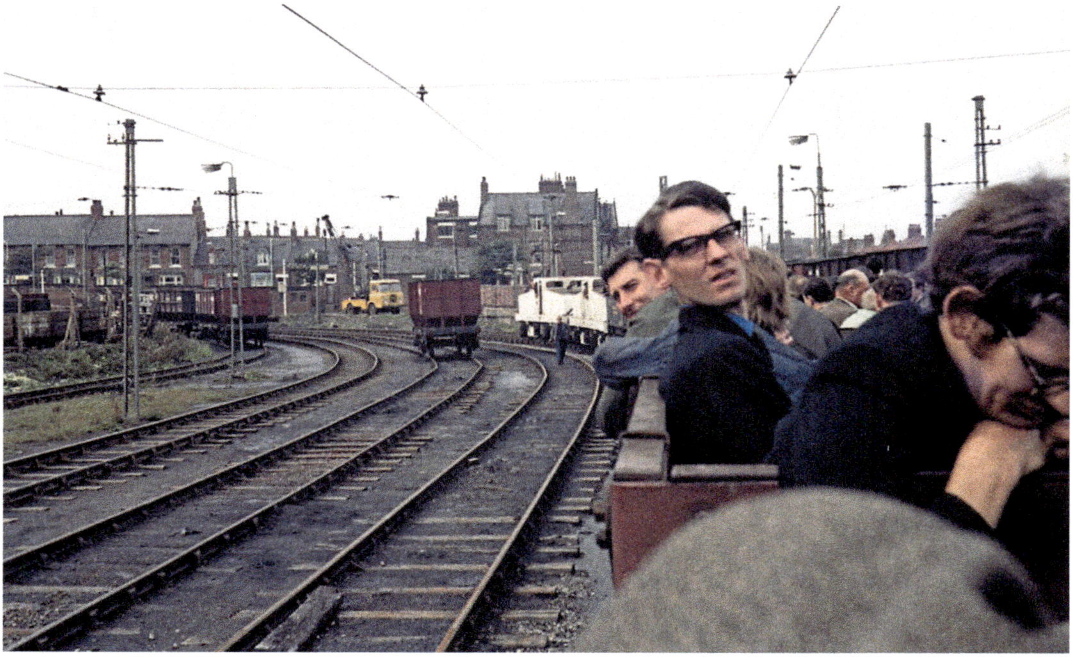

Rail Tour
This part of the tour included a look at the system, with passengers being accommodated on wooden benches fitted into mineral wagons. Erskine Road is visible behind the train. The camera is located in what is now a street of houses called Sea Winnings way.

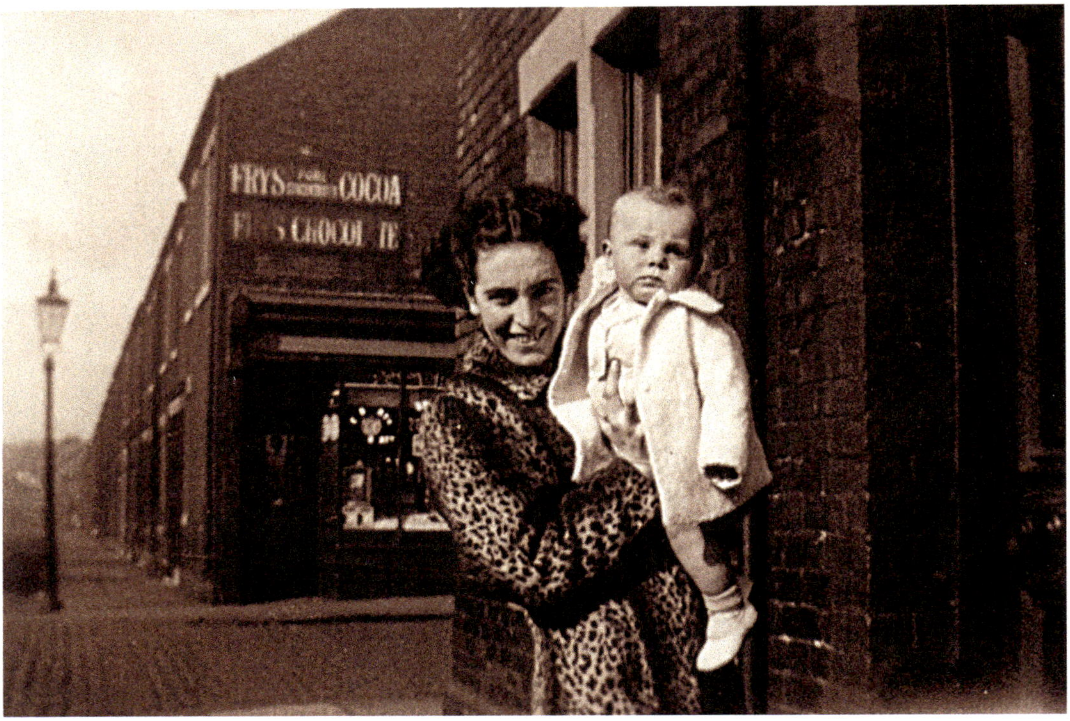

Taylor Street

Margaret Miller (née Ramshaw) with her son Richard outside No. 285 Taylor Street shortly before the Second World War. In the background is Wilkinson's shop in Cuthbert Street.

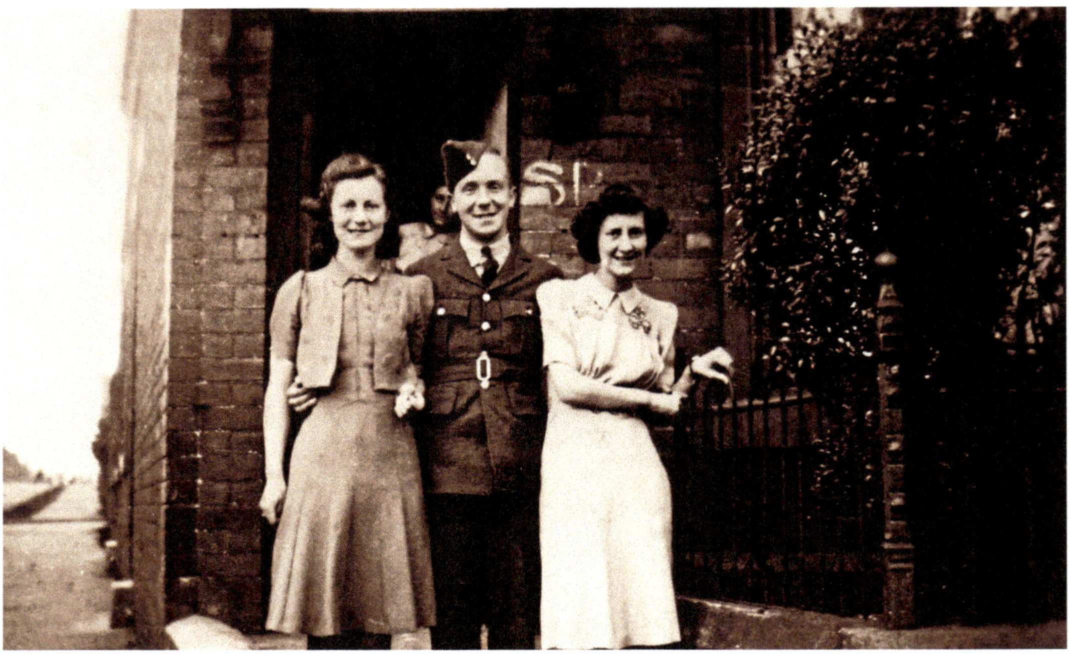

Egerton Road

Ready to go to war. Trevor Tate with Catherine and Margaret Freeman in Egerton Road, 1940.

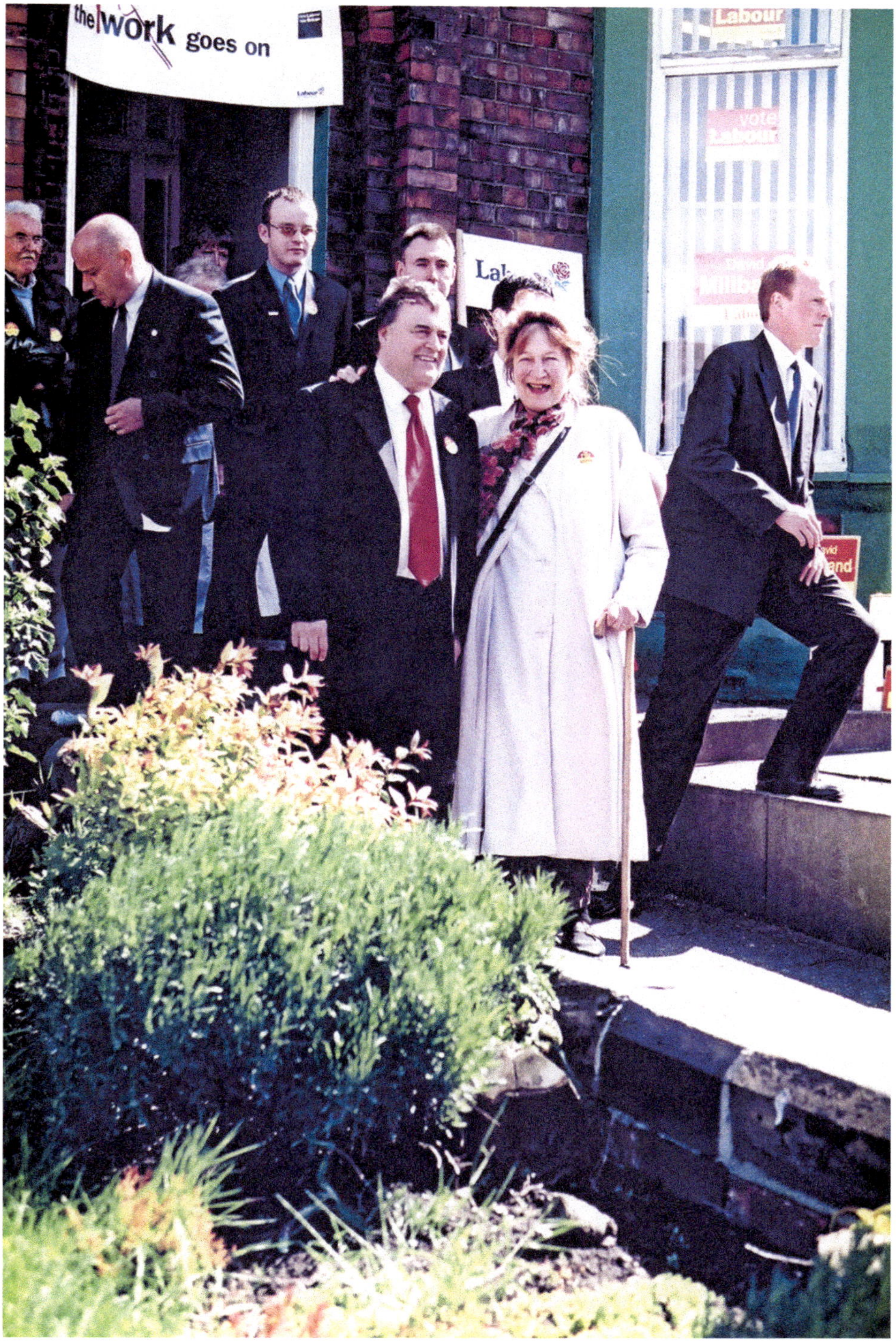

Outside Ede House

Labour Party member Joyce Carlson with John Prescott outside Ede House. This photograph was taken during the May 2001 general election campaign a matter of days after Craig Evans threw an egg at Mr Prescott at almost point-blank range.

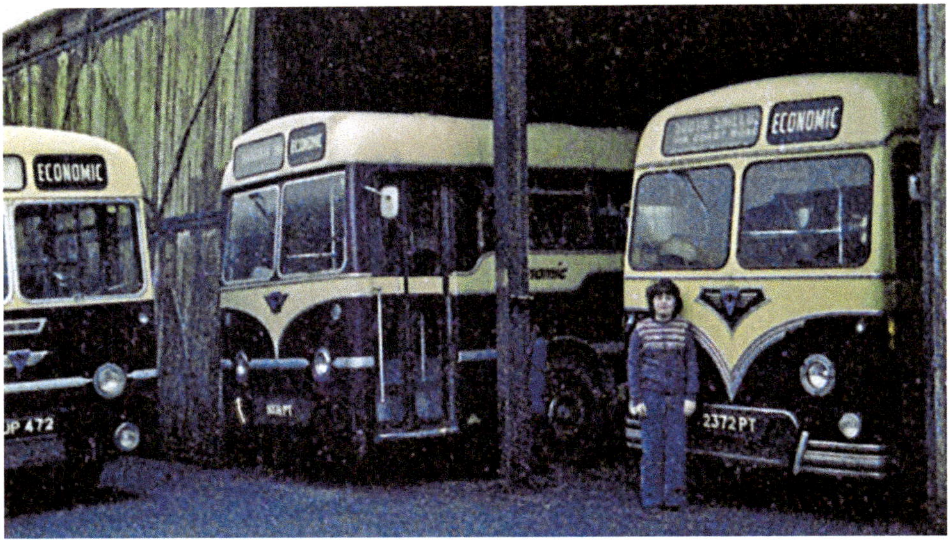

Economic Bus Depot

John Carlson at the Economic Bus Depot outside the former Whitburn Colliery on the Sunday after the old buses had ceased running and were replaced by new passenger transport executive Leyland buses. Economic began operating from Whitburn in 1925 with the new coast road giving them two excellent routes into South Shields. The company was operated jointly by G. R. Anderson and A. W. Wilson. In 1974 both men were bought out by the Tyne and Wear PTE, their garages closed and staff transferred to other PTE depots shortly after. The routes were renumbered as the 538 and 539. However that was not to be the end. The PTE later revived the Economic brand and the services became the E1, E2 and E6 still run by Stagecoach today. Below is a selection of economic tickets.

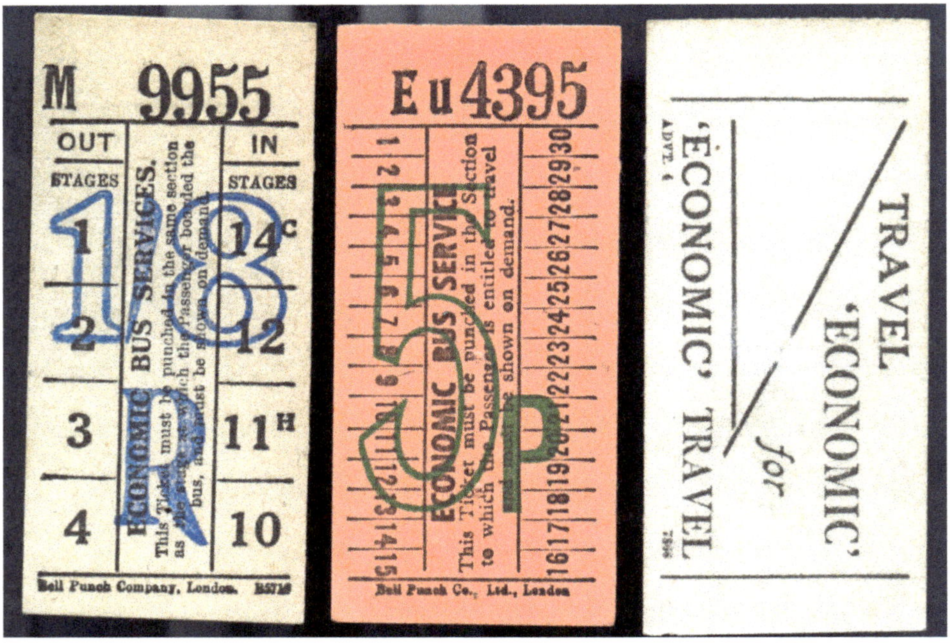

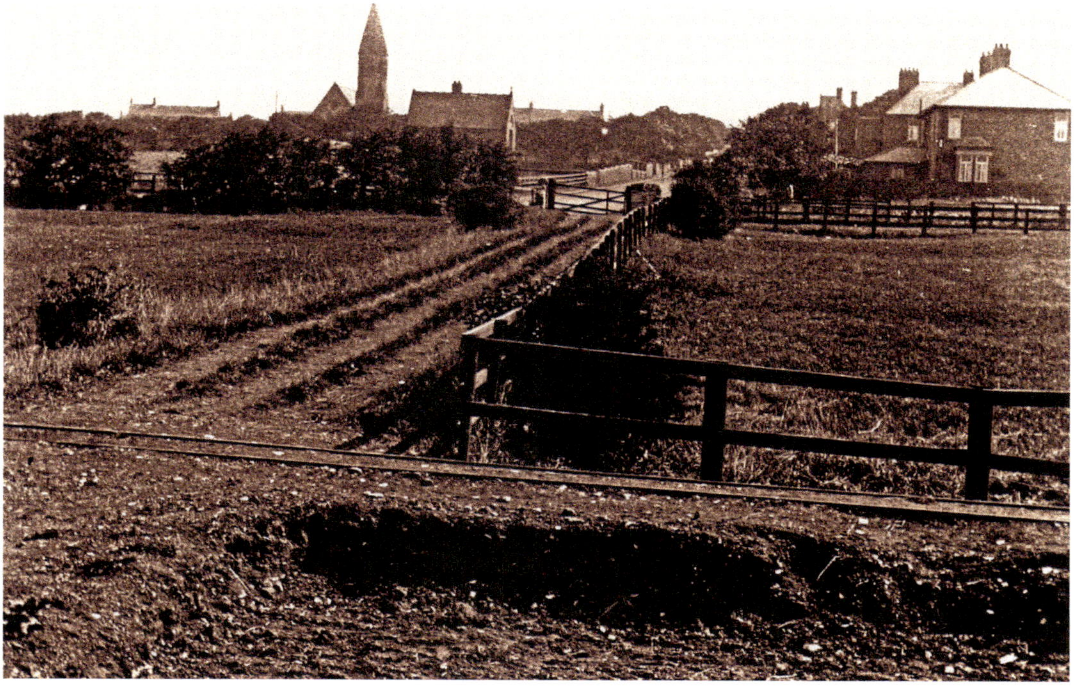

Harton Village

A view of Harton Village looking up Moor Lane from what is now King George Road. We suspect this was taken during King George Road's construction with what seems to be a small light railway in place for moving materials.

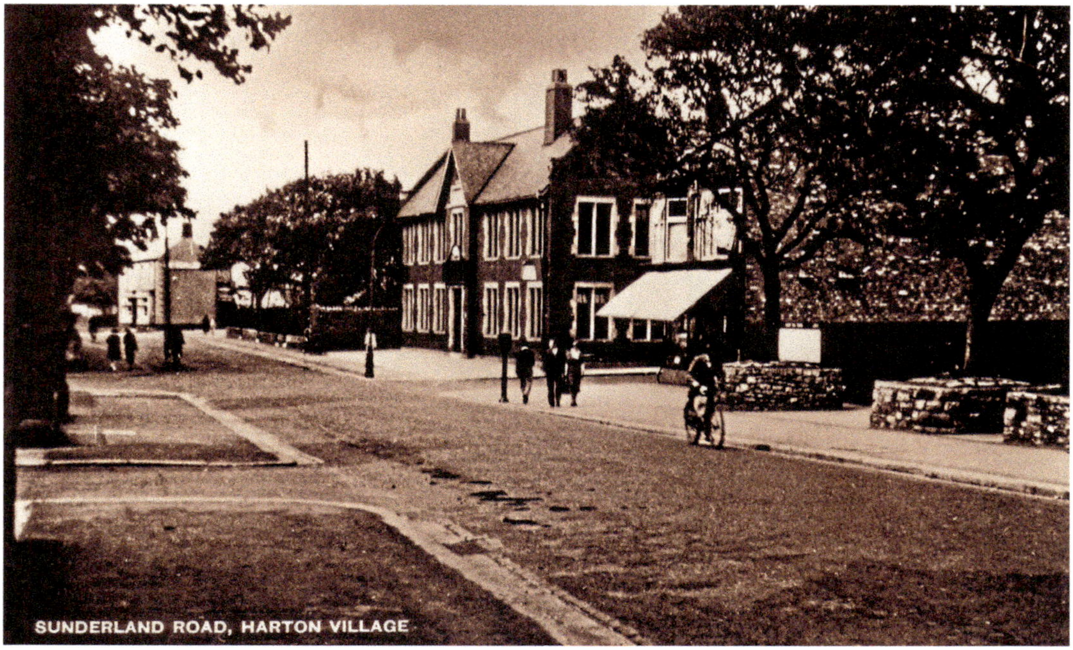

Vigilant Inn

A postcard view of the Vigilant Inn in Harton Village.

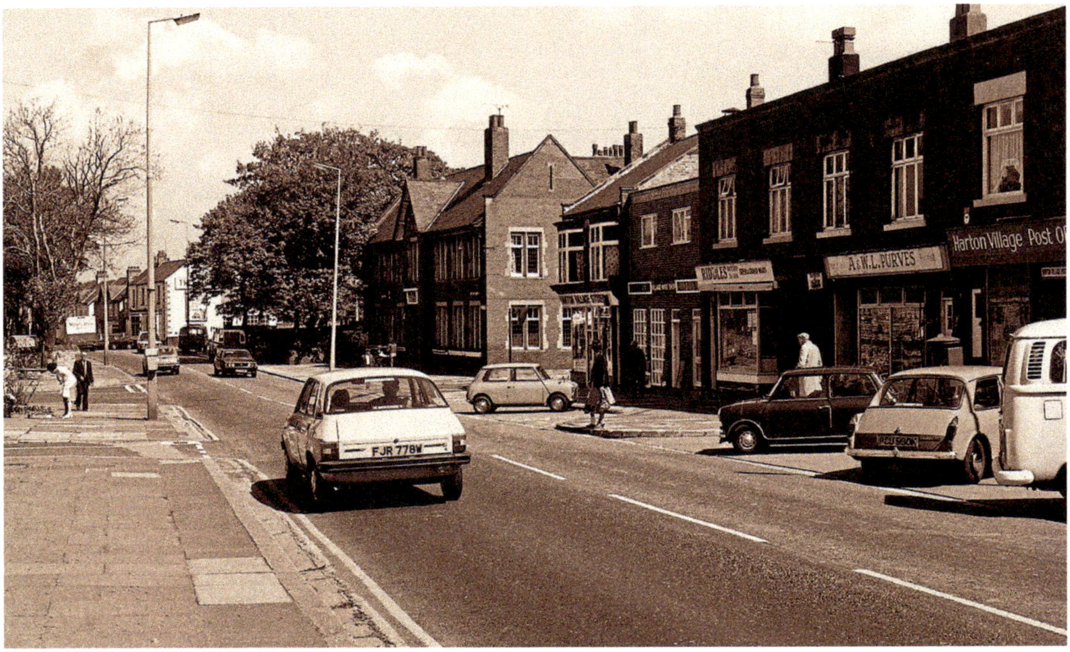

Harton Village

The above view is from the mid-1980s. The trees haven given way to car parking and shops.

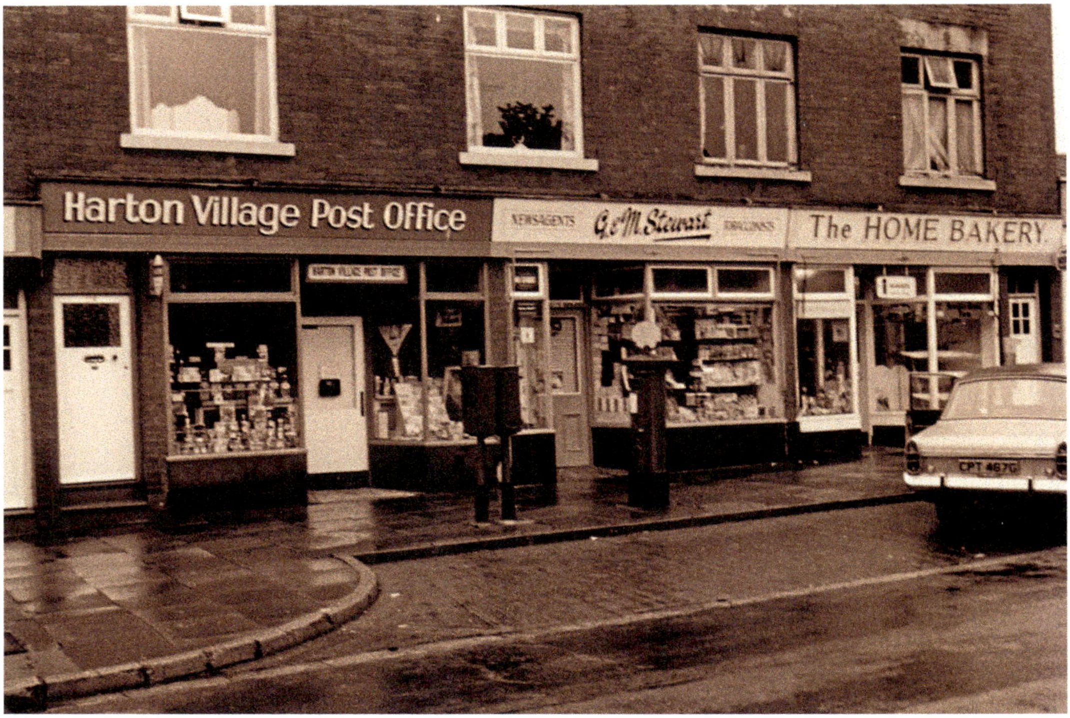

Harton Village

A closer view of the shops in what I believe is the 1970s since this time both the post office and newsagent has gone, but cafés and speciality shops seem stronger than ever.

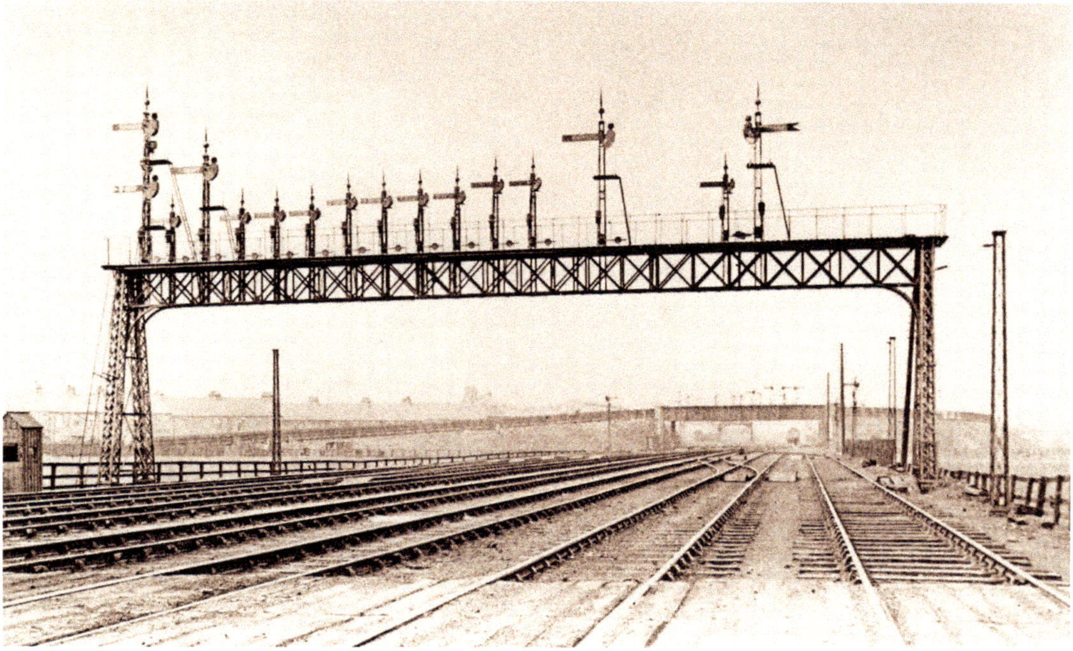

Green Lane

A rather splendid view of the North Eastern Railway signal gantry at Green Lane with the former Green Lane Bridge behind. This area was almost a throat of South Shields with untold numbers of tonnes of coal coming each way along these lines from local collieries and often heading towards Tyne Dock Arches.

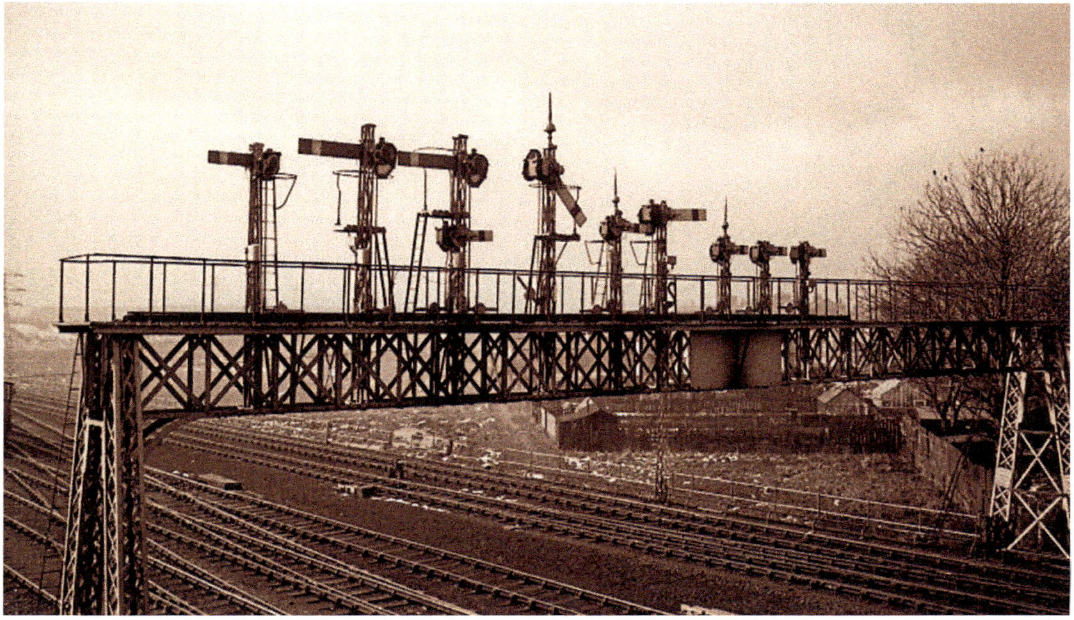

Signalling

More of the vast array of signalling needed to keep control of train movements. The image is taken from Green Lane Bridge.

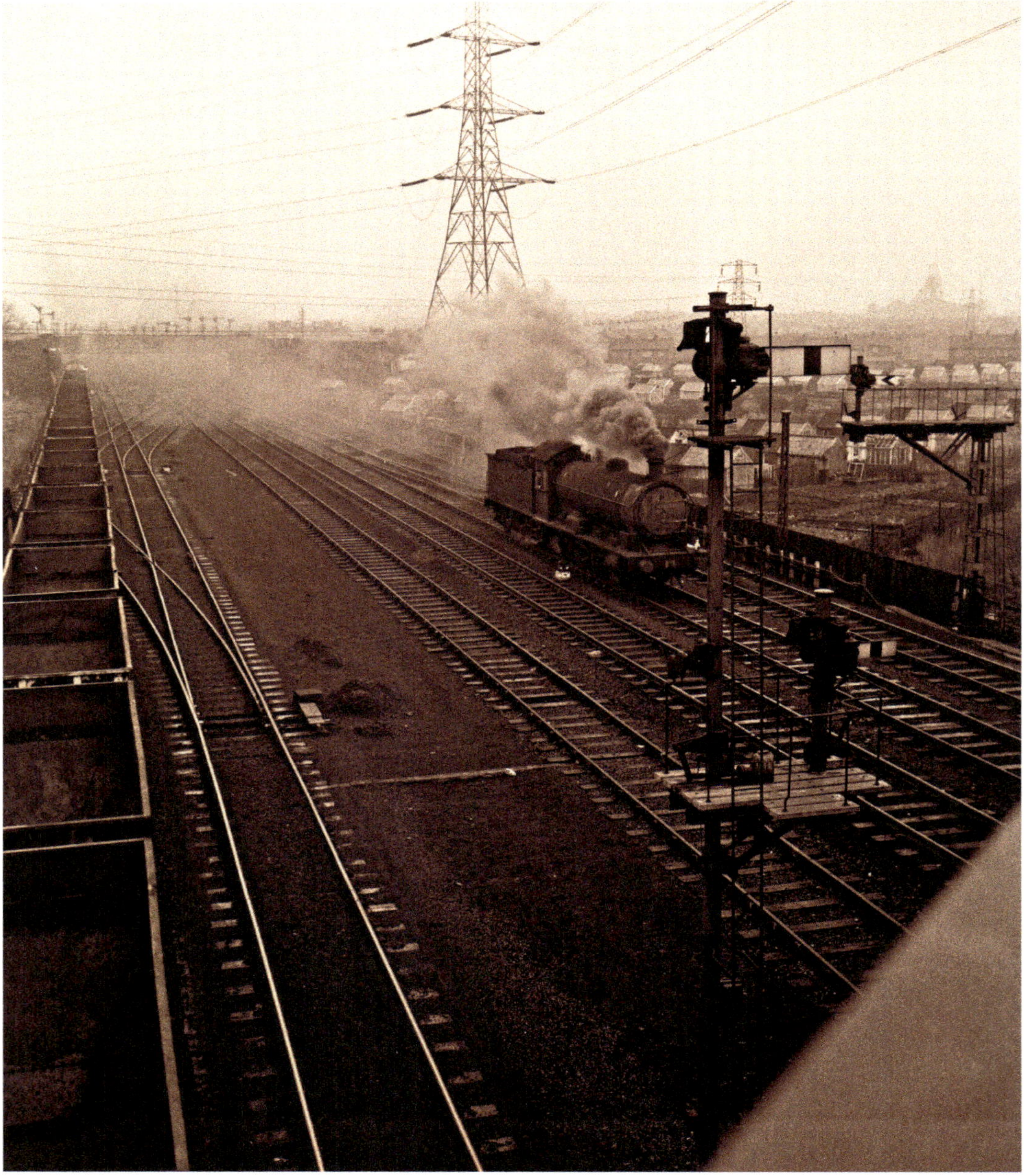

Green Lane
The Green Lane area *c*. 1960.

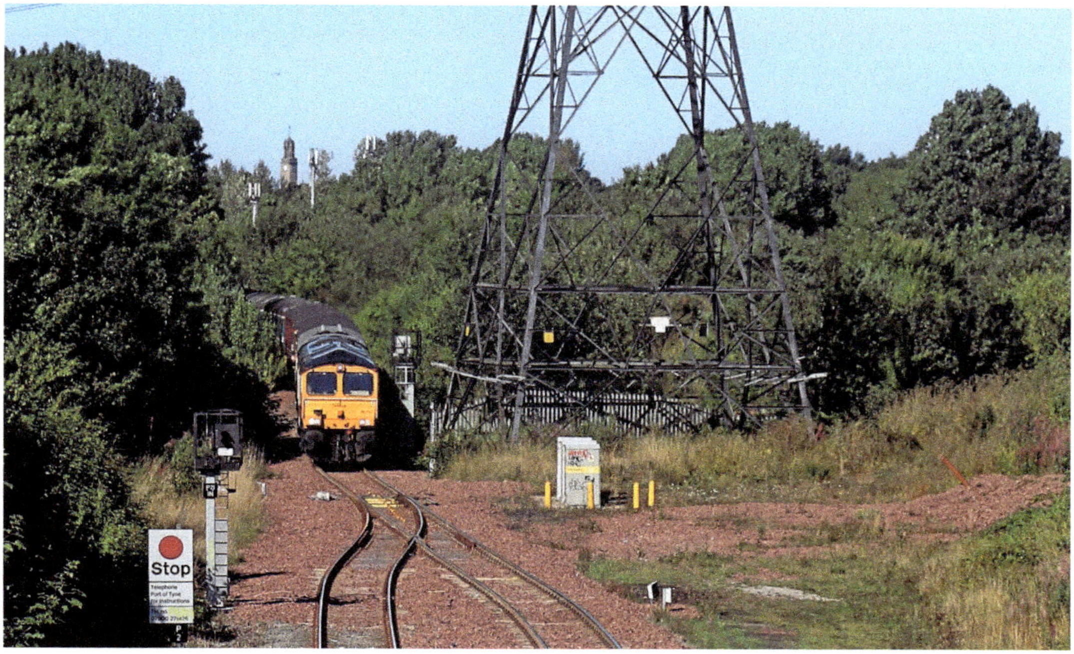

Green Lane Looking Towards South Shields
This image shows the same area as the picture before but now looking towards South Shields. Although much diminished, the existing rail lines are used by modern Biomass trains and the occasional passenger charter.

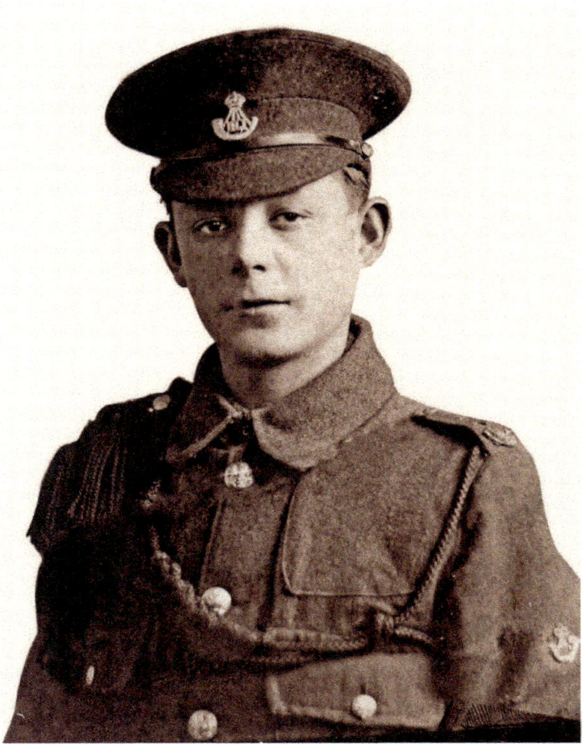

Billy Walker
Billy Walker, who we believe served as a bugler with the Durham Light Infantry during the First World War. I believe his bravery in action was recognised. He later lived in Marsden Road. If you know any of Billy Walker's relatives please get in touch with the author.

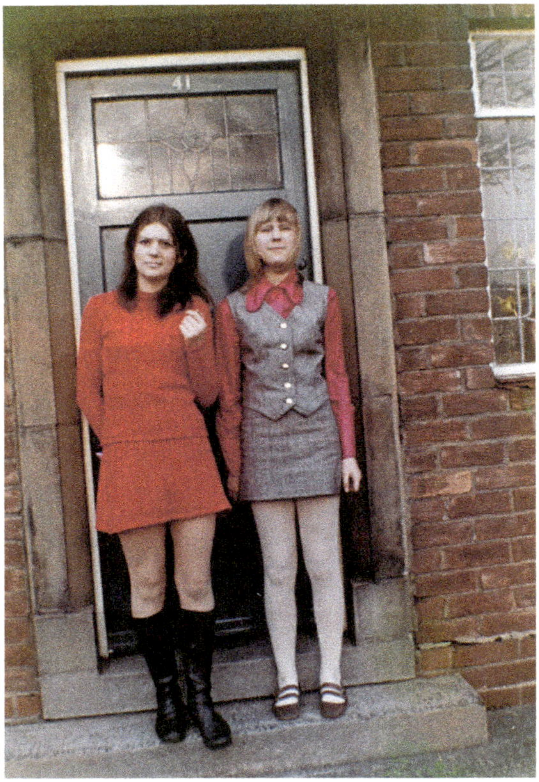

Shields Girls
Two Shields girls in colourful 1960s clothing.

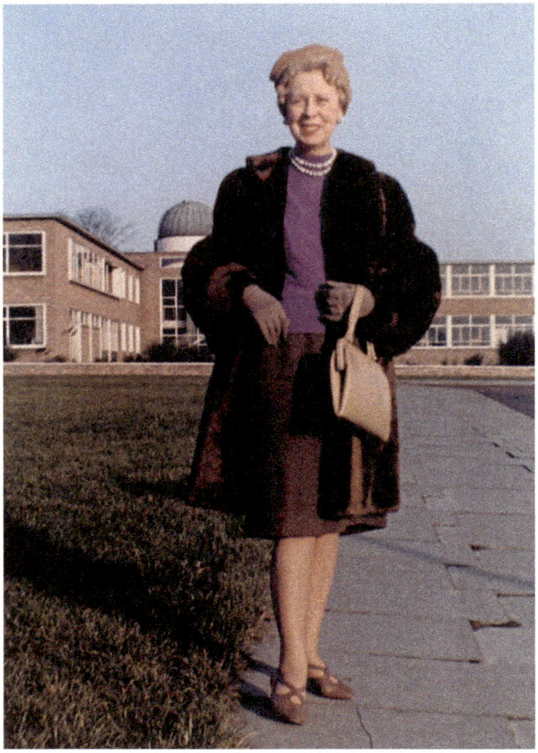

South Shields Marine and Technical College
Gladys Hunter outside of South Shields Marine and Technical College.

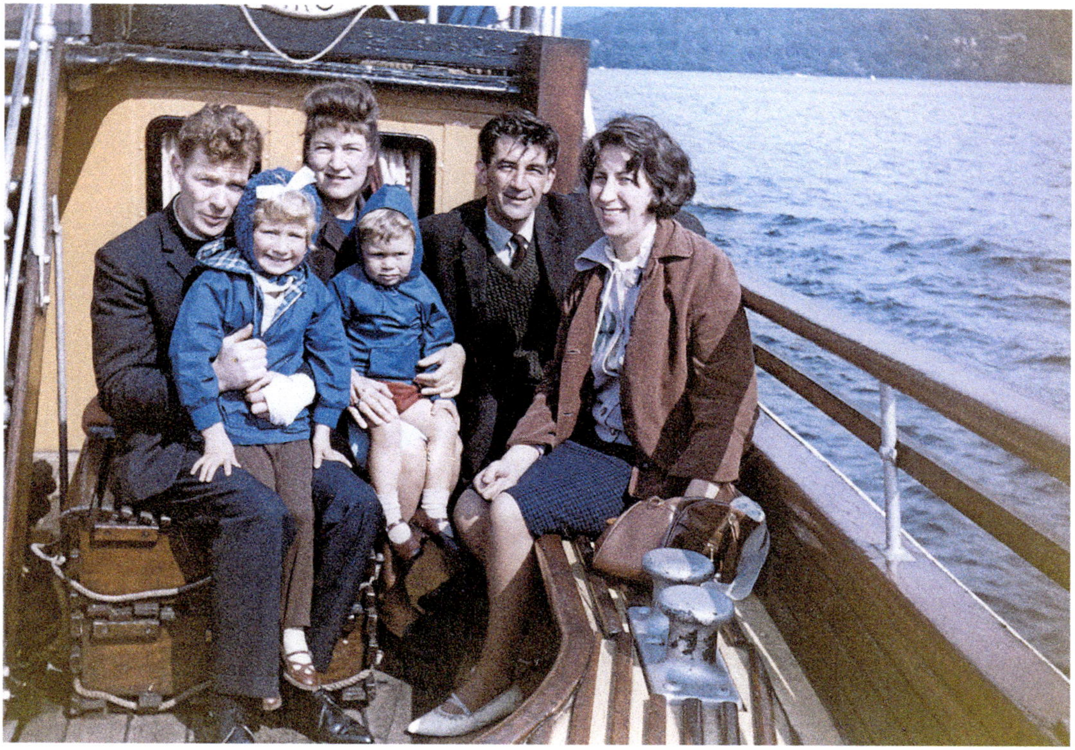

Family Holidays
Tom Peterson, Joyce Carlson, Charles Carlson, and Mary Peterson with daughter Janet Peterson and son John Carlson on holiday in Scotland in the 1960s.

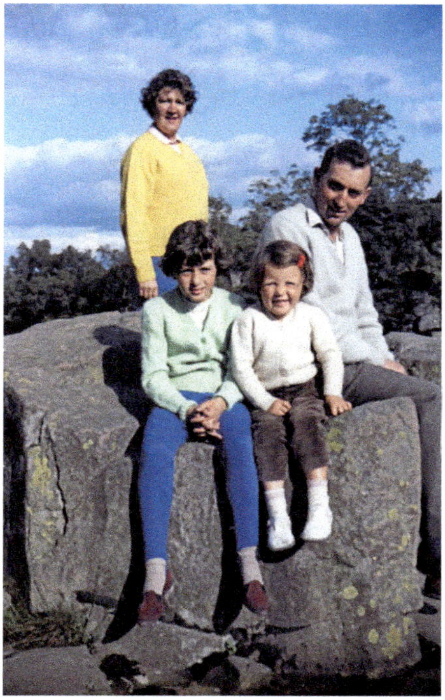

Mary and Jack Thorpe with daughters Judith and Jacqueline.

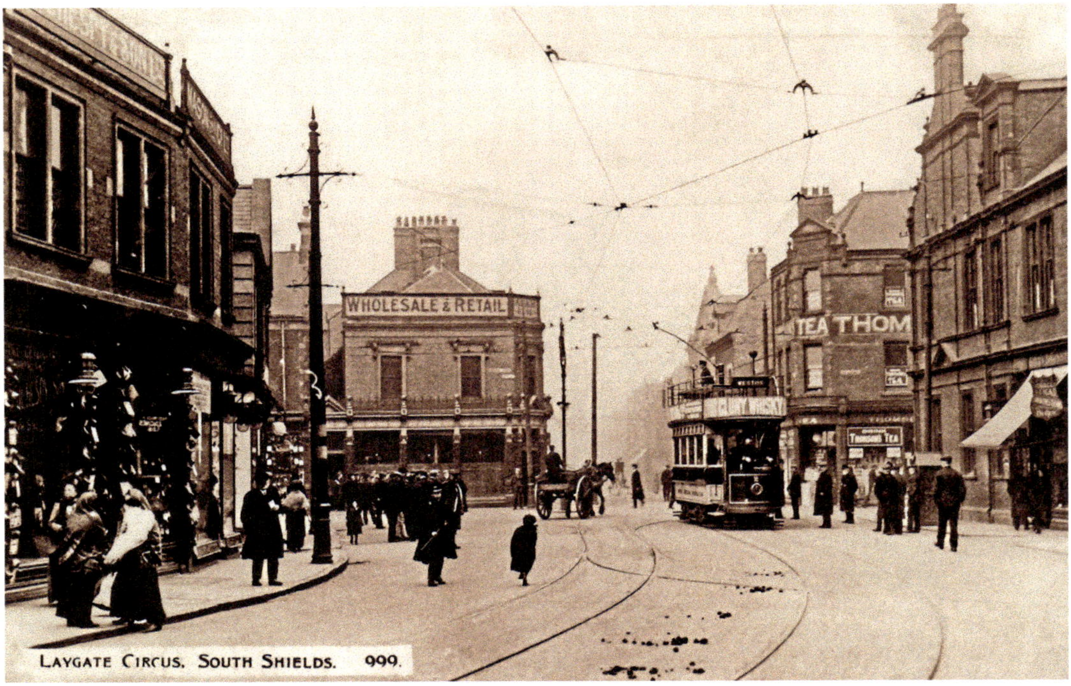

Laygate Circus

Laygate Circus was once an important junction into South Shields but became significantly less important following the construction of Western Approach.

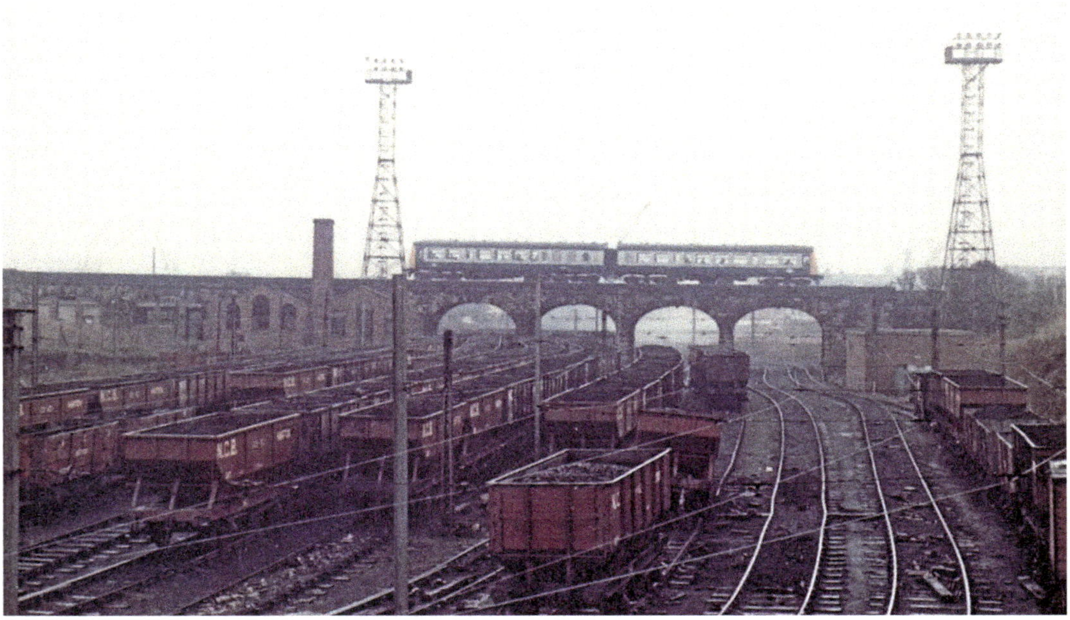

National Coal Board Sidings, Crossgate

This image shows a British Rail diesel train running between South Shields and High Shields stations passing over the National Coal Board sidings at Crossgate. This area has now been redeveloped into the Saint Hilda Industrial Estate.

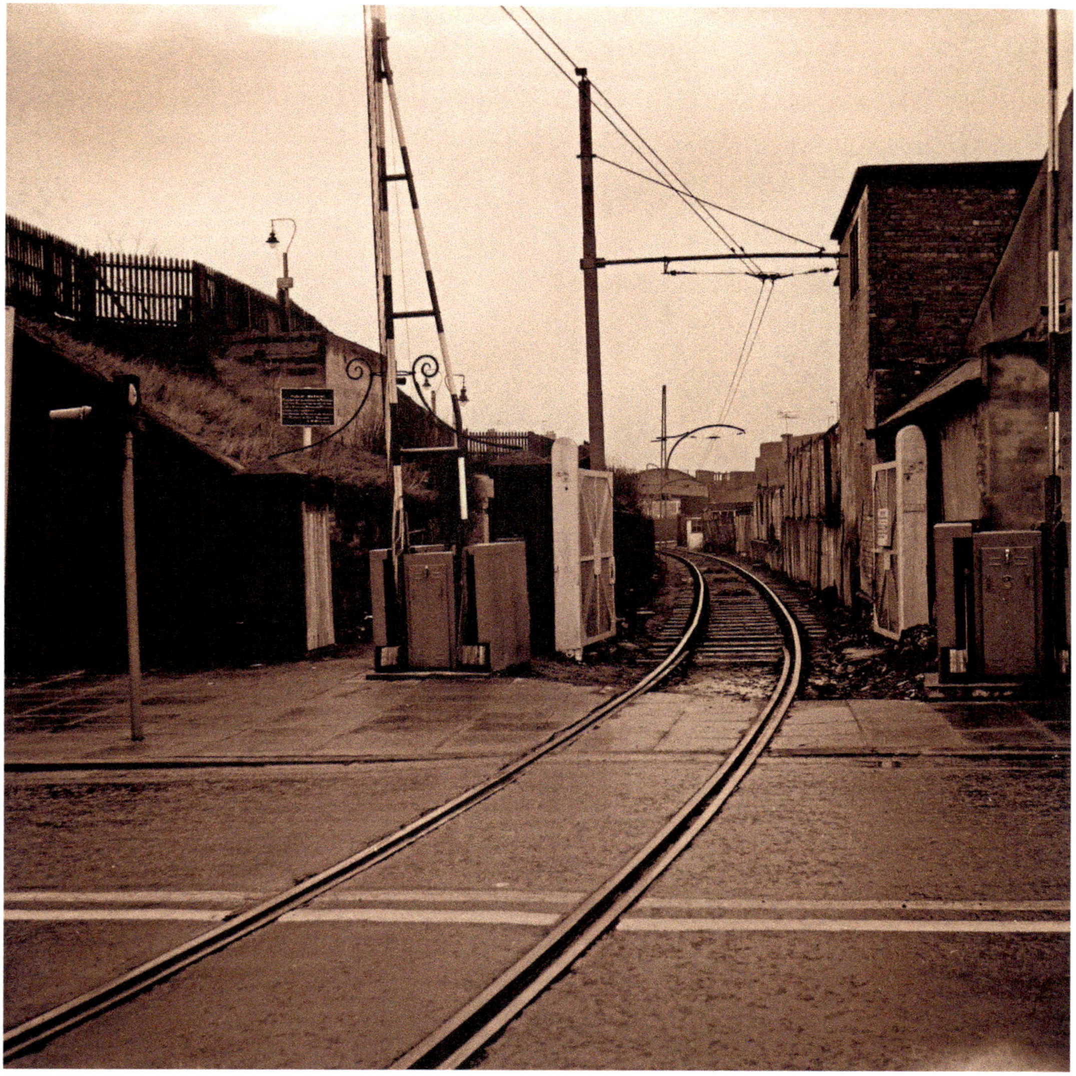

National Coal Board Line at High Shields

The former National Coal Board line at High Shields. This area has now been completely landscaped.

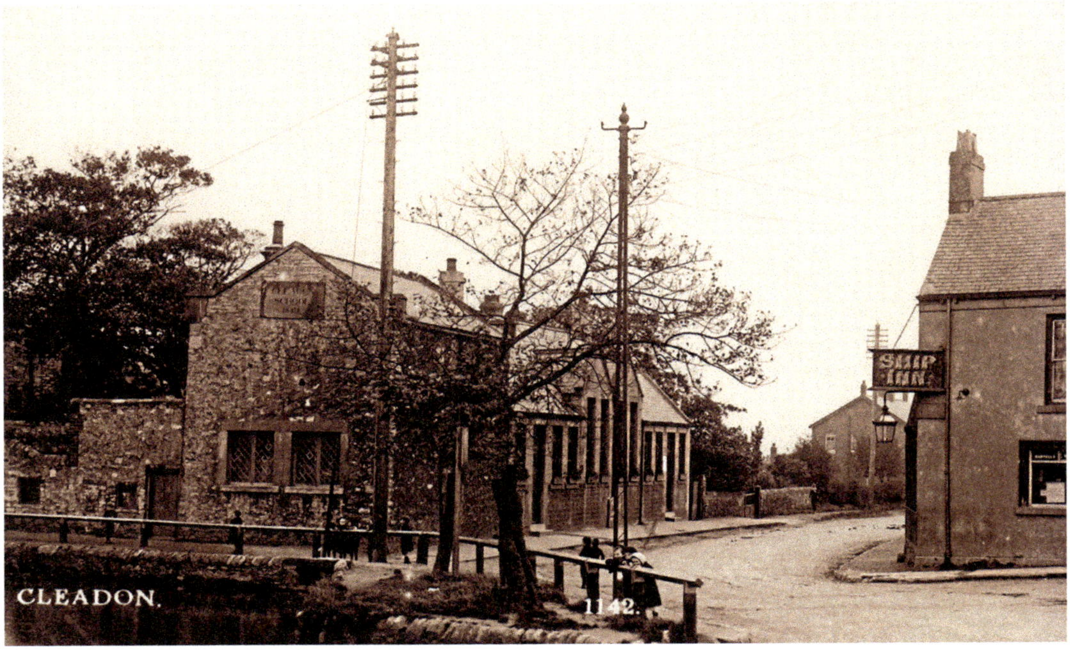

Cleadon Village Pond and School
Although recognisable, the very busy Sunderland Road now passes through the centre of the picture.

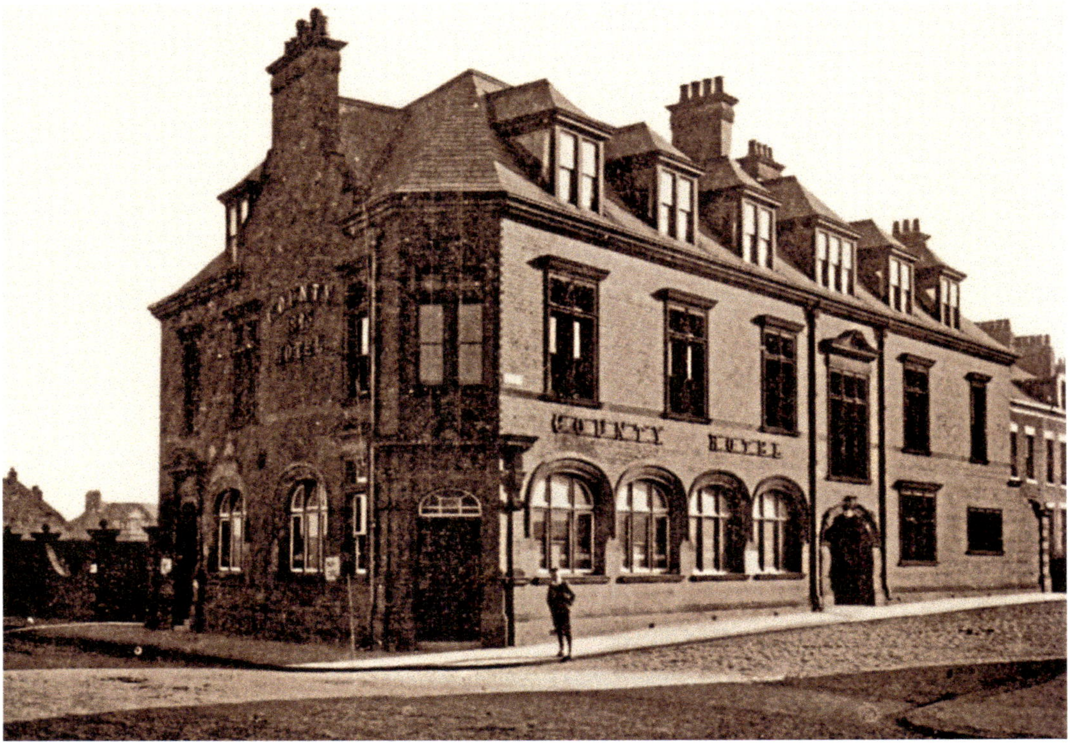

The County Public House
The County public house when very much in use as a hotel.

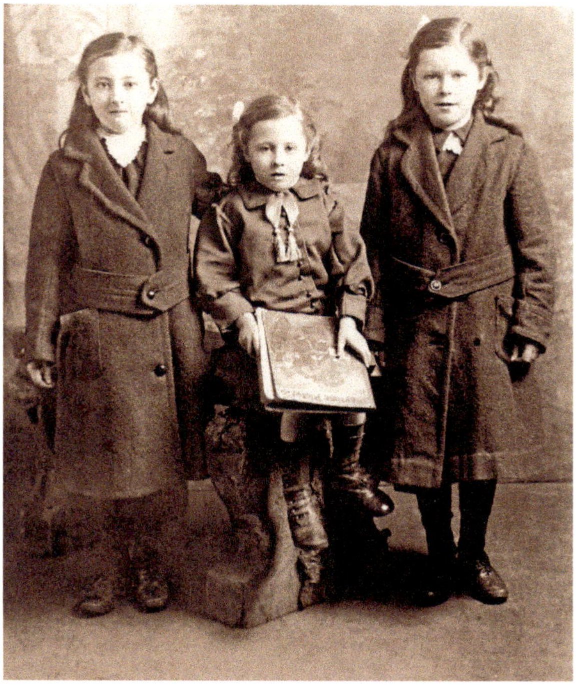

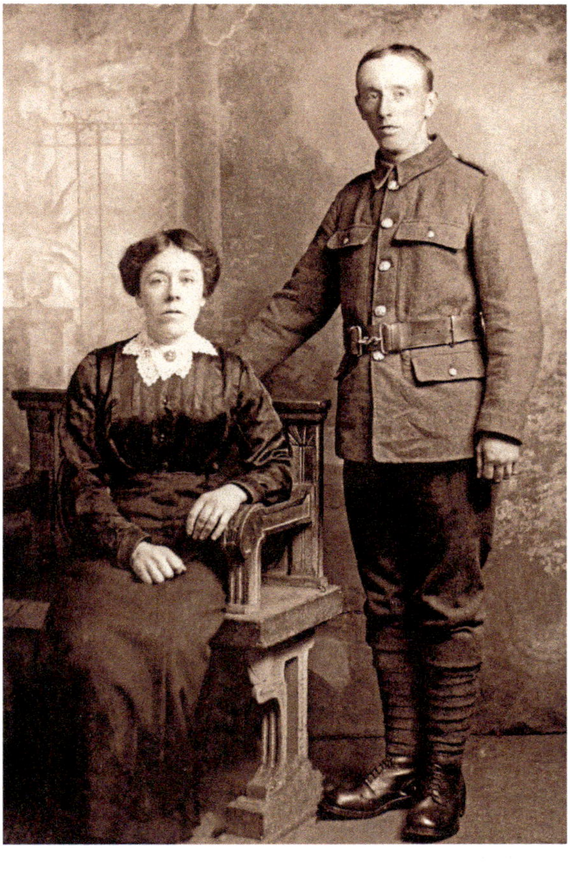

Residents of South Shields
South Shields residents William and Jennie Moore.

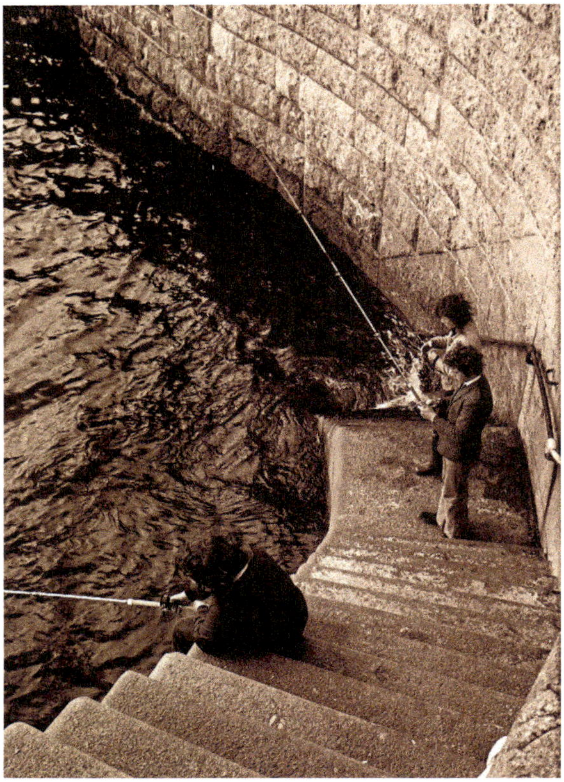

Left: Local Fishing
This image shows a group of children fishing from the pier near the lighthouse.

Below: Parade
A parade passes through King Street on its way to the Bents Park.

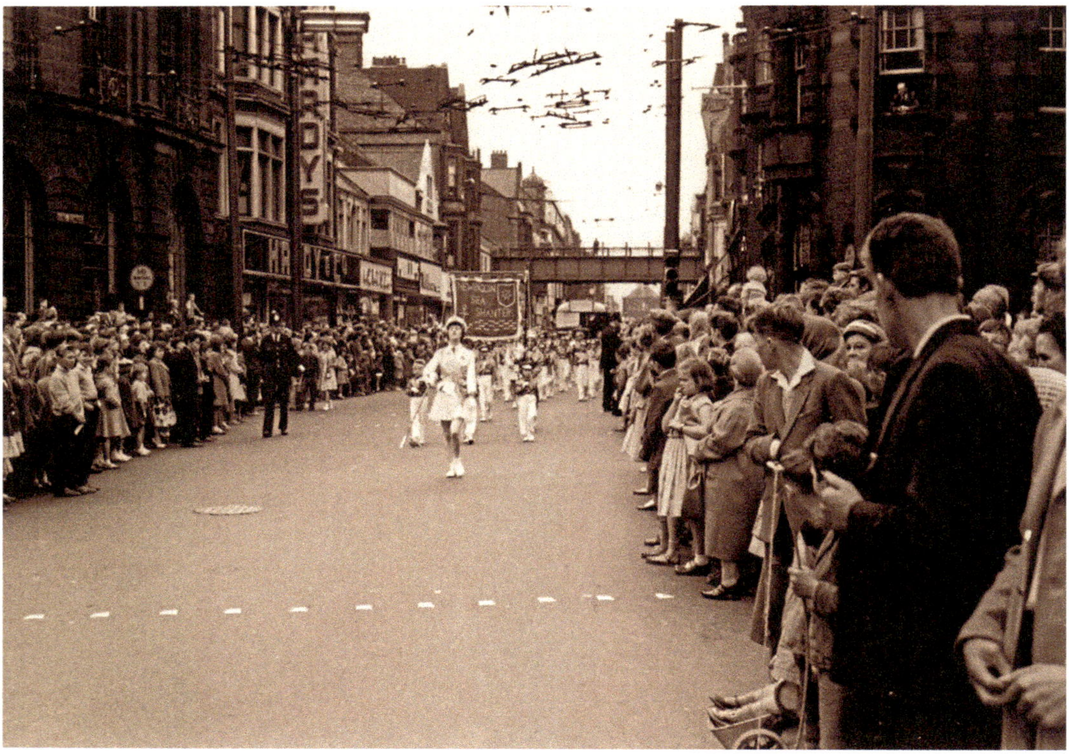

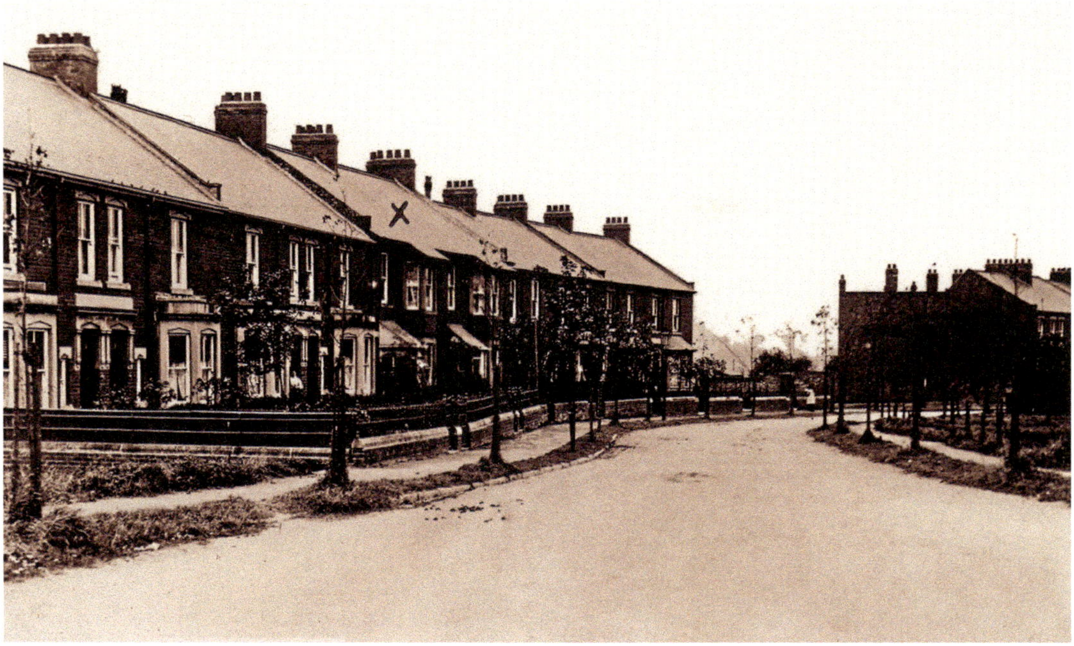

Harton
Harton, near The Nook.

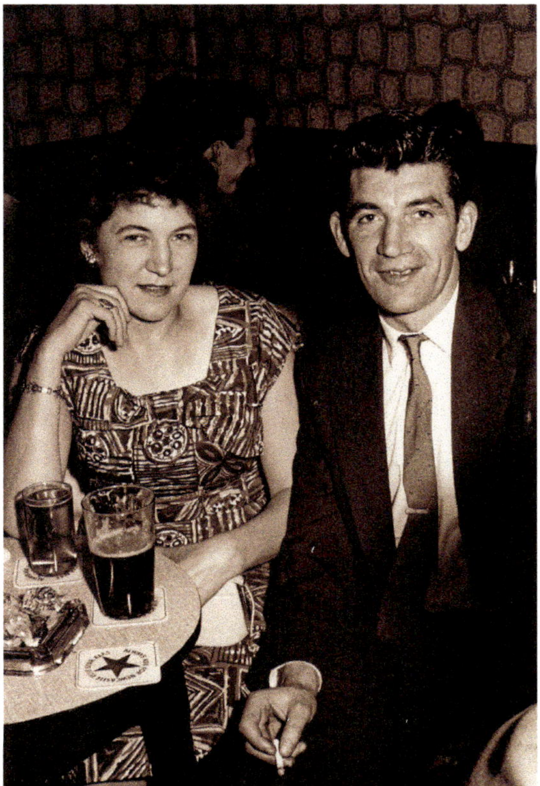

Meet the Locals
Joyce and Charles Carlson *c*. 1960.

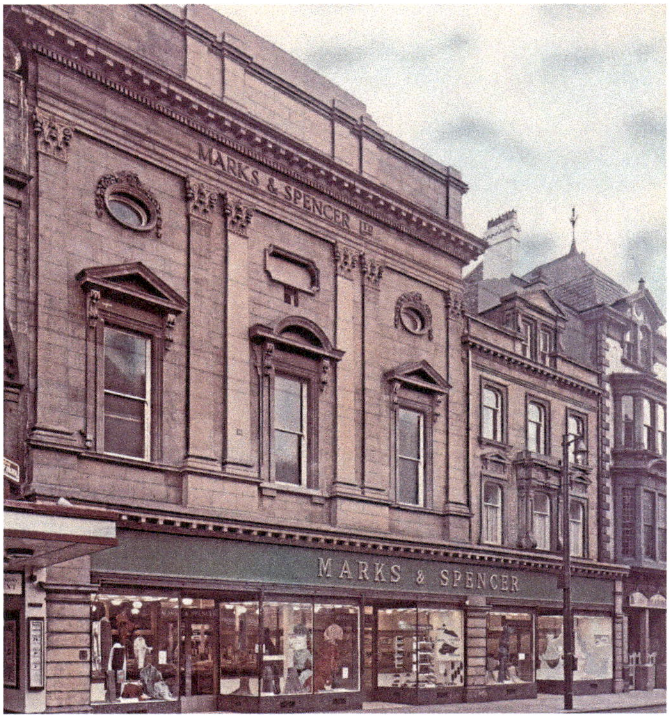

Marks & Spencer
Marks & Spencer, King Street.

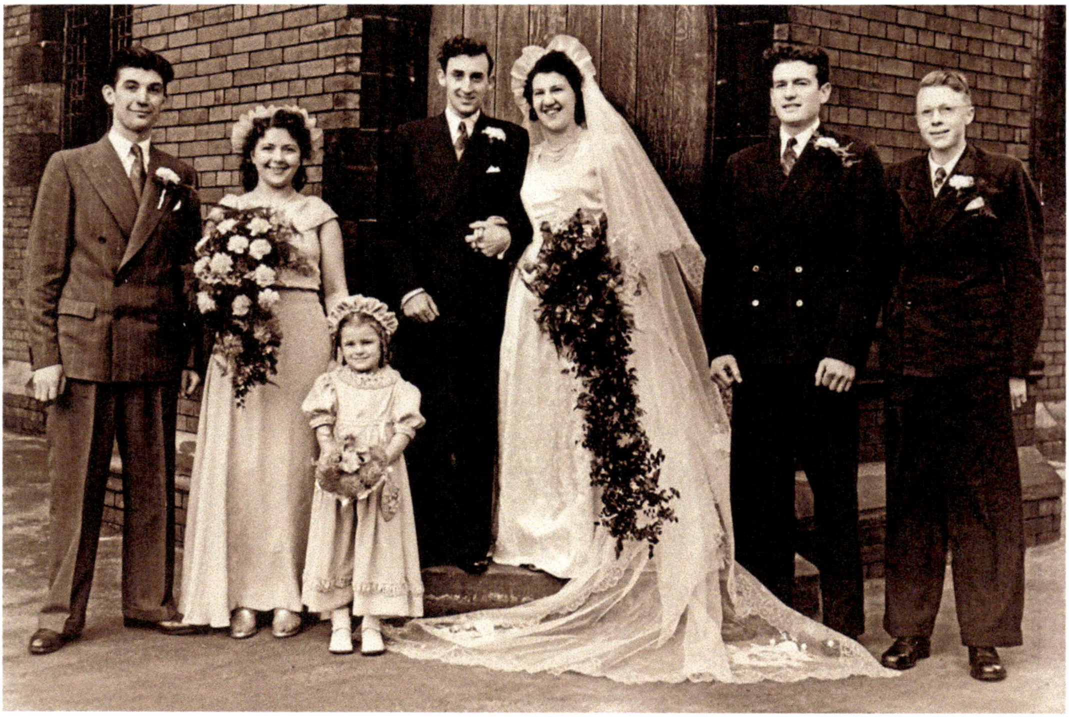

Wedding at St Michael's Church
The wedding of Jack and Mary Thorpe at St Michel's Church. Also present are Marion Young, Matty Young and Oswald Thorpe.

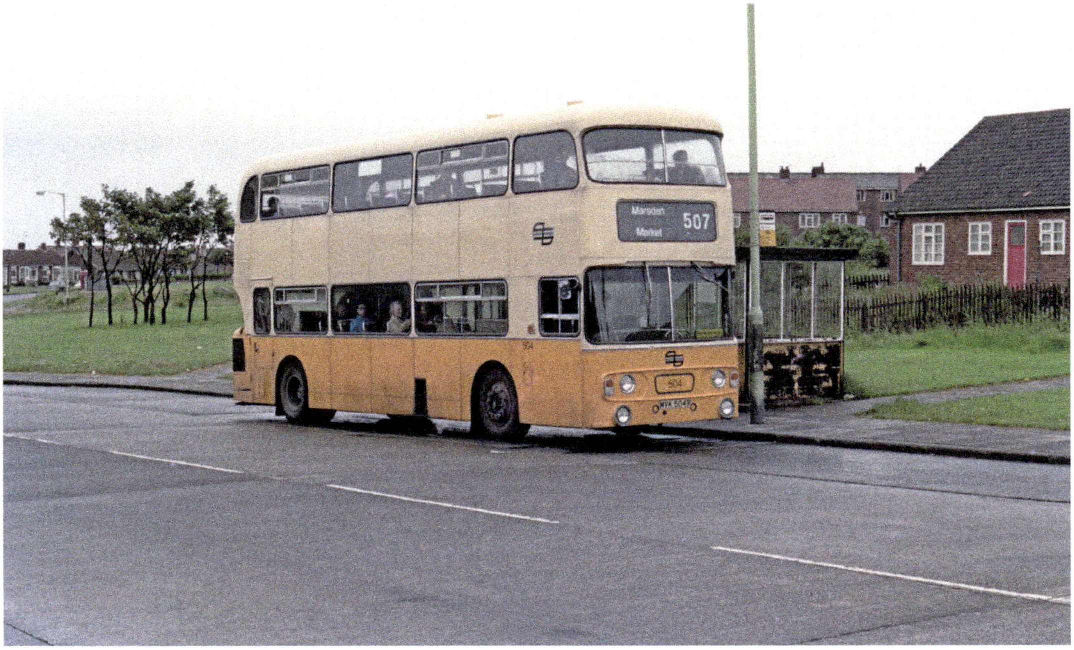

PTE Bus, Marsden Lane
A PTE bus at the top of Marsden Lane opposite the Marsden Inn.

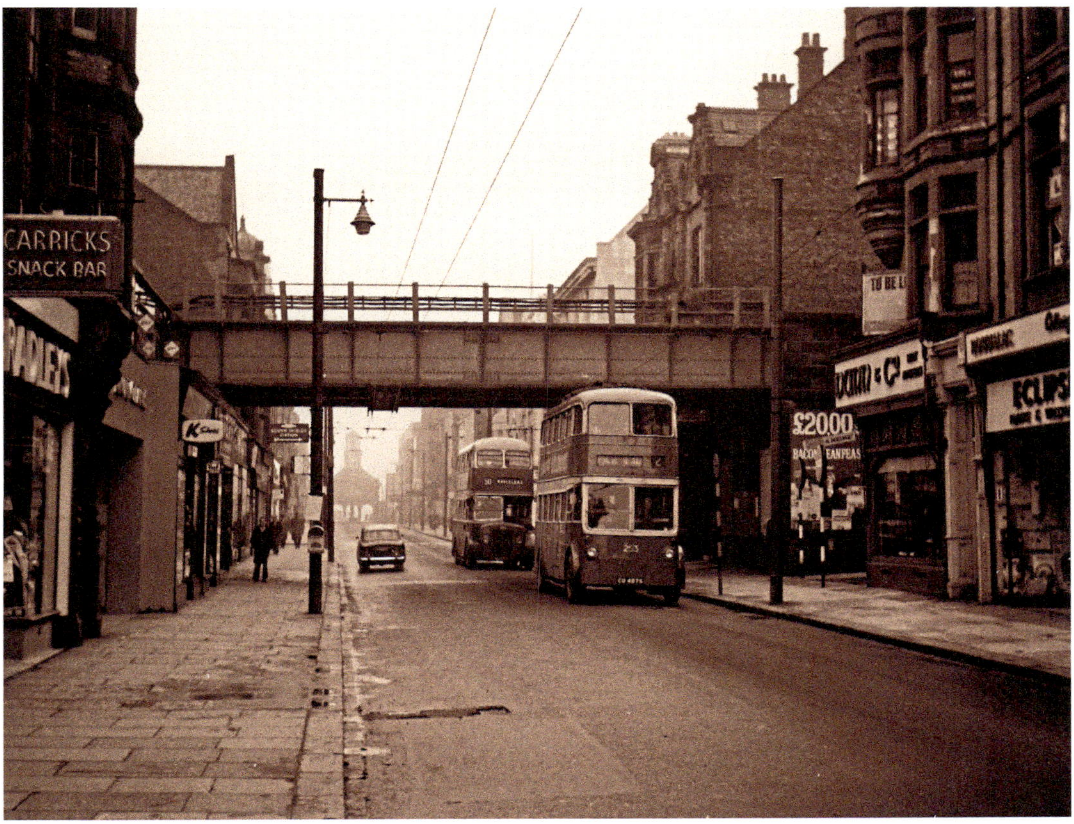

Also available from Amberley Publishing

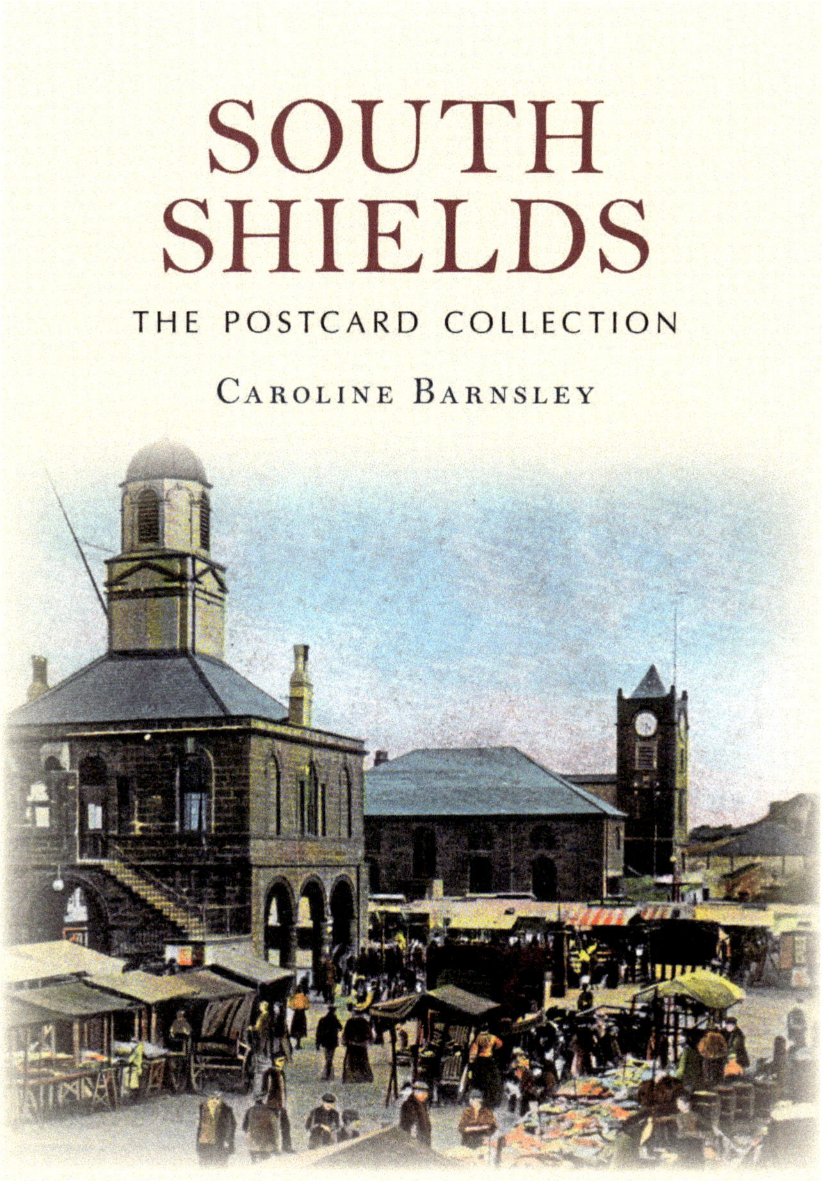

Beautiful postcards capture old South Shields in all its glory.

978 1 4456 3446 3

Available to order direct 01453 847 800
www.amberley-books.com

Also available from Amberley Publishing

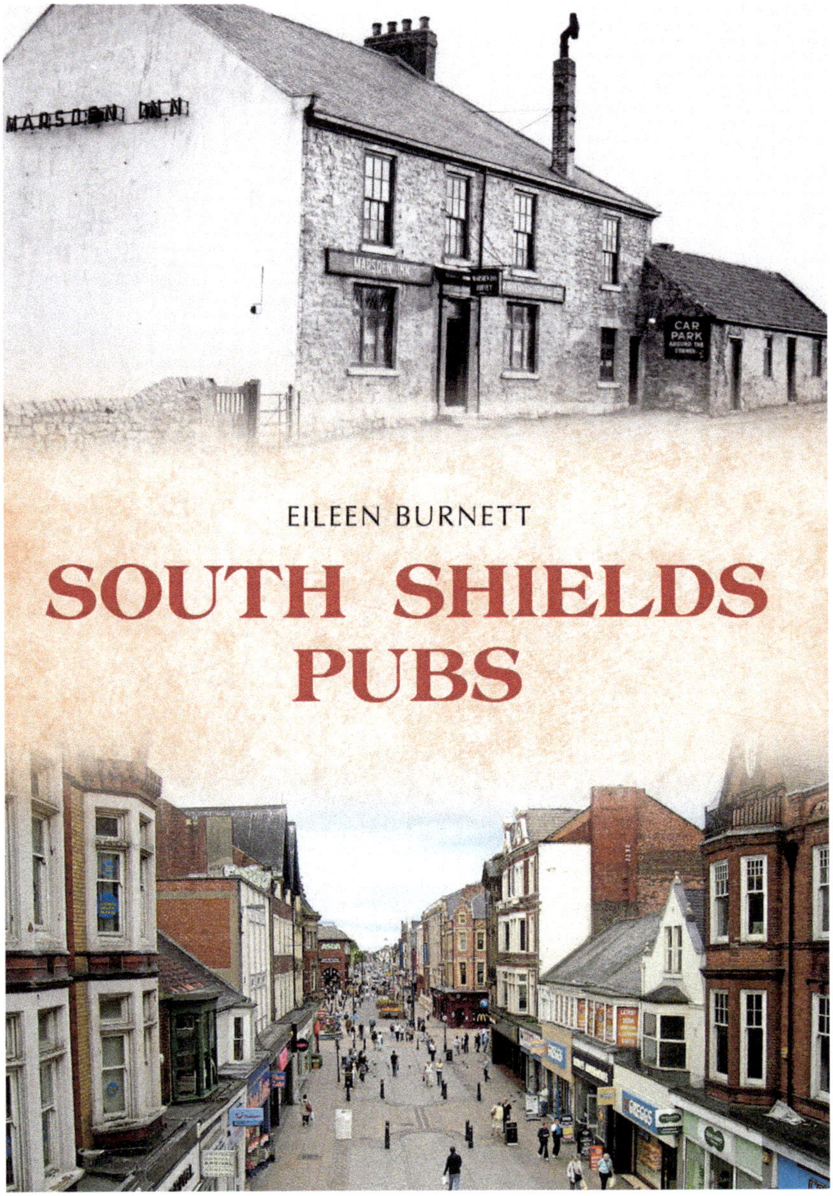

South Shields Pubs gives a unique and fascinating insight into some of South Shield's famous and infamous pubs, taverns and inns

978 1 4456 4200 0

Available to order direct 01453 847 800

www.amberley-books.com

Also available from Amberley Publishing

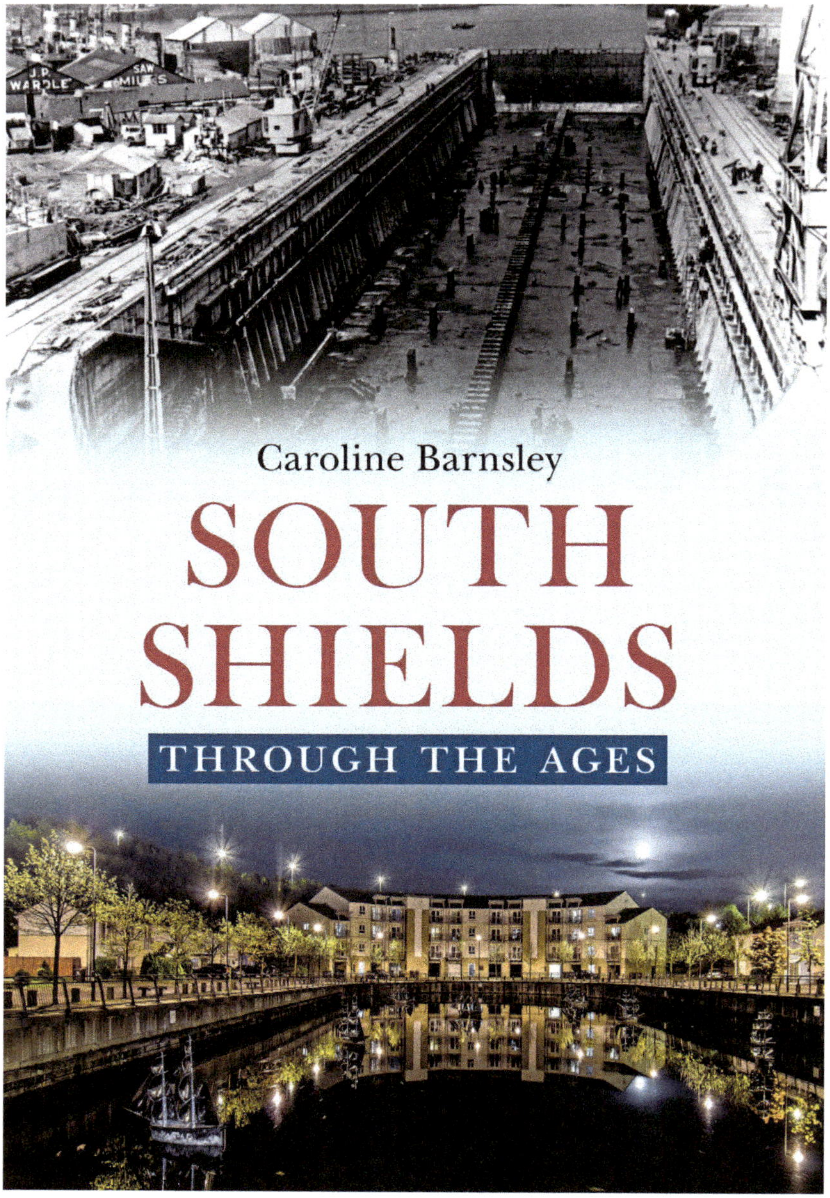

This fascinating selection of photographs traces some of the many ways in which South Shields has changed and developed through the ages.
978-1-4456-4107-2

Available to order direct 01453 847 800
www.amberley-books.com